IN HIS WORDS

Quotes from Sunday School Lessons
by President Jimmy Carter

September 24, 1978: "Facing Life's Tensions"

"Well, it's always nice to come back from a two-week vacation at Camp David.

"I think some of the most unpleasant moments of my life occurred during the last two weeks and, of course, also some of the most pleasant. One of the great things about the meeting was that I was meeting with two leaders who were deeply devout and religious men. Who spent a great portion of their time at Camp David in prayer. Who believe that they and I worship the same God."

———

December 10, 1978: "Forgiveness: A Two-Way Street"

"There have been times in my life when I have been bitterly hurt, at least in my own subjective assessment, by others, either in my political life or sometimes in other ways. And I have harbored in my heart a resentment against those people for years. I've been kind of stingy with parceling out the limited amount of forgiveness that I have to offer. But God, in this parable, through Christ says, 'The amount of forgiveness by me toward you is unlimited,' and I think, with a strong insinuation, that we are not limited in how much we can forgive others."

———

March 4, 1979: "Life in the Spirit"

"If you asked a lot of people in my home church in Plains, what's the worst sin, they would probably say, 'Drinking Tennessee sour mash whiskey,' perhaps, that that's a root of all evil, or at least one of the major roots of all evil. ... But I would think that self-righteousness or pride would be right up at the top among the things that seem to concern Christ most because self-righteousness and pride imply self-reliance in the absence of God."

———

April 29, 1979: "A Cry for Justice"

"Justice is the highest ideal that a government can hope to reach. Justice based on freedom, justice based on truth, but justice is the highest possible achievement of a free society based on truth. What is the highest ideal that a human being might achieve? Love. Love's the word I want. A government, a nation can provide freedom. A government, a nation can provide justice. A person can provide freedom, truth, justice, and love."

———

September 9, 1979: "The Cost of Concern"

"This past week I had at the White House, Rosalynn and I, representatives from religious faiths throughout the world, 45 different nations dedicated to peace ... And I particularly appreciated this international group because they're trying to probe, not for the differences that exist among them—and the differences are quite severe—but they're trying to discern the common ground on which people can worship God in different ways."

———

November 16, 1980: "Grace for Sinners"

"I'm very grateful for a chance to be a member of this church. It's been an exhilarating and a calming, and a satisfying, gratifying experience for us to make friends here who have accepted us, not as special people who live in the White House, but as neighbors and as fellow believers in Christ."

ABOUT PRESIDENT JIMMY CARTER TEACHING SUNDAY SCHOOL

"If you know anything about Jimmy Carter, this may be it: He never lost touch with his home in Plains, Georgia, and he never gravitated away from teaching his Baptist faith. ...

"What might be even more remarkable is that he maintained that grounding even when he was leading the free world, frequently popping up 16th Street to teach a couples' Bible class in the balcony of the First Baptist Church of the City of Washington, D.C. Carter intertwined a first-person, real-time account of world events with his thoughts on the scripture. ...

"In today's tightly controlled media environment, when the fences around the White House keep getting higher and the barricades farther away, it's incredible to think that any parishioner could stand in the balcony of a church and interact with the U.S. president.

"He attended the church regularly, and his daughter, Amy, was baptized there—things I learned after hearing from Christi Harlan, a former reporter who has been a member since the '90s. She showed me the plaque on the ... pew where Carter would sit with his family, in view of a stained-glass window of George Washington Carver, the agricultural scientist who, like Carter, was a peanut farmer."

ZACHARY WOLF, CNN

ABOUT CHRISTI HARLAN AND FIRST BAPTIST, D.C.

"My own clippings about President Carter vanished long ago during various cross-country job changes. Fortunately, the members of First Baptist D.C. were prodigious subscribers and clippers. Copies of my articles in the church archives caught the eye of former reporter Christi Harlan.

"Harlan joined First Baptist 30 years ago, shortly after she began work in *The Wall Street Journal*'s Washington bureau. (She insists that old reporters never retire, so she's using her news skills as the church's communications director.)

"When the 98-year-old Carter entered hospice care in February 2023, a couple of news organizations contacted the church about the former president. Harlan reached out to a few more media outlets and secured coverage on C-SPAN and CNN's website.

"She connected with me soon after that when she took off her public affairs hat and put on her reporter's hat. She is now working to chronicle President Carter's four years as an active member of First Baptist D.C."

JANIS JOHNSON, FORMER *WASHINGTON POST* REPORTER

MR. PRESIDENT,
THE CLASS IS YOURS

*Jimmy Carter's Sunday School
Lessons in Washington, D.C.*

CHRISTI HARLAN

Christi Harlan Media LLC
Washington, D.C.

Published by Christi Harlan Media LLC

www.christiharlanwriter.com

christi@christiharlanwriter.com

FIRST EDITION

Paperback ISBN: 979-8-9902263-0-2

E-book ISBN: 979-8-9902263-1-9

Printed in the United States of America

Cover Photo Courtesy of the Jimmy Carter Presidential Library and Museum

Photo of Christi Harlan by Jay Brousseau

Cover Design by Miblart / www.miblart.com

Book Editing & Design by Booktique Consulting / www.booktiqueconsulting.com

❀ Created with Vellum

For my mother, Barbara

———

Despite our decades of Scrabble games,
I still have words to play.

CONTENTS

INTRODUCTION

The archives of the First Baptist Church of the City of Washington, D.C., contain items dating back to the church's founding in 1802, when Thomas Jefferson was in his first year as president and the swampy land north of the Potomac River was just beginning to be established as the capital of the United States.

First Baptist's archives, like many home attics, basements or closets, contain a lot of "stuff" (i.e., junk). The many duplicates of church bulletins and Christmas concert recordings, along with the minutes of meetings of the groups that govern a Baptist church (Sunday School, church council, deacons, more church council) could probably be disposed of without anyone questioning whether that vote back in 1956 was taken with a true quorum.

But within the "stuff" packed away by 222 years of crazy aunts (and uncles) are true treasures. Among those are 14 recordings—including the original reel-to-reel tapes—of Sunday School lessons taught by President Jimmy Carter while he was in the White House from January 1977 to January 1981.

The recordings were made by Chip Hailey and Ed Fry, both now deceased. For Fry, sound engineering was a side hustle; he was an economist for the Federal Reserve.

By recording Carter's interpretations and discussion of stories from the Bible, Hailey and Fry ensured that an important and little-known part of Carter's life would be preserved. His official speeches and statements as president are safeguarded by the National Archives and Records Administration; his Sunday School lessons as president survive on tapes and CDs with the First Baptist church.

By publishing transcripts of the lessons, I hope to make President Carter's words accessible to as many people as possible and not just to those of us who like to putter in the boxes, file drawers and "stuff" in First Baptist's archives.

The transcripts have been edited for clarity, primarily to close the gaps when class members responded to questions from the President but couldn't be heard on the recordings. Fortunately, Carter repeated many responses, so the gist of the give-and-take is evident. And because the text was originally spoken, it contains repetition and incomplete sentences—rhetorical devices that allow a speaker to emphasize particular points. Certain wording that was common in the 1970s but not acceptable in the 2020s is included as spoken.

The other notable edits involve the Bible verses that underpinned each lesson. Carter frequently asked class members to read aloud the Scripture for the day. Members used a variety of versions of the Bible. Where readings were inaudible, I inserted text from the King James Version of the Christian Bible, whose copyright (if any) lapsed in the 1600s.

The historic context for the lessons comes largely from the public records of Carter's presidency, wonderfully maintained by the National Archives and Records Administration and accessible on the website of the Jimmy Carter Presidential Library and Museum and through public records of other government agencies. Supplemental information comes from contemporaneous news coverage, much of which survives in scrapbooks and folders of yellowed newspaper clippings (more "stuff") in the First Baptist archives.

The full story of President Jimmy Carter's active membership at the First Baptist Church of the City of Washington, D.C., is rich enough to fill another book. For this volume, his words alone will do.

Mr. President, the class is yours.

Christi Harlan
Washington, D.C.
April 2024

THE SUNDAY SCHOOL CLASS

On at least 17 Sundays during his presidency, Jimmy Carter stepped to a lectern in the balcony overlooking the sanctuary of the First Baptist Church of the City of Washington, D.C. There, with his back against one of the concrete pillars that support the soaring neo-Gothic ceiling, Carter faced four long wooden pews beneath the brightly stained glass of the tall Redemption Window.

Shoulder to shoulder in the pews were the adult members of the church's Couples Class, there to hear a Bible lesson from a teacher who just happened to be the President of the United States:

> "About 70 persons attended the first Sunday School lesson taught by Mr. Carter at the First Baptist Church, which he joined a few weeks ago," a correspondent for the United Press International reported on February 20, 1977. "A longtime church member said half the class were visitors.
>
> "Smiling frequently and talking in low, warm tones, Mr. Carter quoted from the Book of Mark. ... Mr. Carter appeared at ease with the class and held its close attention. He asked members to recite from the Bible and then asked for opinions on what the passages meant.
>
> " 'How many of you have been on your knees in the past 24 hours?' he asked. 'I have.' "

Carter's four years as President from 1977 to 1981 would be marked by a series of calamitous events that would bring anyone to their knees in prayer, if not despair. Yet, in his Sunday School lessons and other remarks to the Couples Class and—more importantly—in what he didn't say about the cares of his office, President Carter seemed to find a haven at First Baptist D.C., a church home where he could be just another Christian in worship and study.

"You have made our lives normal lives," Carter said at the Couples Class banquet in October 1977. "A president of our country can be an isolated person. You have taken us in, and we are indebted to you."

The class seemed particularly well suited for the President and First Lady. The Couples Class at First Baptist D.C. began in late 1943 or early 1944 as young married people moved to Washington for jobs during World War II. The war effort required long, irregular working hours that left little time for couples to be together—except in church. With the blessing of the then-pastor, Edward Hughes Pruden, the Couples Class formally became part of First Baptist's Sunday School on January 5, 1945, with 14 members.

By 1977, the class of working couples was integrated by gender and race. Among the members were the Liberian ambassador to the United States; the former executive director of the American Public Health Association and his wife, a nurse; an architect; and a gregarious insurance executive. The membership roll for the class contained more than 50 names in alphabetical order except for those of new members, whose names were noted at the top of the list along with their home addresses. For one pair of new members in 1977, the address was 1600 Pennsylvania Ave., Washington, D.C.

First Baptist D.C., at 16th and O streets, is just under a mile due north of the White House, close enough that President Harry S. Truman would walk to services at the church in the early 1950s. In an era of heightened security, the Carters would get in a motorcade on the South Grounds of the White House and arrive at First Baptist within five to six minutes.

On Sunday, January 23, 1977—three days after Carter took the oath of office with his hand on the family Bible—the official White House diary included this entry:

9:30 a.m. The President and the First Lady attended a Sunday School couples class. The class was led by Fred M. Gregg, Executive Vice President for Marketing, Equitable Life Insurance Company, Washington, D.C.

Gregg, the son of a Baptist preacher, had only recently taken the job and moved his family to a D.C. suburb from his hometown of Chattanooga, Tennessee. Gregg joined First Baptist, became lead teacher of the Couples Class and soon formed a bond with the new President. With equally sharp wits and deadpan delivery, Gregg and Carter often opened the Couples Class trading mock insults about who was the better teacher, sparring in their native drawls of Tennessee and Georgia.

On Carter's final Sunday with the class, January 4, 1981, Gregg described how he wrangled the occasional substitute teacher:

The day that I first met the President, he said, "I'm looking forward to hearing you teach."

I said, "Well, how about you teaching?"

Well, this was only Sunday after the inauguration, and he said, "Well, after all, Fred, I have had a pretty busy week this week," but said, "I will teach."

And he has, and every time that he's taught, he has really blessed our hearts.

1977

Jimmy Carter logged several firsts with his inauguration on January 20, 1977, including the use of solar heat in the reviewing stand and being the first president to walk from the Capitol to the White House with their family after the ceremony.

Carter mentioned the post-inaugural stroll in his State of the Union address in 1978: "[O]ne year ago tomorrow, I walked from here to the White House to take up the duties of President of the United States. I didn't know it then when I walked, but I've been trying to save energy ever since."

The comment was a possibly ill-advised attempt to lighten the country's concerns about energy prices and policy.

When Carter took office, a severe natural gas shortage crippled the northeastern United States, shuttering schools and businesses in a bitter cold spell. The long lines for gasoline throughout the United States were fresh in memories.

In July 1977, an energy crisis born of a natural phenomenon crippled the nation's largest city after lightning struck power lines and infrastructure serving New York City, cutting power for 25 hours and spawning widespread looting and arson.

On August 4, 1977, Carter signed the Department of Energy Organization Act, folding the federal supervision of nuclear power into broader oversight of national energy policies that might reduce reliance on oil imports and keep the lights and heat working in, for example, U.S. homes, businesses and the First Baptist Church of the City of Washington, D.C.

During his first year in office, President Carter attended worship services at First Baptist at least 26 times—not counting his two pre-inaugural services, but including the Sunday his daughter, Amy, then nine years old, was baptized. Carter taught Sunday School classes at First Baptist at least four times that year, but only one was recorded by the volunteer sound engineers of First Baptist.

In the lesson of November 6, 1977, the President described the 1976 annual meeting of the Southern Baptist Convention, with which he—and First Baptist D.C.—were then affiliated. (Both Carter and First Baptist D.C. later split from the Southern Baptists.)

Of the 1977 meeting of the Southern Baptist Convention, Carter merely said, "I was not there. I had other duties to perform this year." Like being President of the United States.

BREAKING DOWN BARRIERS
NOVEMBER 6, 1977
JOHN 4:7-30

FRED GREGG:

We are studying John, and there are some different views expressed by John [from the Gospels of Matthew, Mark and Luke]. One of those is the story where Jesus turned the water into the wine. Another one is the story of Nicodemus, and this Sunday we have the third one, the story of the woman at the well. And it gives me a great deal of pleasure to turn this lesson over to the President of the United States.

PRESIDENT JIMMY CARTER:

Fred mentioned the 1977 Southern Baptist Convention. I was not there. I had other duties to perform this year. But in 1976, I was present, and there was 17,000 or 18,000 people down. Were any of you there in 1976? Fred, you were there.

Well, I was present as a Southern Baptist leader, as a member of the Brotherhood Commission from Georgia and as an ex-governor, and I was invited to speak briefly, only about five minutes. There were three of us who were there to represent the men of the church, and as I looked at the program, I was first very concerned and then immediately after quite relieved because the first speaker in that brief session was Billy Graham. And I saw that I was speaking immediately after him, which caused me a great deal of concern.

And then I saw that the person speaking behind me was a truck driver. And I was told that he was not illiterate, but not a well-educated man, a very rough human and so forth. And I said, "Well, at least I'll look good and sound good compared to him." Billy Graham gave one of his usual very forceful, very inspirational talks.

I fumbled around for about five minutes with my own, and then the truck driver got up and he had never made a speech before in his life. He was completely drenched with sweat. And as I sat there with him on the speaking platform, there were about 50 or 75 people on that tremendous platform. He said, "I don't think I can live through it," he said. "I just cannot do it."

And he got up and said that he was a drunkard and a sinner and that he had found Christ and he didn't know what to do about it. He didn't have many friends, he said, because he had pretty well isolated himself from the rest of the world because of the life he led. The only people he knew were the men like him who hung around the bars in the small town where he lived.

And he wanted to witness for Christ, so he decided to go back into the bars. And, at first, he was a subject of scorn and animosity. That the bartender said, "You're ruining ... our business here." And he kept on going to the bars, and anybody that would listen he would tell them about his change of life and about Christ.

And eventually "They looked forward," as he said, "they looked forward to seeing me come in the bar The men would gather around and ask me questions, and it was almost impossible for me to answer the questions because I wasn't learned in the Bible, and I had to get my new Christian friends around the church to teach me and give me a crash course before I went into the bar."

But he said, "I kept up with them, and if they asked me a question and I couldn't answer it, I went and got the answer and I came back the next time." And he told, I forgot how many, but 13 or 14 of those friends of his accepted Christ.

Well, you can imagine what the highlight of the whole convention was. It wasn't my speech as a well-known candidate for president or an ex-governor. It wasn't Billy Graham's speech. It was a fairly illiterate truck driver. And I don't believe anybody who went to that convention will ever forget that five-minute fumbling statement by this man. And I don't know who it was—an upstanding, successful Sunday School teacher or college professor or insurance executive or business leader—who talked to that drunken truck driver. But it reminds me of the lesson today.

I don't think anybody then could see in that person that in 12 months or 15 months after a personal expression of what Christ meant to that fine, upright, clean, decent, probably a wealthy church member that, that man would be speaking to 18,000 Baptist leaders with effectiveness. But it happened. Somebody bridged a chasm that existed between us fine Christian people and him.

And the same thing happened in the fourth chapter of John. That truck driver became centered around Christ. and he studied and he worked and prepared himself to go among his old friends.

We've, most of us, lived a life with Christ: Sunday School, church, maybe since we were infants. And we come once a week to church, maybe more, and we live a full life during the week preparing ourselves intently for the sale of insurance or to make decisions, in my case, on domestic and foreign policies of our country, or to carry out our daily professional lives or to prepare for final exams in college or to teach.

There's a dedication in our lives to things that we've put paramount. I won't embarrass you by asking how many in this class have read this morning or last night or this week the fourth chapter of John. And how many of you have studied the lesson in the Sunday School quarterly that has been provided for you.

But I would guess that most of the people in this room haven't even done that for the one hour per week when we come to stretch our minds and to stretch our hearts and to learn about Christ. We are part of a struggle that separates the institution of religion—you might say the instinct of religion—from the ministry or the Gospel of Christ. A natural instinct of any religion on earth, including our own, is to acquire security for ourselves, a sense of belonging, the alleviation of fear, finding of a common group with whom we feel at ease.

The Gospel of Christ stands in vivid contrast to that. Where is the security that Christ sought or even his disciples, who fell far short of his example? The lesson this morning touches on that basic conflict, and I think as we go through it today we ought to think about, where do we stand?

Have we created chasms around ourselves that separate us from those who need and hunger for the Gospel of Christ? Is our primary goal in life as Christians to husband to ourselves the mercy of God, the forgiveness of our sin, the knowledge of Christ that gives us security? Or is it to try to tear down barriers, to reach out, to share, to touch other people's lives in a benevolent way, an unselfish way, and at the same time expand our own lives instead of having them narrow down as each year passes?

Not too long ago, Rosalynn and I went to see a superbly performed play, I thought, *The Man of La Mancha*. Maybe some of you have seen it. I know a lot of you have read the book *Don Quixote* by Cervantes. Don Quixote goes into this roadside inn or tavern, and there's a prostitute there. And in his depraved mind or in his twisted mind—depraved toward idealism and the sense that the world wanted to be perfect—he saw in this prostitute a purity and a glory. He called her Dulcinea. And she slapped him away and scorned him and spat on him and made fun of him, and, as he was lying on his deathbed, she appeared later on, and we discover that her life had been transformed. This old decrepit man whose mind wandered had confidence in her much more than she deserved. He exalted her out of her absolute sinfulness, and her life was changed.

Well, I don't know about you, but this has happened in my own life on several occasions where, as a Baptist church member and a deacon at Plains, I went out to witness to people who were looked upon as being alienated from our own churchgoing society. And I've seen their lives transformed, not because of me or even the pastor or the deacon who went with me, but because there was a new awakening in their hearts that they meant something to God, and they meant something to us.

So the tearing down of barriers is one of the responsibilities of a Christian.

It was a natural thing in Jesus' time not to even go through Samaria. If you've looked at the map, you know that Samaria separated Judea from Galilee, and it lay on the western side of the Jordan River. And ordinarily, when Jews had to go from Galilee down to, say, Jerusalem, they would cross the Jordan River, go down to eastern bank of it and then cross back toward Jerusalem just to keep from going through Samaria. It's quite a bit out of the way. But when Jesus and his disciples were traveling just after [Jesus] was baptized, they decided to go through Samaria.

There was an extreme division between the Jews and the Samaritans founded in historical animosity. For eight or ten centuries, the kingdom of the Jews had been divided into northern and southern kingdoms.

Later, the Jews were captured by the Assyrians and taken into captivity. The Assyrians had moved into the area around Samaria and had intermarried with the former Jews, and those who stayed in captivity and came back looked upon the Samaritans as barbarians. And they thought that they had been tainted not only by marriage, but that their religion was destroyed.

When the Jews finally came back into Jerusalem and began to build a temple, the Samaritans came and said, "Let us help you build a temple."

And [the] Jews said, "No. Stay away from us. We don't want to have our temple defiled." So the Samaritans went back up very near where Jesus stopped at the well and built a temple.

And then, about a hundred and fifty years before Christ, the Jews, who had then become quite strong in Jerusalem and formed a kingdom, went up into Samaria and destroyed the Samaritan temple. So there was a very intense hatred between the two.

So it was a shock to the disciples, I'm sure, that Jesus even wanted to go through Samaria. But then when they did decide to go, and Jesus met the Samaritan woman, we have a well-known story that illustrates some very important points for us.

What were some of the things that separated Christ from the Samaritan woman other than the hatred between the Jews and the Samaritans? Anybody recall?

CLASS MEMBER:

Speaking to a woman in public.

PRESIDENT JIMMY CARTER:

Absolutely. It was strictly forbidden that any religious Jew would even speak to a woman in public. So there was a sex chasm or discrimination there that existed that was quite strictly observed. Anybody else think of something?

CLASS MEMBER:

Race.

PRESIDENT JIMMY CARTER:

Race. You're right. The Samaritans were, I guess, a dark-skinned people, and they were looked down upon as racial outcasts and of not being worthy, not even being in the same category as human beings by some of the more fervent racists, I guess you'd call them, among the Jews. ...

When Jesus got to the well, he was thirsty. His disciples went into Sychar to buy food. ... And what time of day was it? Anybody remember? It said the sixth hour. I think the interpretation of that is probably noon. She was the only person around the well. Who had put the well there?

It was Jacob's well, that's right. A well-known well, in fact. Jesus had gone there knowing it was Jacob's well. But nobody was there when he arrived except this woman. And what do you think the normal pattern of life would be to and from Jacob's well?

If you were living in a nearby town, say, Sychar, a couple miles away, and you were a woman, and one of your duties was to bring water from the well, what would you ordinarily do, you think?

You'd get with a group of women, right? And every evening, perhaps when it got cool or when the field work had been done, women would walk along toward the well in a spirit of friendship, talking about the day's events.

It would be a social thing to go to the well and get water, which was a mandatory act in the life of those people. So there's a significance about this woman being by herself. ...

She was an outcast. If somebody had asked in the little village of Sychar, who's the most sinful person in Sychar, the chances might be that they would've said, "This woman is the most sinful one of all."

So here was Christ, perfect, pure, without sin, confronting a woman who was the epitome of sin.

The vivid contrast is something that's there for us to study. Did Jesus know about this woman's character when he spoke to her? Sure he did.

What did he ask her for?

CLASS MEMBER:

A drink of water.

PRESIDENT JIMMY CARTER:

A drink of water. Did he have a cup with him or a dipper? No. So what was he going to do? He was going to drink what? Out of her bucket, where her lips had been and where her hands had been. He was going to drink out of the same vessel that she used to drink from with her prostitute's mouth.

And she couldn't believe it. She said, "Why are you talking to me? Why do you speak to me? You're a Jew and I'm a Samaritan. You're a man. I'm a woman." So the encounter was one that was a bridging of a tremendous chasm or gap. And Jesus' disciples, when they returned, were quite surprised. And perhaps their opinion of Jesus fell some, that he would associate himself with this kind of woman. What was the woman's reaction to Christ after she said, "Why are you talking to me?"

Surprised. That's right. What else? She was embarrassed. I think so. She didn't know quite how to handle it. And what was Jesus' point in the encounter that he pursued? Was it to get a drink of water? What was it?

Forgiveness. Living water. To challenge her in her life.

She had a lot to conceal, didn't she? She didn't want Jesus to know. She knew that he knew that she was a Samaritan and a woman, but she had a lot more to hide. And Jesus tested her, didn't he? What did he tell her that tested her, do you think? He said, "Where's your husband?" And what did she say? "I don't have a husband." She said, "I don't have a husband."

And Jesus then said, "That's right, you don't have a husband, because the man you're living with now is not your husband. And you've lived with five other men before this."

Did she run away? No, she didn't. I think a natural thing for a woman like that to do would be to maybe cover her face with a veil and to take her bucket and leave, because it must have been excruciatingly embarrassing for her. Why do you think she stayed there?

The Holy Spirit was working with her. I'm sure God's hand was on her. She was astounded that he knew. I mean, that was certainly an intriguing thing for somebody like a fortune teller to say, "That's right. You've done this in your life," and she knew she never had seen him before. A feeling of hope, okay. What else?

Fear, that's right. I think because there was an unknown quantity there, and she probably wanted to say, "Well, what is this power that this man has or this trick that this man has?" But there was something else. She saw that he was a prophet. That was her guess. She said, "What are you, a prophet?" There was something else. What is it?

CLASS MEMBERS:

She wanted to know him more. … She was lonesome.

PRESIDENT JIMMY CARTER:

I think the reason she didn't run away at first was she didn't have any friends. She was a lonely woman. None of the other women who were self-respecting would speak to her. I'm sure the women that went to church every Sabbath wouldn't speak to her.

And I doubt if she had anybody to talk to her except men who wanted her body. She had been a despised person, and perhaps she was filled with her own lack of self-respect and worth and her own sinfulness. I think she probably felt dirty. And here was someone who really transformed her instantly, and the fact that he said, "You've had five men with you before," was significant. Not only because he seemed to be a fortune teller or a prophet, but what else? Because he had spoken to her knowing it.

If he had thought she was a pure woman, she could understand how he could speak to her and ask her for a drink of water out of her bucket. But I'm sure the thought went through her mind, "This man asked me for a drink of water out of my own bucket, and he knew who I was. He knew what I was."

So there was an instant realization in her own mind that at least one person on earth thinks I'm somebody and thinks I can be at least a transient friend. And she wanted to go into it a little bit more, so she said, "What are you, a prophet? You think you're as good as Jacob, our forefather, who gave us this water to drink?" Somebody tell me the next part of the conversation.

CLASS MEMBER:

He gave her the living water.

PRESIDENT JIMMY CARTER:

Yes. Jesus said, "Jacob gave you this water, yes, that's true, but I can give you living water." He said, "You don't have to come."

She said, "You mean I don't have to come to the well every day to get water? I don't have to be embarrassed by coming here by myself?"

And Jesus said, "I can not only give you water that's still that you can drink, but—what? Living water that wells up like a spring."

And she said, in effect, "Nobody could do that." Except who? Except the Messiah. And Jesus said what?

Jesus said, "The man you're talking to is a Messiah."

I'm not a good historian about it and I don't understand it, but I'm not sure that Jesus had ever told his fellow Jews that up till then. Had he? I'm not sure. Why do you think he would tell her, "I'm the Messiah," and he really hadn't told his own disciples that in just so many words? He certainly hadn't told the priests in the synagogue, even the good ones who were studying to genuinely learn about God. He never had got on a street corner and said, "I am Christ, the Son of God. I am the Messiah." Why do you think he told her that?

CLASS MEMBER:

Up until that time, salvation had only been for the Jews, and now he was saying it was for the whole world.

PRESIDENT JIMMY CARTER:

Yeah, but why do you think he singled her out to tell her something that he didn't even tell the Jews who were eligible for salvation?

CLASS MEMBERS:

So she could bear witness.

PRESIDENT JIMMY CARTER:

But I think that some of the Jews with whom he talked could also bear witness. I'm trying to draw a distinction between her and the Jews. Yes.

CLASS MEMBERS:

She was more open, and she brought up the subject. She asked him. She needed it.

PRESIDENT JIMMY CARTER:

She needed it. She really needed it. If anybody ever needed it, she did.

She moved from [an attitude] of alienation and consternation to one of a casual conversation. To one of a realization of friendship, at least to drink out of the same bucket. To one of saying, "Are you a fortune teller or a prophet?" To a realization that, in spite of her sins, he cared for her. To the belief that he might be as great as Jacob, to a hope that he might be the Son of God.

There's another difference, too, that I wouldn't have known about had I not studied the lesson this morning. And that is there was a difference in how the Samaritans looked upon the Messiah compared to how the Jews looked on the Messiah.

What kind of Messiah were the Jews looking for? A king. Somebody like David, who would come in and lead them and cast away the Romans and set himself up as a religious and a temporal ruler together. That's what the Jews wanted, and that's what Jesus did not want.

But the Samaritans, now what about them? What were they looking for in a Messiah?

Instead of a ruler, kind of a teacher, right? A religious teacher to explain the mysteries of life that concern people, about sin and redemption and salvation and how to bridge the gap, not between two people, but between me and God.

That's what the Samaritans were waiting for. Not like David, but like whom? Moses. They wanted to be delivered. They wanted to be taught. They wanted to be brought back to God. They wanted to be saved, spiritually.

And Jesus recognized in this woman, a representative of the Samaritans, who wanted the kind of Messiah that he was, not somebody who was looking for a Messiah to strike down the Romans with a sword, to ride on a white horse. So he said, "The one that you're waiting for, the Messiah is the man you're talking to." And the disciples came back then, and what did she do?

She went into the town. What kind of attitude do you think she had? Joyous, right? She was excited, wasn't she?

[S]he forgot her bucket. She forgot her water jar. I doubt if she owned very much. I would guess that one of the precious things that she had, speaking about material things, was her water bucket, and she ran off and left it.

She had, in two or three words in John, she had already recognized in a demonstration by her action, which I'm sure she didn't think about, that distinction that Christ drew between giving you a drink of water and giving you eternal living water. She forgot about the water bucket, and she ran into the village knowing about her reputation. And what did she tell the villagers there?

She didn't run in and say, "I have met the Messiah." She said, "I've met a man that knew about my life." And she said, in effect, "Is it possible that this man might be the Messiah?"

I think she knew that he was. I believe that. But if she had gone in and said, "I've met the Messiah." ... She didn't want to be rejected, and she might very well have been rejected, but the way she expressed it kind of created a mystery: "I've met a fortune teller, a prophet or somebody that can tell me about all my background. I've never seen him before. He's never been around here before. Can this possibly be the Messiah?"

And she kind of created an attitude among the people who lived in Sychar that let them take the initiative, to let those big shots in Sychar say, "Let us go and find out if this is the Messiah."

And she created in their minds an inquisitive attitude, and not an attitude that they were students and this prostitute was teaching them. She used some very good psychology. So they came out and met Christ. And what was the result?

Many of them believed. And so what did Jesus do? Leave? He stayed there a couple of days. He stayed there a couple of days. In his short life, he spent two days in that little tiny village, not as a healer, not as a preacher, not as a teacher, as what?

As the Son of God, as the Messiah. At least in that little tiny part of the world for those couple of days, there's a general sense here that they talked to him and listened to him, at least many of them believing that he was the Son of God.

So that was a special demonstration of tearing down divisions that exist between us and our neighbors, us and those we despise, and a human being and God. And the disciples were filled with consternation. They couldn't figure it out.

They were looking on down the road, I'm sure, as you know, many of them knew that he was the Son of God, but they were saying that this is a precious bit of information we have. "We know the Messiah. And someday in the future, we're going to really tell people about it."

And what did Jesus say about the harvest? Does anybody remember?

He said, "Here's the harvest. Why do you want to wait four months?" Here it is right here. This woman is a harvest. These despised Samaritans are the harvest. You don't have to wait until I'm gone. You don't have to wait until next month. You don't have to wait till we get to Canaan or Galilee, where he was going. Here it is, right here.

The person that you work with every day, the student that sits in the next desk, the members of your own family. Here it is, right here. What are you waiting for?

Does anybody see a lesson for us? It's quite obscure, but does anybody see it? [*Carter laughs.*]

Absolutely. We break down the barriers sometimes in a highly publicized way. We've made a lot of progress in our country between Black and white people.

And there's a tendency on our part to say, "Well, gee, the Civil Rights Acts and Martin Luther King Jr.'s life's work has solved that problem once and for all." Right? No, it's a continuing thing.

And we have a tendency to kind of rest on our laurels and say, "Well, we've done our part. We weren't there, but there were people that were there, and it was my Congress that passed the law. And so we've broken down those racial barriers, so I don't have to worry about that anymore. And we've broken down the religious barriers.

We permit under our constitution, Catholics and Jews and Muslims and even atheists to live without persecution."

So I, as an American citizen and as a Christian, I don't have to worry about religious barriers anymore because, you know, that's been taken care of. We don't have quite as easy a time about the barriers of good versus bad, pure versus defiled.

I'm sure when I say that, almost all of us say, "Well, he means that I'm good and that I'm not out witnessing to the defiled or the sinful."

Sometimes the church creates a barrier in itself because it tends to encapsulate us in a mantle of respectability and security and good-ness and decency and religious commitment. Amos said, "I hate, and I despise your feasts and your institutions." He was talking about the church of his day. He said, "Let justice roll down like water and righteousness like an ever-flowing stream."

Now, it was hard back in those days for justice and righteousness to roll down like water out of the church. And it's hard today. Where is the water? Where is a church filled with righteousness and mercy? Where is that water?

Ourselves, we are the rivers of water. We are the overflowing and ever-flowing stream, dammed up.

Is that stream dammed up by the church? Is it dammed up by our feeling that since we are secure, since we are part of God's commu-nity, since Christ does love us, since we read the Bible, that we can become still and at peace and avoid suffering or exploration?

Most of us have that attitude. We've got it made; therefore, we must be specially blessed. Why should we spoil ourselves or soil ourselves by coming in contact with those who are different, whose lives are filled with drunkenness or prostitution or alienation or crime or sinfulness or just people who are different? So we form still waters and maybe become stagnant because of it.

There's another interrelationship between Christ and this woman. There's something that they had in common. What was it?

CLASS MEMBERS:

They were alone. They needed water. Sorrow. Grief.

PRESIDENT JIMMY CARTER:

Grief, suffering. Right? Okay. Frustration. Christ could look forward in his own life and see what? Sorrow, grief, alienation, suffering. So they were tied together with not only a common hope, but also a common human experience.

Christ knew as vividly as though it had already occurred about his future filled with despair and suffering. And that's why Christ reached out to Mary Magdalene, to others who were despised. He didn't do it from up here, reaching down, did he? He said, in effect, "I'm one of you."

And sometimes that's the hardest thing for a Baptist deacon or a Sunday School teacher or a preacher to do, is to say, "I'm one of you." Not "I'm better than you are, and I feel sorry for you. And I'm here to give you a part of my own goodness and my own favored position in God's eyes. I'm here to share with you my superiority."

But it's almost impossible not to have that attitude knowing that God loves us unless we remember how Christ felt about this woman at the well. Did he love the local rabbi or priest more than he loved this woman? No. I think in a personal way, he loved her most of all because she was the most sinful. She needed it most.

Christ gave us a lot of parables to illustrate this: the woman who had 99 coins and lost one, or 10 coins and lost one; the man who had sheep and lost one, he went out and searched for the one that was lost. And he said, "Doctors don't need to worry about well people, they need to worry about sick people."

But we tend to gather around ourselves as Christians—charged with Christ, with a direct responsibility—the well people, the ones that are like us, so that we're safe and secure and we don't have to shatter our lives or our concepts. We don't have to stand in danger of being embarrassed.

One of the most fearsome things is to be embarrassed … to get yourself out on a limb and have it chopped off or to be publicly scorned or rejected. We are kind of reluctant when we go to a convention or something to reach out to somebody and say, "My name's Jimmy Carter. I'd like to meet you." Because we're not quite sure if that person will respond in a friendly way or be rude to us and reject us. And everybody needs to have a sense that we are accepted and so forth.

So we are reluctant to be that courageous for Christ, to go to somebody and say, "I'm here as one of you, a sinner like you, loved by God, to share with you my knowledge of Christ and my suffering." Because we might be rejected. And wouldn't that be terrible to be rejected?

But some of us will live out the rest of our lives—five years, 15, 20, 25, 30, 40 years—and never break through the obstacles that separate us from those that Christ tells us to go to. And in a sense of timidity, we directly violate the will of Christ.

Now, all of us are different, and we all have different responsibilities in different ways, but it takes a lot of strength for someone to admit "I myself am sinful. I'm not blessed with God's forgiveness because I'm good. I repent of my own sins daily. I confront my own sins daily. And it puts me naturally in a position of equality or understanding or comprehension or compassion or love with those that don't know Christ."

You can't witness to somebody from an ivory tower. You've got to be one of them. And it's not an artificiality because we are one of them. We are not better in God's eyes than the prostitute at the well. We're sinful in the eyes of God. We're not saved because we're good. We're not better because we come to church in the eyes of God. All of us are sinful.

And we don't deserve God's mercy just because we're church members. But it takes a lot of courage, and it takes a lot of comprehension of others, and we can't do it by ourselves. There's too much for us to do by ourselves.

So the closeness with which we live with Christ is what makes it possible for us to reach out and to let our own lives be a beneficent factor. When that woman felt close to Christ, she reached out and said, "Look what I've got. Look what I've found. My life's been changed. I forgot my bucket, but I wanted to tell you about it."

So the Samaritan woman had the same experience that we've had. She learned Christ and she had an experience after that that we ought to emulate if we are as good as she is. She had to tell somebody and exemplify in her own action what Christ was, what she saw in him.

Well, this is a good and an interesting lesson, I think. It's one that is quite pertinent to us. We didn't even read the Bible. I'm sorry I didn't read it this morning. ... And the last point I want to leave you with is, where are the barriers created? [S]omebody else doesn't build barriers around us. We're the ones that build the barriers to protect ourselves. And we are the ones that have to tear down the barriers.

And if we get on our knees when we get home and say, "God, show me how to tear down the barriers that separate me from you, and let me tear down barriers that separate other people from you," then I think God will do it. Thank you.

FRED GREGG:

Aren't you glad you were here? If you enjoyed it, say, "Amen."

Mr. President, if I ever teach that lesson again, the subject's going to be "She Left Her Bucket." That was a tremendous job. Let's all stand and be dismissed.

Our Father, we thank you for this day. We thank thee for the privilege that we have to come into thy house and to study thy word. And Father, we thank thee for the teacher today, and we pray that thou would guide and direct him. Give him special guidance this week. Be with our First Lady as she goes about doing her duties. We pray that thou will be with our pastor. May this be a glorious Lord's day and whatever's accomplished, we'll give you the praise because we'll ask it in your name and for your sake. Amen.

1978

The Sunday School lessons for the Couples Class at First Baptist D.C. were spelled out in the curriculum, including the Scriptures and titles for each lesson. In retrospect, the titles for the five lessons taught by President Carter in 1978 were apt.

The first lesson, "Jesus and the Holy Spirit," on January 29, 1978, contained something of a self-assuring message for Carter's second year in office: "[W]ith Christ, with the Holy Spirit, we're given the strength that's adequate to meet the responsibility put on us by God, and that's a big responsibility."

President Carter taught "Resources for Facing Opposition" on March 12, 1978, and the regular Sunday School teacher, Fred Gregg, closed the class with an unusually specific prayer request: "I want to ask all of you to get on your knees during this week, because this is a very vital week, when decisions are going to be made that could greatly affect this country. And I want everybody to be very much in prayer that the right decisions will be made."

After worship at First Baptist and lunch at the White House that Sunday, Carter worked the phone—hard. Between 3:45 and 7 p.m., Carter spoke with 15 U.S. senators—Republicans and Democrats, including Barry Goldwater, Bob Dole, Richard Lugar, Ted Stevens, and Dennis DeConcini—lobbying for their votes for the treaty that would transfer control of the Panama Canal from the United States to Panama.

Carter, and maybe a few kneeling Baptists, got the first part of the treaty through the Senate four days later, on March 16; the second part was approved a month later.

Carter was back at the Sunday School lectern on June 25, 1978, teaching a lesson titled, "The Growth of Concern." He wouldn't return to teaching at First Baptist for three months, although he attended worship services at the church twice in August and again on September 3. On September 4, Carter left D.C. for the presidential retreat north of Washington

Carter was scheduled to teach at First Baptist September 17, but let Fred Gregg know that he had some business to wrap up. When Carter took the lectern on September 24, he was wry: "Well," he said, "it's always nice to come back from a two-week vacation at Camp David."

On December 10, 1978, in Oslo, Norway, the leaders of Egypt and Israel, Anwar Sadat and Menachem Begin, received the Nobel Peace Prize for the accords achieved during the 13 days in September at Camp David with President Carter. Carter would receive the prize years later, but on that Sunday in 1978, he was teaching the weekly lesson for the Couples Class titled, "Forgiveness: A Two-Way Street."

JESUS AND THE HOLY SPIRIT

JANUARY 29, 1978

JOHN 14:15-31

PRESIDENT JIMMY CARTER:

Fred [Gregg], I thank you for your friendship and what you mean to me. It's good to have a Sunday School teacher that becomes an instant part of your personal and family life, particularly when you are living in the White House and you've severed a lot of your relationships back home that provided stability for you. Our pastor and our Sunday School teacher have performed that function in the life of my family.

He always seems to pick out the difficult subjects for me to teach. This one's "Jesus and the Holy Spirit." And there are a lot of people here present this morning that could do a much better job of teaching this lesson than I can, but I'm going to call on them for help.

Paul Tillich said that, for a Christian, just having to live and to face a certain death creates enough anxiety for a human being, and that a church, in its teachings about Christ, should not add anxiety to a person's consciousness.

We have enough anxiety as it is. The ministry of Christ, the relationship between us and Christ, should not be built on a fear that's deliberately instilled in our hearts, of God or of Christ.

Another theologian that I read every now and then is [Reinhold] Niebuhr. He says that anxiety is a basis for all human creativity.

That's a very far-reaching statement. And I wonder if anybody can see what Niebuhr is trying to say—that anxiety, which is a kind of a negative word, is a basis for all human creativity. Anybody have a thought about that?

How about someone who struggles always to improve oneself through praying, through learning, and then attains a worthy objective? What's the general reaction to that in our lives?

That kind of person, you can imagine them. Maybe that's the way to describe you. When you're setting a goal for yourself and work hard and then achieve it, what's the normal response?

Preparation for the next goal. Not to sit back and say, "Well, I'm 25 years old. I've graduated from college. I've graduated summa cum laude. I've got a good job. Now, I'll relax the rest of my life."

In fact, the kind of person who's driven to take advantage of opportunities—to stretch one's mind, to stretch one's heart—ordinarily will not, at an intermediate point in life, stop. So there is an urging. And when you see how much you can stretch your mind or heart, and if you can achieve an intermediate goal, it creates in your mind an inclination to look higher, to set another goal, and to work.

Well, that setting of goals that are doubtful of achievement creates an uncertainty, an anxiety, a doubt—that's a challenge. How about as far as a Christian life is concerned? What is there within a Christian's life that creates an anxiety that might lead to higher accomplishment or creativity?

A desire to do God's will.

We read the Bible. We study the life of Christ. We probe our own consciousness. We have frequent confrontations with God or encounters with God. And the despairing aspect of it is that we as Christians know what? As we measure ourselves against God's will, what?

CLASS MEMBER:

Fall well short.

PRESIDENT JIMMY CARTER:

We fall well short. And I think one of the things that Christ talked about more than any other subject—I haven't analyzed it word for word—is self-satisfaction. Pride. I've accomplished what I ought to as a Christian, which implies perfection. I'm perfect. I'm equal to God.

Well, that's the very thing that Christ warns us about. And the most notable example is a Pharisee prayer, "I thank you that I'm not like other men." And Jesus said that guy was praying to whom?

CLASS MEMBER:

Himself.

PRESIDENT JIMMY CARTER:

To himself, yes. To himself. He wasn't even praying to God. So the failure of all of us to measure up to God's expectations and demands and laws creates a predictable and a beneficial anxiety or concern that we are not measuring up to God's standards.

One of the easily explained definitions of that anxiety is an awareness of one's own sin, which is a prerequisite to the redemptive plan of God. If we don't see that we have sinned, then there's no way that we can be submissive or ask forgiveness or turn away from sin and be redeemed.

On one of the missionary visits that I have made in my life, we went in to see a woman. And as we started to explain the plan of salvation, the first part of it was all have sinned, and she said, "No, sir. Not me." That's where the witnessing broke down, because she would never acknowledge the fact that she had committed sin.

So anxiety is not necessarily a bad word. It creates a tension within ourselves, which is an inspiration, a challenge, and a basis for self-condemnation or self-acknowledgement of inadequacy or sin. Well, we try to overcome those anxieties, but in effect, we merely change one for another. We substitute one for another.

This is not bad, because we ought to be anxious about our shortcomings. We ought to be anxious about our lack of knowledge of God. We ought to be concerned about how much more we could know about the world or about people around us. But that's just part of it. That's maybe beneficial.

But there's some other concerns or worries that we have that preoccupy us that are not of concern to God. What is one of the major, all-pervading worries of human beings?

CLASS MEMBERS:

Health. Money. Success. Death.

PRESIDENT JIMMY CARTER:

Right. And our concern or our overconcern about human death is a result of our elevating in our own mind the importance of our own human life. If we think that our existence on earth is the most important thing of all, then to lose it is one of our most important losses. And of course, this was not at all in accordance with the teachings of Christ. The most important single theme of the New Testament is what?

CLASS MEMBER:

Eternal life.

PRESIDENT JIMMY CARTER:

Eternal life. Demonstrated or proven by what? The resurrection of Jesus. And Paul has said that without the resurrection, there would be no purpose in his teaching or the witnessing of the disciples. Christ's death and resurrection proved to us that there's life after death, but it also proved to us that a preoccupation with this present human life should not be ascendant in our own consciousness. But still knowing that, we are concerned about death.

Last weekend, we were at a funeral for my uncle, who was almost like a father to me. He was my daddy's only brother. And all of us experience that repetitive sorrow in our own lives, the deaths of our parents, the death sometimes of a child, the death of our spouse. And it's a time of crushing despair or sorrow. And the Bible passages today are the ones that are most often read at a funeral, at a time of death.

Well, I think that at that moment, one of the characteristics of that loss is exemplified by one of the first experiences in the life of a little child. All of you who've had children or who've nursed grandchildren and so forth know that a frequent dream of a young child is demonstrated when the child wakes up screaming in the middle of the night, and the parent goes to comfort the little baby. And the baby says, "I thought you were gone. I thought you had left me." And the mother says, "I'm right here and I'm with you." So when we lose a loved one, there's a sense of abandonment or loneliness or an empty space in our life.

And this is what Christ is talking about because this is one of his final messages to his disciples who loved him, who cared about him, who couldn't understand the interrelationship between a human existence and the thrust of Christ's ministry in his life. And he's trying to explain it to them. He says, "In a little while, I'm going to be gone, and I won't return later. I will return temporarily." But he's trying to convince them and us that we need not ever be alone, that we are not ever abandoned, that God always loves us.

Let's turn to John 14. And if someone would, in the King James Version, read the 15th verse. Anybody? It's also in your Sunday School book.

CLASS MEMBER:

[15] If ye love me, keep my commandments.

PRESIDENT JIMMY CARTER:

If you love me, keep my commandments. Right? All right, now somebody read the same thing in the Revised Standard Version.

CLASS MEMBER:

[15] If you love me, you will keep my commandments.

PRESIDENT JIMMY CARTER:

Okay? There's a difference in it. The person says, "If you love me, keep my commandments." That's the King James Version. The Revised Standard Version said, "If you love me, you will keep my commandments." They're not in conflict, although they have a different emphasis. But here in the initiation of one of the final speeches or talks of Christ to us, he's trying to show what love is. And one of the remarkable demonstrations of love is what?

CLASS MEMBER:

Obedience.

PRESIDENT JIMMY CARTER:

Obedience. To keep the commandments of Christ. "If you love me ..." If you and I love Christ, we will what? Keep his commandments. If we don't keep his commandments, that's a demonstration of an absence of our love for him.

And we can talk and come to Sunday School and sing hymns and put on a pious attitude and claim to love Christ and not keep his commandments and prove thereby that we are liars, that we don't really love Christ, we love ourselves. We love the approbation that comes to us from Christians as we pretend to love Christ.

So the keeping of Christ's commandments is a necessary proof of whether or not we love Christ. It doesn't matter which one you prefer. "If you love me, keep my commandments. If you love me, you will keep my commandments." They really kind of strengthen each other, those interpretations.

So Christian love obeys. There is a constant interrelationship or interplay between two things. One is the demands of God on us, and the other one is the grace of God. The demands of God and the grace of God. The demands of God are quite stringent. How can we be perfect? Christ said, "Be perfect." That's the demand of God. In not being perfect, we sin.

The grace of God means regardless of our sin, we're forgiven. With Christ, with God, we can overcome a temptation and we can reach great heights of achievement. We can experience a genuine meaning of love. We can overcome our innate human selfishness.

By ourselves? No. With Christ? Yes. And God gave us a will. He didn't make us automatons so he can say, "This is Jimmy Carter and I'll make him do this and that, and he has no will of his own, therefore he'll be perfect because I control it." I have the power, the authority to reject God, if I wish.

Love is not a quiescent thing. It's not something that just kind of floats around. ... Christ's life is a demonstration of love because of what he taught or said—that's just a very particular part of it.

It's because of what he did, what he actually accomplished, his actions. And one of the things that Christ is teaching us in his life as an example is that love is an active thing, a demonstrable thing. We could isolate ourselves, not do anything, not hurt anybody. That would not be an expression of love.

And love is a difficult thing. It's a precious thing. And as almost every other kind of precious thing, it has a lot of counterfeiters, a lot of false kinds of love that we tend to substitute for the more difficult kind.

The difficult kind of love is when we act in concert with God to improve the life of others. We kind of form a partnership with Christ to improve the life of others, and that's a demonstration of love.

In the process, with Christ's help, we can forget about ourselves. We can even forget about getting credit for helping others.

We don't have to pray on the corner of the street. We don't have to drop our money in the collection plate with a great clatter so everybody sees us. We don't have to draw attention to the fact that we love others.

If it's a genuine love, and to overcome those human temptations for self-recognition, it has to be with and through Christ.

But the bad thing about it is that almost 2,000 years ago, Christ died. And his disciples who loved him, knowing that he was facing death, were bereft of consolation, and they felt that they were going to be abandoned.

So here is where Christ spoke to reassure them and to reassure us. Let's read the 16th and 17th verses.

CLASS MEMBER:

[16] And I will pray the Father, and he shall give you another Comforter, that he may abide with you for ever;
[17] Even the Spirit of truth; whom the world cannot receive, because it seeth him not, neither knoweth him: but ye know him; for he dwelleth with you, and shall be in you.

PRESIDENT JIMMY CARTER:

Okay. Now, here is one of those mysterious kinds of statements that Christ made that we have studied and learned and which we cherish and which gives us an assuaging concept for our own lives. The Greek word was *"parakletos,"* and we have a modern word, "Paraclete." Does anyone know what "Paraclete" means?

"Para" means at one's side as a helper. A paramedic is one who's at the side of a doctor to help him. The *"kletos"* part means to call. So to call to one's side to help. Jesus said, "I'm going to ask God, or God will call someone to be at your side to help." At Jimmy Carter's side, at Fred Gregg's side, at Paul's side, at Peter's side, there's going to be someone at your side to help.

What are some of the characteristics of the Paraclete or the Holy Spirit as we call him? What are some of the functions of the Holy Spirit? He's an advisor. He's a counselor. What else?

CLASS MEMBERS:

A comforter. An advocate for us to God. A convictor. Teacher. Ever present.

PRESIDENT JIMMY CARTER:

Ever present. That's a distinction with Christ himself, right? Christ pointed out, "My time on earth is limited." He's ever present … and he is not only here forever, but he can be everywhere, right? Christ was subject to death, right? At least in the physical form. His presence with the disciples was limited.

The Holy Spirit, Jesus said, would be here forever. He can't be killed and separated from us. He's a consoler and, someone said, a teacher. Quite a remarkable entity for us and the person in the Holy Trinity about whom we speak least of all. He's an extension of God's redemptive presence on earth after Christ. These are some of the most remarkable and gratifying characteristics that we could hope for.

The Holy Spirit is a personal reality that lives in the disciples of Christ and lets the word of Christ continue and prevail through us. What did Judas, not Iscariot, ask Jesus? Does anybody remember?

Judas asked perhaps the same question that we would ask. Why didn't Jesus, just in a constant blinding demonstration of godliness or all-powerfulness or miraculous presence, convince all the nonbelievers?

I think Jesus saw several things there that we didn't cover in this lesson. What could you do that would be more miraculous than to call and say, "Lazarus, come forth from the tomb where you've been dead four days" and have Lazarus walk out?

Or heal the blind or give the most exalted teaching on earth or demonstrate in miraculous terms, almost, that meekness could inherit the earth, that love could be all pervasive. That purity of life could actually be demonstrated by a human being. Now, Jesus in his ministry there had performed these remarkably shocking things, and many had rejected him. Jesus.

How many of you have seen the movie *Oh, God*? How many of you were disappointed or repelled by it? I thought it was one of the best movies I've seen, and I dreaded it. I thought it was going to be terrible. I was afraid it would be sacrilegious to have George Burns be [God].

But I would advise you and all Christians, if you have a chance, to go and see it. And I won't cover all the movie at all, but the thing that I would like to point out is that I would imagine that the rejection of George Burns in this movie was fairly similar to the rejection of Christ when he was on earth. And I don't say that in a sacrilegious way.

But I imagine it was just as hard for people back then to believe in Christ as an actual Son of God, as it was for John Denver and others to believe that this could actually be God, and it explains it in a subtle, in a thought-provoking way.

But the rejection of Christ in one three-year ministry was the most dominant human reaction. If you ran a public opinion poll in Israel during the time of Christ's life and say, "Do you believe that Jesus is the Son of God, is the Messiah?" it would probably be lower than the number of people that supported the Panama Canal treaties a year ago [1977], lower than 8 percent. There just wasn't an overwhelming recruitment of broad thousands of people to Christ.

It was a very difficult thing. Let's read the 18th, 19th and 20th verses. I want to get through prayer time.

CLASS MEMBER:

[18] I will not leave you comfortless: I will come to you.

[19] Yet a little while, and the world seeth me no more; but ye see me: because I live, ye shall live also.

[20] At that day ye shall know that I am in my Father, and ye in me, and I in you.

PRESIDENT JIMMY CARTER:

Jesus knew that death was real for himself, physically; for his disciples, that the fear of death was there and that tragedy in a Christian's life even was always a possibility, in fact, a likelihood.

And those disciples and those of us who think that just because we are Christians, we believe in Christ, that we're going to be immune to fear or trepidation or tragedy, we're sadly mistaken.

Christ himself who was perfect certainly was not spared tragedy. And I think almost all the disciples met a tragic end.

So for us to search or to rationalize the ordering of our lives, to avoid tragedy, to avoid conflict, to avoid embarrassment, to avoid disappointment is kind of an un-Christian thing to do.

And so Jesus is trying to tell the disciples that you're not going to be comfortless, you're not going to be desolate, unless you depend entirely upon human things. If you depend upon wealth, if you depend upon social status, if you depend upon an unending human existence, if you depend upon the constant presence of all those you love without interruption in that relationship, then your life is going to be tragic in its totality.

But if you wipe out all those things as frivolous, as superficial, and substitute for it the very important relationship between you and Christ, you and God, you and the Holy Spirit, then your life can be fulfilled in spite of human tragedy, which is inevitable.

It was kind of a shocking thing for the disciples to try to correlate physical loss—that Christ was going to leave them—and the grace of God, the love of God, the permanence of Christ's influence. How could a man be dead and gone and still have an influence that would last through eternity?

And Jesus said, "This is the way it's going to be." The Holy Spirit is coming. The Paraclete is coming, the comforter is coming, the consoler is coming, the teacher is coming, the spirit of myself is coming.

Part of the presence of God is coming to be with you, permanently. It's not an intangible thing. The tangibility of it, the realness of it exists in our receptivity, our willingness to accept the Holy Spirit, our willingness to let the Holy Spirit come. And where did Christ say that the Holy Spirit would dwell, would live, where? In us!

It is going to live in you, going to dwell in you. It's going to be there as an extension of myself, inside of you, in your heart, in your mind, in your presence, in your prayers, with you. I don't think the disciples quite understood it. I never have understood quite why. But when Jesus came back after being resurrected, what kind of people saw him?

Just people who believed in him. There weren't any nonbelievers who saw him so far as we know. And that's why Judas was so concerned. The ones you want to reach are the nonbelievers. Why come back just to us? And what was Jesus' answer to that?

CLASS MEMBER:

For those who love and obey me.

PRESIDENT JIMMY CARTER:

For those who love and obey me. Right. Let's read the 21st through the 24th verses that will bring in the part about Judas. Listen to the conversation now.

CLASS MEMBER:

21 He that hath my commandments, and keepeth them, he it is that loveth me: and he that loveth me shall be loved of my Father, and I will love him, and will manifest myself to him.
22 Judas saith unto him, not Iscariot, Lord, how is it that thou wilt manifest thyself unto us, and not unto the world?
23 Jesus answered and said unto him, If a man love me, he will keep

my words: and my Father will love him, and we will come unto him, and make our abode with him.

[24] He that loveth me not keepeth not my sayings: and the word which ye hear is not mine, but the Father's which sent me.

PRESIDENT JIMMY CARTER:

Jesus returns again to what word?

CLASS MEMBER:

Love.

PRESIDENT JIMMY CARTER:

Love means what?

CLASS MEMBER:

Obedience.

PRESIDENT JIMMY CARTER:

Obedience. Love, obey. You've sung the hymn a lot of times. But that's one of the most difficult ways to demonstrate love, isn't it? To obey. But Christ said that through the Holy Spirit, for those who love me, who keep my word, God will love them.

And in their existence, in their influence, down through the ages, the nonbelievers can be reached through Judas, not Iscariot, through Peter, through John, who else?

Through us. And here's a charge that Christ gave to his own disciples that applies directly to us. We're weak, we're sinful, we're doubtful. We're anxious, we're lonely. We're not influential. We're insecure by ourselves, but we need not ever be alone, and we need not ever be doubtful. We need never be filled with anxiety. We need never be fearful nor weak because with Christ, with the Holy Spirit, we're given the strength that's adequate to meet the responsibility put on us by God, and that's a big responsibility.

But I'll repeat myself: with the Holy Spirit, with Christ, the presence of God, we are strong enough, forceful enough, competent enough, brave enough to meet the responsibilities put on us by God. We can carry out God's purposes, with him. We can't carry out God's purposes against him. And, with that presence of God, with that partnership that we ourselves have to form on our own initiative, we can be rewarded. Let's see how. Let's read the 25th and 26th verses. … Let's read the 27th, too.

CLASS MEMBER:

25 These things have I spoken unto you, being yet present with you.
26 But the Comforter, which is the Holy Ghost, whom the Father will send in my name, he shall teach you all things, and bring all things to your remembrance, whatsoever I have said unto you.
27 Peace I leave with you, my peace I give unto you: not as the world giveth, give I unto you. Let not your heart be troubled, neither let it be afraid.

PRESIDENT JIMMY CARTER:

Very fine. Jesus said, "The holy comforter is coming in my name, in the name of Jesus." the Holy Spirit is with us. [When] torn by anxiety and fear … and by disappointment and loneliness and by a sense of abandonment like an orphan. Jesus said, "In spite of all those things, peace I leave with you."

You'll never see me again except just briefly after my resurrection, but peace I leave with you. My peace I give unto you. There was a peace that existed all over the earth right then known as the ... I can't pronounce it, Pax Romana.

Under the Romans, the subjugated people had lost the spirit to rebel, and their physical needs were pretty well met, so there was peace. Is that the peace that Christ was talking about? No. He says, "Not as the world giveth, give I unto you. Let not your heart be troubled, neither let it be afraid."

This is a very difficult lesson to understand, but it's a very consoling lesson, and it also puts a responsibility on us. Jesus didn't just spread oil on troubled waters. He just didn't rub balm on us to make us impervious to tragedy or disappointment.

He said those kinds of things—if the Holy Spirit's in your heart—are just superficial, they're almost inconsequential. As a matter of fact, those trials, those tribulations, those testings can bring you closer to God, closer to the reality of life, closer to personal fulfillment, closer to happiness, closer to real peace.

A lot of people identify our present age as the age of anxiety. One of the things that causes us anxiety is we measure what we have against the TV or movie image of people that have more in a physical sense, and it creates in us a sense of inadequacy. Why am I not as rich as that person? Why am I not as famous as that person? It must be because I failed.

And we measure failure by human standards or human measurements and forget about the fact that God's standards for Christians are quite different, and in this lesson is spelled out five standards for God who gave them to us by which we can measure ourselves.

These are tests of a Christian that I jotted down. First of all, a Christian must demonstrate obedience to God's commandments—not easy.

Second, the measurement of a Christian is the presence of the Holy Spirit. There's not a Christian here who at some time or another has not felt in a tangible way, a provable way, perhaps even a miraculous way—I know I have—the presence of the Holy Spirit, but it takes a deliberate opening of our heart. In time of trial or tribulation or testing or the performance of God's will, there comes a time when you've got to have some help, and you can feel it when it comes.

The third thing is a growing understanding, with the accent on growing, which means that all through our lives, we ought to be searching for a deeper relationship with Christ through the Holy Spirit, a deeper relationship with God through the Holy Spirit, a deeper relationship with our fellow human beings through the Holy Spirit.

And if we ever reach that plateau where we think this is it, I have measured up to God's requirements—my life is a success, I'm an adequate Christian—that's when we lose something precious, and the thing that we lose is a requirement for a Christian to search more, to dig more deeply, and to grow an understanding of God.

The fourth thing is that our life's work be consistent with Christ's life. This is also very difficult, and when we read in the New Testament what Christ actually did, what his life meant, and then measure ourselves against it, we can't obviously meet the perfection of Christ, but the thrust of our lives, the philosophy under which or through which we live, our attitude to other people ought to be consistent with the life of Christ as we know it.

And the fifth characteristic of a Christian is an inner peace. It's not something you can will on yourselves. You can't say, "Tomorrow I'm going to start and have an inner peace in my heart." It slips away from you. It's not something that's guaranteed to you just because you want it.

It comes with the first four. If we subjugate our will to God, if we open our hearts to the Holy Spirit, if our life is consistent for the purposes or examples of Christ, if our dependence is upon a partnership with God and our relationship with him and others, then we will have an inner sense of peace. That's part of the process of being born again, born as a child of God.

So this lesson is one that shows us, in a sense of offering or gift or grace on the one hand, a sense of tough demands on the other, what our life is and should be and can be after Christ died and was buried and was resurrected and joined God in heaven.

It wasn't the end of the Christian era when Christ left this earth because—in us, through the Holy Spirit—Christ's word can still be heard, Christ's actions can still be witnessed, Christ's purposes can still be realized—through the Holy Spirit, yes, but also through us.

FRED GREGG:

If you enjoyed that, let's say, "Amen."

CLASS MEMBERS:

Amen.

RESOURCES FOR FACING OPPOSITION

MARCH 12, 1978
JOHN 15:18 & 16:33

PRESIDENT JIMMY CARTER:

This is a lesson that I've been looking forward to for several weeks. … It's one that I think exemplifies, in a more personal way, the thing that afflicts us all.

We start out our life as an aware person as soon as we can understand the English language, hearing fairy tales. And there are two phrases that are typical in almost every fairy tale.

Does anybody know what they are?

CLASS MEMBER:

Once upon a time.

PRESIDENT JIMMY CARTER:

Once upon a time. And what's the other one?

CLASS MEMBER:

Lived happily.

PRESIDENT JIMMY CARTER:

Lived happily ever afterwards. That's right.

Well, it kind of gives us a false impression, but maybe it's good when you're two, three, four years old to think that eventually after trials and tribulations and troubles, conflict, testing, sorrows, dangers, that when that episode is over, that "they lived happily ever afterwards" always comes.

And then later on in life, we find that that part of the fairy tale doesn't come true. And this morning we're going to study about the fact that "they lived happily ever afterwards" is something that's not easy to discern.

If you think about Jesus' life and his relationship with people around him, what would be the one word that would come to your mind? I know there'll be a lot of different words, but just call out a few that ... just one word. What?

CLASS MEMBERS:

Love. Caring. Friendship. Compassion. Concern. Servant. Devotion. Sacrifice.

PRESIDENT JIMMY CARTER:

Okay. Sacrifice. All those are very, very good, inspiring, mostly pleasant words, right? Friendship, compassion, love, devotion.

Anybody else? Think of a word that doesn't quite fit into that category.

CLASS MEMBERS:

Suffering. Betrayal. Sorrow. Sacrifice. Light. Treasure. They sought to kill him.

PRESIDENT JIMMY CARTER:

Sought to kill him. Okay. Nobody's got to the word that I want yet.

CLASS MEMBERS:

Joy. Death.

PRESIDENT JIMMY CARTER:

Death? Okay. How many of you studied your lesson? [*Class laughs.*] Okay, but there's a word that describes this lesson today.

Jesus' relationship with the world around him, which is also the disciples' relationship with the world around them after Christ's death. It also is a word that describes the relationship between us as Christians and the world around us to the degree that we commit our lives to Christ.

Conflict. Conflict.

When Jesus was encapsulated or surrounded by his own disciples who believed in him and who loved him, and who were blessed by God with some inspiration and some understanding, there was harmony, there was friendship, there was love.

But almost every time when Jesus reached out and came in contact with the outside world, which was close to him, but not part of his inner circle, the word that characterized almost every time was conflict.

He created tension and he created debate, and he created disharmony and he created misunderstanding. And he created the opposite of love, which was what?

Hatred. Hatred.

It's hard for us in the 20th century to look back on Christ's time when he was living on earth as a man. And it's hard for us to understand: How could anyone have hated my savior? How could anyone have hated Jesus Christ of Nazareth, whose life was epitomized by the words that came out first: love, compassion, understanding, friendship.

But hatred as it focused on Christ among the broad populace was probably a more accurate description of feelings toward Christ than the word "love."

Jesus didn't respond with hatred, but he recognized that it existed. And he suffered because of it, as we know, to the utmost degree.

Why? Why did Christ's life bring out animosity and conflict and hatred? Anybody?

Jesus told us in this lesson. Everybody got their Bibles, turn to John 15. And we'll read three verses, which are not part of the lesson text: 22, 23 and 24. Anybody who has it, would you read it please? Somebody with a strong voice?

CLASS MEMBER:

[22] If I had not come and spoken to them, they would not have been guilty of sin.

PRESIDENT JIMMY CARTER:

Okay, let's stop there for a moment. That's the 22nd verse. Read that again.

CLASS MEMBER:

[22] If I had not come and spoken to them, they would not have been guilty of sin.

PRESIDENT JIMMY CARTER:

Who said that?

CLASS MEMBER:

Jesus.

PRESIDENT JIMMY CARTER:

Jesus. We're all Bible students. We've been studying the Bible since we were three or four years old. How many of you understand what that means? "If I had not come and spoken to them, they would not have been guilty of sin." What do you think it means?

Instruction that they would not otherwise have had about evil and sin.

It's easier to live by the admonition "An eye for an eye, a tooth for a tooth," right, than it is to live by the admonition if someone slaps you on the face, "Turn the other cheek." And it's easier to live by the admonition "Thou shall not kill," than it is to live by the admonition "You shall not hate—or despise or criticize—your brother."

Jesus presented to the world what? A new spirit, a new covenant, a new standard. A new standard for what is right and what is wrong, what's acceptable in the eyes of God and what is not acceptable in the eyes of God.

And you got away from the listing of all kinds of little tiny things that you did on the Sabbath day or exactly how you handled the tithing of mint and spices that grew in your garden to the genuine significance of a life acceptable in the eyes of God.

And Jesus spoke with authority, that there was something about Christ when he witnessed to people either individually like the woman at the well or in vast multitudes like the Sermon on the Mount. And quite often it says, "And they went away perplexed," because this man apparently spoke with authority, apparently spoke directly from God.

And what he said, although it was hard to believe, it was hard to ignore. There was kind of a personal aspect of it that touched individual people's hearts.

People even like Nicodemus had his life transformed; he couldn't forget what Christ told him. So Jesus came into a kind of a complacent religious world where people prided ... themselves on their inner relationship with God's house, God's church, God's rabbis. And all of a sudden, their complacency was torn apart; it was destroyed.

And they had to reexamine the standards that they had set for themselves, and they were not willing to face God's facts in their own lives.

Instead of setting a set of requirements where you very carefully molded them to meet what you were willing to do and then judging other people by those requirements, Christ said, "This is what it means to be a child of God. And this is what you must do to be accepted by God, and this is what you must do to have eternal life. You must repent. You're a sinner."

And a lot of those people said, "I'm not a sinner. You know, I follow all the little laws." Remember the Pharisee said, "Lord, I thank you that I'm not like all these other people. I tithe everything I do. God, thank you for letting me be acceptable in your sight."

And Jesus said, "That man did not go away justifying," but the recognition of one's own sinfulness is a shock. When Christ was alive, there was a shock when his disciples inherited the mantle of speaking for God.

And it's a shock today. And whether we like it or not, we tend to do the same thing that the people who lived around Christ did 2,000 years ago. We tend to make for ourselves a set of rules that suit our own nature, our own incarnation, our own system of priorities.

If we are not tempted by a particular thing, we elevate it to one of the most important requirements of God. If we have temptation and we yield to it, we tend to forget about that or move it from our mind.

And so we build for ourselves a definition of what is acceptable in God's sight that creates a sense of euphoria for us, or complacency for us, or assurance for us, that in God's eyes, we as Christians, we as Baptists, are acceptable.

And when Christ talks about sinners, he's really not talking about me. I know it says, "All are sinners," but he's really not talking about me because I know what goes on in my own heart, and when I do sin, I know the reasons for it. I know the temptations that confronted me, and I know what that other person said that really made me so angry and filled my heart with hatred.

And I know how it is because there are certain worldly responsibilities that I have that might be in conflict with a pure commitment to God, but I understand the circumstances that made me want to take care of my family first. And it's good for my business to be cutting a corner here and cutting a corner there. I understand, and I'm sure God understands also.

But Christ said no. And to the extent that we adhere rigidly to Christ's pure principles, we'll experience conflict.

We're a complacent church. We're a complacent denomination. We're complacent Christians because we've modified the standards of God to suit our own lives.

And it's hard for us to apply to ourselves the phrase, "For all have sinned and come short of the glory of God," and "The wages of sin is death." Surely this doesn't apply to us. We know all the good things we do. We know all the times we pray.

When Jesus said these words, his disciples couldn't quite understand because they had not suffered very much.

Jesus had been the cutting edge of the new spirit, the new setting of standards. His disciples were there with him. They gave him support, but I never have understood quite the reason that they were not brought into all of the comprehension of what Christ was and what his ministry meant that they later learned.

Jesus spoke to them in parables. He spoke to them in riddles. They didn't quite understand exactly what went on, and they were left out of the abuses that were heaped on Christ, even when they walked the dusty roads with him.

Later, they began to feel those problems during the last few hours of Christ's life. The most vivid example that comes to my mind is Peter, who when he was just pressed with the possible condemnation of the authorities, political and religious authorities, he denied his own savior, whom he knew was the Son of God. Just because some serving maid came up to him as he was standing there by the fire and said, "Aren't you one of those people that was with Jesus?" "Oh no, no, I never heard of him before." He did it three times.

That was the first tangible experience of the pressures that fell on the disciples. And Jesus is saying in this lesson, "It's going to come to you." And he also said it's inevitable.

[Nonbelievers] hated Jesus for that reason. And in the process, they hated God whom they professed to love and worship.

Jesus came as a savior, but he also came to judge [and] to condemn their way of life, and that made people uncomfortable and filled with hatred. Let's hear John 16:1-6.

CLASS MEMBER:

[1] These things have I spoken unto you, that ye should not be offended.

[2] They shall put you out of the synagogues: yea, the time cometh, that whosoever killeth you will think that he doeth God service.

[3] And these things will they do unto you, because they have not known the Father, nor me.

[4] But these things have I told you, that when the time shall come, ye

may remember that I told you of them. And these things I said not unto you at the beginning, because I was with you.

⁵ But now I go my way to him that sent me; and none of you asketh me, Whither goest thou?

⁶ But because I have said these things unto you, sorrow hath filled your heart.

PRESIDENT JIMMY CARTER:

Jesus is saying that this is the inevitability or the certainty of conflict and sorrow and condemnation, and he also went on to predict very accurately what was going to happen among people who were religious leaders. The second verse, read that one more time.

CLASS MEMBER:

² They shall put you out of the synagogues: yea, the time cometh, that whosoever killeth you will think that he doeth God service.

PRESIDENT JIMMY CARTER:

Right. Using the voice of God, the people who killed the disciples would say, "I'm doing this because of my faith." And Jesus said, "This is what you're going to have to suffer."

Now, what had occurred by the time this Gospel was written, all the Gospels were written? Absolutely. When John wrote this, he knew that Jesus' prediction had come true. When Jesus said it, they couldn't quite understand.

But by the time this was written, 80, 90, 100 years later, whatever it was, I don't know, it had come true.

The Roman officials had outlawed the church, and the disciples had been excommunicated. They had been kicked out of the church. It was not an easy thing for them to accept. It was a heart-rending thing.

And as you read through the Acts and through the messages of Paul to the early churches, you see how difficult it was for Paul and Peter and John to accept the proposition [that] we are no longer part of the synagogue, we are no longer part of the existing church.

They did not cast away all of their historical religious beliefs.

They wanted to have their intense faith in Christ transported into the existing church, but the existing church said, "No. This is incompatible with anything that we can accept."

So the disciples were excommunicated. They did not consider themselves a pure, separate part of God's kingdom who were renouncing everything that had gone before. They wanted to be part of the existing church and to change the existing church to be compatible with Christ's teachings about love and compassion and understanding and friendship and sinfulness and redemption. But the church said no.

And almost all the disciples, I understand, were actually killed. They lost their lives because they believed in Christ and because they were willing to express their beliefs in spite of the condemnation and the hatred of the world around them.

We have a tendency to rationalize, and maybe it's a salvation force. I don't know. It blunts the sharp edges of conflict. I know quite often ... a lot of the questions that come into the Oval Office are the ones that are most difficult to resolve.

If a person has a problem and he can't resolve it, generally it's handled by the family. Or if the family can't handle it, maybe by city hall or maybe at the county courthouse or maybe at the state legislature.

And if it can't be resolved any of those places, it eventually gets up here in Washington and gets on the desk of Congress members and gets on the desk of the president. And quite often in my Oval Office there is finally focused the resolution or possible resolution of an intense conflict.

And I've seen how hard it is for someone talking to me and for myself to bring ourselves to recognize that difference in all its unadorned sharpness.

We both tend to rationalize what we hear. We screen out the rough phrases, and we try to find some compatibility there. We try to make things mesh in together when they actually don't mesh.

I've seen this happen in my dealings with foreign leaders, and some of it's been publicized.

The last time Prime Minister [Menachem] Begin came over, he presented a very complicated 26-point program without interruption, I might say. And then afterwards I said, "Well, I think that's a good step toward peace." He later went back to Israel and said that I had adopted his entire program in its entirety because he wasn't trying to lie or mislead anyone.

His hope was that the President of the United States would accept what he put forward. And my hope was not to alienate Prime Minister Begin so much that he would abandon the good offices of the United States in seeking a Mideast peace.

We both wanted to hear the part of the conversation that confirmed our own position and minimized conflict or disagreement, and that's the way Christians are.

We want to hear the part of the Bible, we want to learn the parts of Christ's teachings, that are not in conflict with the way we want to live. But Jesus said you can only go so far with that. Eventually there comes a time of decision or rejection, acceptance of Christ's teachings or turning away from them. And this created the conflict in the world.

Read John 15:19, anyone.

CLASS MEMBER:

[19] If ye were of the world, the world would love his own: but because ye are not of the world, but I have chosen you out of the world, therefore the world hateth you.

PRESIDENT JIMMY CARTER:

Very good. This is the only time that phrase "of the world" is used in the Book of John. What does that phrase "of the world" mean to you, anybody?

CLASS MEMBER:

Acting like the run-of-the-mill, worldly people.

PRESIDENT JIMMY CARTER:

Acting like the run-of-the-mill, worldly people. What do you say would be a characteristic of a run-of-the-mill person?

Selfishness. We tend to build our life centered on what? On

ourselves. And that's a human trait that Christ recognized. But when we figure out how to build our lives and how to establish our priorities, the most powerful inclination is to build those priorities around what's best for us.

What's best for me must be what's best, because God created me a special person, an individual, and surely he must have wanted me to have a good life. So if I build my life around what's best for me and the ones that I love and depend on me, surely that's a very high and noble concept.

And that's the way of the world. That's the way of the heathens. That's the way of those who despise other people. It's the way of those who've never heard of Christ. It's the way of Christians. All have sinned. That's the way of the world.

And Jesus said, "When you're of the world, you can live in peace and harmony with your neighbors." But when you're not of the world, you're going to be hated and despised, cast out, even killed.

What's the distinction now between those who are of the world and those who are not of the world? Those who are of the world build our lives around ourselves, right? Those who are not of the world build our lives around what?

Christ. That's the difference. A self-centered life or a Christ-centered life. And this presents an almost hopeless distinction. How can you bridge this terrible chasm between me and Christ, a sinner and perfection?

Jesus told his disciples, "That's what you got to do." And they despaired about the resolution. They knew already when this conversation took place that Jesus was going to die. He had already made that plain to them.

Read 15:20. Jesus had just told his disciples that I'm choosing you out of the world. I have chosen you out of the world. I've made you separate from the world. Now read John 15:20.

CLASS MEMBER:

[20] Remember the word that I said unto you, The servant is not greater than his lord. If they have persecuted me, they will also persecute you; if they have kept my saying, they will keep yours also.

PRESIDENT JIMMY CARTER:

Strange thing in this lesson: At the Last Supper, in the last few hours with his disciples, and he got down on his hands and knees and did what?

CLASS MEMBER:

Washed their feet.

PRESIDENT JIMMY CARTER:

Washed their feet. And the essence of that was to show what?

CLASS MEMBER:

Humility.

PRESIDENT JIMMY CARTER:

Humility. And Jesus said that those who are servants are the greatest. He said that many times. And here he's drawing another different kind of relationship.

He says, in effect, "I am the master. You are the servants." What did he mean by this? It seems to me to be in conflict with what he had previously said. What did he say? What did he mean?

To abbreviate the conversation so we can move on, Jesus is saying in effect, "Your being a servant makes you great. My greatness lies in my service to other people. And you should not be proud and seek an ascendant position when you get to heaven or argue about who's going to sit on my right hand and who's going to sit on my left hand. Who's going to be the greatest among you? You're not better than other people simply because I love you and your sins are forgiven."

But "I am the Son of God," Jesus said. And my teachings, you must repeat, and there are things you don't understand. You're still in a questioning part of your life, and you have to accept that my words come from God, and when I'm gone, I want you to remember what I said because I am the master. I am the teacher. You are the student. You are the servant.

And your loyalty to me, your love for me, should permit you to overcome these inherent conflicts between a self-centered life and a Christ-centered life and let you act in accordance with God's teachings.

You can't on your own initiative as a fallible, sinful human being, create a theology or an explanation of what God thinks, what God means. You can't create your own God and put him in a box and say, "This is a God I worship because it's compatible with me." You've got to take God as he is. And the perfect exemplification of what God is, is I myself Christ.

Jesus said that there's a limit to the equation of a disciple—John, James and others—with me because the truth comes from my lips. It's given to me by God. And when I'm gone, you take my word, which is God's word, and let that be the guiding light in your life, not create your own God to suit yourselves.

[T]hen Jesus goes on to give them some assurance. He said, "It's not going to all be negative. I've given you a bleak picture about alienation and being despised and being killed and being excommunicated, but it's not all going to be bad."

He said, "Look, I was by myself, a carpenter from Nazareth, and I spoke and I was despised and I was hated, but there were some who listened. You, my disciples listened. Others who are not here listened.

"Part of the world hated me because they listened, and the word of God has been strengthened. What happened when you observed my life is also going to happen when other people observe your lives. Don't be hopeless. Stand firm in your faith, and your voice will be heard."

And to ensure that that is going to happen, what? How will you be strengthened? How will disciples be strengthened?

CLASS MEMBER:

The Holy Spirit.

PRESIDENT JIMMY CARTER:

The Holy Spirit, [Jesus] said, "I will have sent from God."

Jesus said, I'm going to be the one that goes to God and gets him to send the Holy Spirit. And with the Holy Spirit permeating your soul and your heart, preferably on a permanent basis, but certainly on a transient, temporary basis when it's crucial, your voice will be magnified as you speak my words. Don't be hopeless.

You'll be strengthened. You won't be abandoned. And you may suffer physically and you may be an outcast and you may be despised and you may be alienated and lonesome among men and neighbors, but you won't be alone because I will be with you through the comforter.

And the comforter is an extension of whom? God himself. God will live in you through the comforter.

Let's read that very briefly in John 15: 26 and 27, just two verses, anyone.

CLASS MEMBER:

[26] But when the Comforter is come, whom I will send unto you from the Father, even the Spirit of truth, which proceedeth from the Father, he shall testify of me:
[27] And ye also shall bear witness, because ye have been with me from the beginning.

PRESIDENT JIMMY CARTER:

That's a very interesting thing, the 27th verse there. What does it say? Yeah, and people will probably listen to you more.

If you've actually known a great teacher personally, when you speak that teacher's words, you're likely to be heard and people will give weight to your voice. I was there. I know what happened. I heard him when he said this. People will listen.

I've been in many meetings with Andy Young among Black audiences, and when Andy says Martin Luther King did this or Martin Luther King said that, the audience listens because they know that Andy was there. And when King was thrown in prison, Andy was there. When he walked the streets, Andy was there. When he was stoned, Andy was there.

And it gives an authenticity to Andy Young's voice when he talks about the civil rights movement or what it means to be despised, what it means to struggle for rights, that transcends what Andy has in himself had he not been with Martin Luther King Jr. during those trying days.

Well, Jesus is saying the same thing, that because you knew me in the beginning, you can be assured that people will listen to your voice not because of your own strength of character, not because of your own oratorical skills, but because they will know that you speak for me.

Again, a parallel. "People listen to my voice because I was with God in the beginning," Jesus said. In the beginning was the word and the word was God, and the word was with God in the creation of the universe. Christ was there.

He spoke authentically because it was an extension of God, and the disciples who walked dusty roads with Jesus were an extension of Jesus, as are we.

We are the present-day extension of Jesus to the extent that our lives are Christ-centered, to the extent that our souls and our minds are permeated by the Holy Spirit, to the extent that we don't try to identify and worship a God that we create to be compatible with what we are and what we'd like to be. To the extent we've patterned our lives after the perfect example of Christ.

The disciples were sinners. So are we. Other people watch the disciples, listen to the disciples, saw them make mistakes. They watch and listen to us as Christians, and they watch us make mistakes just like the disciples [did].

But as the holy comforter, the Holy Spirit sustained and strengthened the disciples, so the Holy Spirit and the comforter sustain and strengthen us if we let him.

Pride, which comes from a self-centered life, can close the door on which Christ is knocking. If we think we are self-sufficient, there's no way really for God's spirit to come in and combine with our own and give us a strength that's important in the eyes of God.

We might be important in the eyes of our neighbors or the world, but without the Holy Spirit, without these very teachings that Christ is describing, our lives are insignificant in the eyes of God as a Christian witness.

Read the 20th verse of the 16th chapter somebody.

CLASS MEMBER:

[20] Verily, verily, I say unto you, That ye shall weep and lament, but the world shall rejoice: and ye shall be sorrowful, but your sorrow shall be turned into joy.

PRESIDENT JIMMY CARTER:

That was kind of a riddle, wasn't it? ... He said, "You will be sorrowful, and the world will rejoice." At the same time, right? And then "Your sorrow will turn into joy." What does he mean by that?

This radical has been destroyed. Our safe, secure life has been protected. We've rooted out this cancer in our midst that caused so much trouble and tribulation and disturbance, that shook up the church. We've gotten rid of him finally, and the world rejoiced.

I imagine ... special prayers [were] said in the synagogue that day: "God, thank you for letting us get rid of this troublemaker." And his disciples were cast into the depths of despondency and sorrow. And then what happened?

Then Christ was raised, right? And the disciples rejoiced again. They didn't understand this. They were still in a questioning mood. They hadn't got into the comprehending mood yet.

And Christ said, in effect, "I'm teaching you in riddles right now. I know you don't quite understand. But later I'm going to speak to you in very frank terms, so that you and the world can understand what's meant by these extraordinary happenings created by God."

And then he gave them one of the most vivid and easy to understand expressions that I've ever seen in the Bible. Somebody read the 21st verse. I'm sure there's not a woman here that won't understand this one.

CLASS MEMBER:

[21] A woman when she is in travail hath sorrow, because her hour is come: but as soon as she is delivered of the child, she remembereth no more the anguish, for joy that a man is born into the world.

PRESIDENT JIMMY CARTER:

I don't think there's any more vivid description of a time of Christ's death and crucifixion, and in his being raised from the dead, than to draw the parallel with a woman in childbirth. It's something that a man can't understand.

But the physical dread and torture, and discomfort, and intense pain, that I'm sure almost creates a lack of faith and a rejection of maybe one's husband, and the family, and the responsibilities of motherhood. After the birth comes, and a new life is created, there's a flood of joy.

And the pain is remembered, but not with rejection. The pain becomes perhaps a part of the pride and a part of the love. I went through suffering because of this little tiny baby. It's part of me now, and I'm part of it.

And that's what happened in the death of Christ. And then the world gave birth to Christ all over again. And a new life was created for him and for us. And the disciples' faltering faith was strengthened.

And I'm sure they remembered, John and all the rest, of what Jesus ... said: "You're going to be sorrowful. The world's going to be joyful. And later on you're going to be joyful."

And Jesus didn't say, he didn't create a perfect balance there. You notice that? He said the world's going to be joyful, you're going to be sorrowful.

That's half of it, and the other half is you're going to be joyful. Jesus did not say the world's going to be sorrowful, right?

Because with the disciple's life, evoking in the rest of the world a renewed faith in the relationship between God and man that could be bridged, the world was not cast into sorrow because Christ lives.

CLASS MEMBER:

Mr. President? You told us once, in a lesson, that we were all there and a part of the crucifixion. Now you're telling us we are all part of the Resurrection and the spirit that went forth from the tomb?

PRESIDENT JIMMY CARTER:

Absolutely. We are part of both the resurrection and the death of Christ. And we know that part of the anguish of Christ on the cross was because of the sins of Jimmy Carter and Fred Gregg, John White, and others.

Jesus was tortured because I sinned, and when he was raised from the dead, it gave me the assurance, not the belief, but the assurance, that in spite of my own sinfulness, I can also have eternal life. Let's read one more verse, the 22nd verse, 16th chapter.

CLASS MEMBER:

[22] And ye now therefore have sorrow: but I will see you again, and your heart shall rejoice, and your joy no man taketh from you.

PRESIDENT JIMMY CARTER:

That's right. Jesus said that you're going to have this joy, after the Resurrection. And you need not be worried about people taking it away from you. Because it was given to you by God, and people cannot take it away.

One of the great things about Christ, God, is the means through which this conflict is resolved. What characteristic of God resolves this conflict between a self-centered life and a Christ-centered life? Between hatred of the world and love of the world? Is it the power of God? It's not just the exertion of God's power to twist, but it's what?

CLASS MEMBER:

The Holy Spirit.

PRESIDENT JIMMY CARTER:

The Holy Spirit is exemplified by what?

CLASS MEMBER:

Forgiveness.

PRESIDENT JIMMY CARTER:

Forgiveness, yes. But what's the shortest, what's the earliest Bible verse you used? God is love, right? Divine love is more powerful than worldly hatred.

And it's the exemplification of what God is, not a punitive God, but a God that through grace gives us a redemption from our own sins. Christ proved it with his well-described life, written down by John and Matthew and Peter, and others. And the parallels that are drawn between Christ versus his disciples, and Christ versus you and me, is almost absolute.

The responsibilities that Christ put on his disciples are exactly the same ones he puts on us. We are indistinguishable from Christ's disciples.

The one sobering thing today is that we don't experience the conflict and the punishment and the abrupt confrontation with the outside world that was created by Jesus' disciples 1,900, 2,000 years ago.

And I'm afraid that one reason is that we conform too much to the world. We don't draw the distinctions. We don't set the standards in our lives and in our teachings, in our public utterances, that Christ told us to. The instantaneous communication with all the outside world tends to kind of absorb us into it.

Standing alone is much more difficult now, perhaps. Or at least we say it is. Individuality is kind of sapped away. Even distinctions in speech that were preserved for hundreds of years in isolated parts of the United States, or regions, are now being filed away and those distinctions are being minimized.

But Christ told his disciples: Center your lives around me. Don't modify my teachings. Don't be afraid because the standards of the world are not important. The standards that I've given to you are important.

Well, I think this is a lesson that's both sobering and also encouraging, because the sum total of it is, the crisis, in the end, the conflict will be resolved. Perhaps with personal physical suffering, perhaps with alienation and loneliness. But with the presence of the Holy Spirit, and with the knowledge of me and my example and my teachings, and with the grace and forgiveness and love of God, the ultimate consequence of a Christ-centered life is not suffering, but joy. Not pain, but peace. Not hatred, but love.

FRED GREGG:

Thank you, Mr. President. And I remember one of the lessons you taught earlier. You asked how many had been on their knees in the last 24 hours, and a few raised their hands. I want to ask all of you to get on your knees during this week, because this is a very vital week, when decisions are going to be made that could greatly affect this country. And I want everybody to be very much in prayer that the right decisions will be made. Let's stand and be dismissed.

THE GROWTH OF CONCERN

JUNE 25, 1978
GENESIS 37:22-36 & 42-45

FRED GREGG:

[L]ast Sunday [President Carter] did such a beautiful job with a spontaneous question on highlighting the life of Joseph that I said, "Mr. President, you've earned the right to teach the final lesson in Genesis on Judah." So I'm happy to tell you that President Carter is going to teach the class this morning.

Mr. President.

PRESIDENT JIMMY CARTER:

I just came back from two days in Texas, and it's always a thrill to me to get out of Washington into the other parts of our country, to just restore my own knowledge of different communities, revisit people who have come to be so close to us.

And I know that Texas is not different from many other states in this respect. But one of the extraordinary things that happens to me when I go out and shake hands with literally thousands of people is the frequency with which people shake my hand and, with perhaps their one and only contact with a president in their entire lifetime, think of the most important thing on their mind to say.

And I would say the most prevalent comment is "God bless you."

And the second most prevalent comment is "I'm praying for you." And this is very reassuring to me because they could say something that was important to them and would benefit them personally, because it is a rare thing to have that direct relationship with the top political person in the country.

Who would like to guess which group of people, on an average as observed from my perspective, has the most frequent reference to God or to prayer when they shake hands to me? Would anybody like to make a guess?

CLASS MEMBERS:

Ministers. The poor. Spanish. Ordinary people. Young adults. Baptists.

PRESIDENT JIMMY CARTER:

That's a good guess. I'll say in Texas you would be right because it seems to me most of the people in Texas are Baptists. No, you haven't got it right yet.

CLASS MEMBERS:

Democrats. Blacks. Women. People who are in trouble.

PRESIDENT JIMMY CARTER:

People who are in trouble, that's hard for me to discern.

The military.

When we were first elected, and in fact, I think the second day I was president, we had a reception for all the key military officers and enlisted men in this area. And Rosalynn and I stood in the receiving line and shook hands with probably 2,000 people, maybe even more. And it was an overwhelming surprise to us that this occurred: Almost every top military person, whether it was a master sergeant or a general, referred to their faith in God—God give our country peace; God be with you—which I haven't figured out why, but I thought you might be interested in thinking about it yourself. Maybe you can figure out why.

But I would say of all the groups that I meet that are identifiable, the military has the most constant reference to the fact that they want my decisions as President to be guided by God, and they want me to have God's blessing. Which brings us to the lesson, strangely enough.

Quite often we tend to categorize people in our own minds from our own limited perspective as being either good or bad. And I would guess if you had listed for a couple of hours the particular group that might be referring to God most often in a spontaneous way, military would be one of the last ones you would think of. They might want better retirement benefits or better pay or more frequent change of assignments and so forth.

But the tendency we have as Christians, as human beings, is to either stigmatize somebody with a condemnation based on flimsy evidence or sometimes overly exalt someone on flimsy evidence, particularly if they happen to be compatible with us. We tend to think that folks that are like us are better than other people. We Americans tend to think that Americans are better than other people.

And since I've been President, I've had a chance to travel around a lot and to learn the unique perspective of others. And I've begun to see that Americans are legitimately subject to tough criticism because quite often we preach Christian principles about being so concerned about those who are poor, destitute, deprived, illiterate, inarticulate, and when we start putting it into practice, we are not too good at it.

I had a meeting the other night with about 75 or 80 members of Congress, key members who were interested in foreign policy. I had the Secretary of State, Dr. [Zbigniew] Brzezinski, and Harold Brown, the Secretary of Defense, there with me, and we just sat on a little raised platform and answered questions. The session lasted three hours. And the strongest condemnation I gave to the Congress was their attitude toward foreign aid.

Ordinarily, stalwart, courageous members of Congress, when they're put under the slightest bit of pressure, will vote against foreign aid. We spend a tiny amount of our total budget, of our total gross national product, in helping others. Quite often that's the best investment we can make. It's a peaceful way to meet the challenge of alien philosophies, communism, and so forth. It doesn't cost us anything. When we give another country a little bit of money to help them have a better agriculture, a better industry, or build dams or have better health, we get enormous benefits back.

But that is a target for people who want to be demagogic. And we suffer because of it. We have the least foreign aid toward other people of any developed country in the world—three tenths of one percent of our gross national product. And countries like Sweden or the Netherlands or France or Germany or Great Britain even, some of whom are in trouble financially, are three times more generous. And this is not compatible with the American character, I don't believe. But it's a truism. And other nations know it. But we tend to think we are better than other people.

The same way with biblical characters. If I mention the word "Jacob," what would be your right reaction? Good or bad? Just one word. What's your general impression of Jacob? Good. How did Jacob get his original dominance?

He lied to Isaac. Isaac was a father who loved him and who cared for Esau. Esau and Jacob were very different. And [Jacob] disguised himself as his brother and came to the old and feeble and almost blind father, who was giving his blessing, one of the most important and significant actions in the life of a man, particularly in those days, particularly in one's aged time. And as he blessed him, put his hand on him to give in fact God's blessing through his father, there Jacob was a liar, to his own father, and benefited greatly from it himself. He didn't do it in an altruistic way. He stole something that was Esau's. He wasn't all good.

And later on what was his relationship with Esau? I'm sure Jacob, once he got the material blessings or benefits from that stolen blessing, he began to think about what he had done. And do you remember the next encounter that Jacob had with Esau?

When Jacob knew that he was coming into Esau's territory, he didn't know what to do. He was just so afraid that Esau was going to wipe him out and kill all his children and kill all his wives, steal all of his livestock and kill Jacob himself. He sent out messengers to Esau. In fact, he sent two different groups of messengers so if he killed all of one group, the other group could come back and let him know so he could escape, matter of fact.

And he offered him great wealth and a kind of goodwill gift. But the fact was that Esau, who was ordinarily considered by many people to be a scoundrel, you kind of think where "Esau" has bad vibrations, the word "Jacob" has good vibrations. But Esau said, I don't need your gift.

How about Joseph? What's your natural reaction to Joseph? Good, right? Was Joseph all good?

CLASS MEMBERS:

He was selfish. He curried the favor of his father, too.

PRESIDENT JIMMY CARTER:

That's right. He curried the favor of his father. One episode the Bible describes is that he was out in the grazing lines, and his two, I think four, of his brothers did something that was wrong. And Joseph immediately went back and tattled on his brothers and got them in trouble.

And when his father obviously liked him best of all, Joseph didn't accept it in a quiet way, adequately rewarded because he knew his father loved him, from a sense of security, showing generosity to others, which is what we would admire.

He did just the opposite. He kind of rubbed it in the face of his brothers. He flaunted his cloak of many colors. And when God blessed Joseph in that tender age—16, 17 years old—with the ability to dream dreams that we know later came true, he didn't accept that in a quiet way and go to his father and say, "Father, this is something I've dreamed. What do you think it means?" He went and bragged in front of his brothers, first of all.

Do you remember the first dream he had? Sheaves of grain, right? And what happened? There were, I think, 12 sheaves of grain, and 11 of them bowed down to the other one, and he was obviously the one to whom the others bowed down. And his brothers became irate, and he had another dream. Do you remember what the other dream was?

About the stars and the moon deferring to him in a manner of worship, which meant his own father, in effect, was going to bow down to him. And it hurt Jacob's feelings. And he didn't quite know how to deal with it. And Jacob pondered in his heart about what Joseph was saying, but Jacob had a feeling that Joseph's dream might come true.

How about Reuben? Good guy, bad guy?

Reuben, yeah, pretty good. What did Reuben do that made us think he was good? ... All the brothers together plotted against Joseph when they saw him coming from a distance. And Reuben was the one that said, "Let's don't kill him." A lot of people think that was Judah, but it was Reuben. Reuben said, "Let's don't kill him. We'll put him in the pit, and then we'll tell our father that he was killed." And I guess the original intent even then was to let him die in the pit. Who decided that they shouldn't leave him in the pit? Judah.

And we're going to talk about Judah a little more today. Was Judah a good guy or a bad guy?

I would say good, yes. Because the impression is that Judah's descendants created an entity in God's eyes that was blessed, and therefore he must have been good. .... But it's kind of hazy about what Judah did until you get down and kind of pick out the verses in the Bible that refer to Judah directly. Why do you say Judah was good? What happened there when Joseph was 17 years old? What did Judah do? Who remembers?

Kept his brothers from killing him and suggested what? ... That [Joseph] be sold. To save Joseph's life, you think?

CLASS MEMBER:

To make money.

PRESIDENT JIMMY CARTER:

Reuben, I think it's accurate to say, did not want Joseph killed. I'm not sure about Judah. Now, that's just a matter of opinion. The way I read the Bible—and I read three different versions this morning of the same passage—it looked to me like Judah was trying to make money. He never expressed any sentiment that was interpreted as being compassionate or concerned about Joseph himself. It seemed to me like he said, "What will it profit us if he stays in the pit? But we can get 20 pieces of silver if we sell him as a slave."

And there is some feeling among even biblical characters and among us today that slavery and death are almost equal punishments, permanent lifetime of a slave. I would guess that those who lived in Israel—in those days, Canaan—were very fearful of the Egyptians and those who lived about them, because there'd been a great deal of slaying and war and bitter hatred when entire races were wiped out. And to sell someone into slavery, into an alien society, was not a beneficent thing to do.

So no one knows really what was in Judah's mind. But there's no evidence that he was trying to be compassionate or concerned about Joseph. It's as though he was avaricious, wanting to get some money back.

To make a long story short, we've got mixed emotions about people. And we can see in this little brief listing of people that sometimes we tend to judge others on superficial evidence, who are biblical characters. And we tend to do that in the modern day too. Not only the military.

Since I've been in the White House, I've read a lot of biographies, long and short, about my predecessors there. I could go back down the list of presidents, some of whom are condemned ferociously, some of whom [are] looked on as heroes. And when I read the history of what they actually did in the White House and what they tried to do, what they failed to do, the good things that weren't publicized, the bad things that were exploded out of all proportion in the public's mind, you can see that I think without exception, as far as I know, certainly in recent history, they tried to do a good job.

Some of them are condemned in retrospect because of one incident in their lives as president, over which they had not too much control. I just came back from Texas. Lyndon Johnson comes to my mind. I don't think there was ever a president who worked harder or who had a greater, more generous heart, or who cared more and did more for people who were persecuted and deprived and who felt the stigma and the punishment of racial hatred and prejudice and discrimination. But when you think about Lyndon Johnson, now, you don't think about freedom. You don't think about an end to discrimination. Don't think about voting rights acts nearly so much as you think about the Vietnam War. But Johnson was always trying to do things to make a better community, better cities, better highways, better life for people.

And still, he's not one of those presidents, at least yet, who's recognized as big-hearted, great-hearted, concerned about others.

He's kind of a guy that used to twist arms in the Congress and so forth.

But the point in this lesson is that we need to judge people as little as possible. Let God judge them and learn from their lives, their mistakes, which are equivalent to our mistakes, their good deeds, which are equivalent to our good deeds and see how we stand in the eyes of God. God had an overall purpose apparently in this history of a family that was torn apart.

Jacob. How many children did Jacob have? Anybody know? ... 12 sons. Was it two daughters? I remember one daughter. What was his daughter's name that was kind of famous? ... Dina. And Dina was a beautiful girl, apparently, who brought great tragedy. And how many of his sons, anybody remember where his sons came from? His ugly wife, Leah, his cross-eyed wife, had how many? Leah had six sons. She had four and then she quit for a while. [*Class laughs.*]

And then don't you remember, Rachel's handmaiden was taken into Jacob, and she had two. And then Leah thought the idea was pretty good, so she had her handmaiden go in and her handmaiden had, I think, two. And then Leah came back and had two more. And then how about the other two?

Rachel had Joseph and Benjamin. Rachel didn't know Benjamin. Why? She died when Benjamin was born. And who was the one of all those women that Jacob loved?

Rachel, from the very first time he ever saw her, he loved her. And there was a violence in the family that Dina precipitated, the murder of a whole tribe because she was sexually assaulted by a man who loved her. And Jacob's sons went and wiped out a whole tribe. So, the point is that this was a violent time. When we look back on this, selling one's brother into slavery and so forth, it's hard for us to translate this episode in the Bible over a continuing period of years into our own lives.

Well, we all know now that Joseph was sold into slavery, and we learned last week that he became a great leader of Egypt. The leader, really. He said that God had made him ... what relationship with Pharaoh? Does anybody remember?

The Father. Joseph finally told, sent word back to Jacob in the end, he said, "God has made me the Father of Pharaoh," which meant that he was a powerful figure, but also a very influential figure. Then the famine comes, and I think after the famine's been going on for about two years, the people in Canaan began to starve, too. What happened then? We'll move pretty rapidly.

Jacob sent for grain. Who went?

CLASS MEMBER:

All the sons except one.

PRESIDENT JIMMY CARTER:

All but one. Which one didn't go?

CLASS MEMBER:

Benjamin.

PRESIDENT JIMMY CARTER:

That's right. That may have made his brothers feel bad too, because Jacob in effect said, "I'll send the rest of you into this dangerous territory to get food, but I'm not going to send Benjamin." Is there any evidence that the brothers resented that? No. I think that's a good indication that in that period of time, after they had committed this horrible crime against Joseph and against their father, that they had had a change of heart. I think, in effect, they understood why Jacob loved Benjamin and Joseph so much, because of his special relationship with Rachel. So when he kept Benjamin back to protect him and let his brothers know that he was doing that, they did not resent it. They left and went to Egypt. What happened when they got to Egypt?

They met Joseph, who was obviously the leader of Egypt, who was distributing food out of profit, I'm sure, for the Pharaoh, and Joseph immediately recognized his brothers. They did not recognize him. He did not speak Hebrew to them. He spoke Egyptian. He was clean shaven, which Egyptians always maintained as a very intimate, physical characteristic. I think the Canaanites probably grew beards, and so he was quite different from them. So what did he decide to do, Joseph?

He wanted to test them. I would guess that Joseph wanted to be reconciled with his brothers, but he had a legitimate complaint, right? He had a legitimate reason to hate his brothers, and I don't think he immediately forgave them. He wanted to discern whether or not they were worthy of forgiveness. I think this grew on him, but he finally figured out some way to test them. So he accused them of being spies, right?

They denied it. They said they were true men. What did they say? What did they kind of blurt out to show that they were true men? They told Joseph about their family. What were two items of information they gave to Joseph about their family?

They had a good father in Canaan. What else? ... Yeah, [they] said we've got a young brother at home. So they were family men, and they had a close-knit family. They did not come as separate members of the society in what's now Israel, but they came as a cohesive part of one family. Had they been spies of a foreign government coming to disrupt and to steal, the chances are they would've been from a broad range of families.

They said this is just one family. We've just come because we're hungry. We've got a father at home and a young brother who trust us and are looking for us to come back home. We didn't come here to bother you.

What did Joseph say? He said, "I'm not sure whether you're lying or not." He said, "You say you've got a young brother at home. Let's just see if you're telling the truth. Why don't you go back and bring your brother here?"

They didn't want to do that. Why?

They knew how Jacob felt, right? At this time, Judah had pretty well become the leader of the group. I don't know why he was dominant over Reuben, but the Bible says at one place, Judah and his brothers. Which shows that although he was not the oldest son, that he had become kind of a leader. In the Bible, they identify him as a leader by saying that. Does anybody remember offhand who was Judah's mother? It was Leah. He was the fourth son of Leah, but he had become the dominant person there.

He said, "We don't want to go back and get my youngest brother."

Joseph said, "Well, I want you to leave someone here." First, he said he is going to lock them all up, and he locked them up for three days. He swore on the Pharaoh's life that he was going to keep them there, but then later he decided he would keep one. He kept, I think, Simeon. In effect [he] told the rest of them, we'll abbreviate this, to go back and bring the other brother. Then what happened? Very quickly, it's an interesting story. Does anybody remember what he did to his brothers?

He put all the money that they had paid him for the grain back in their own sack and hid it, and had his Egyptian helpers seal up the bags. Then what happened?

[T]hey went on back to Canaan. When they got there, they found that all the bags had the money in it. They told Jacob what had happened. Jacob was quite concerned because they had brought the money back. He was quite concerned that Simeon was in prison. He was adamantly opposed to Benjamin being sent to Egypt. So I think they did a strange thing then.

What did they do after they got back to Canaan with the food, with Simeon in prison? How long did they wait? Yeah, they just left Simeon in jail, and they didn't go back to Egypt until the food ran out. That's exactly right. It was a strange thing to have happened, since the whole family apparently had changed character and were all quite concerned about each other in this new life of theirs. They forgot about Simeon until they ran out of food, and then came the dramatic, in effect, a confrontation between Judah and Jacob.

He said, "If I fail to bring Benjamin back, my life, in the eyes of you, my father, Jacob, and in the eyes of God, will be condemned forever." He, in effect, put up not only his life but his soul as a warranty that he would not lose Benjamin.

So to make a long story short, they returned back to Egypt with Benjamin. ... [A]t first, [Joseph] recognized Benjamin, and he was so excited that he told his servant, "Bring these men into my own house and we'll have a banquet."

And the brothers were fearful at first. They said, "Gee, he's going to bring us out of the street and kill us all." But he had beautiful food put in front of them, a lot of wine apparently. And when they served the brothers, he gave Benjamin five times more than he did anyone else. And Joseph was so overwhelmed with love that he had to go off by himself and weep. And then he washed his face with cold water, the Bible says, and came back.

And eventually when he saw what he thought was a glimmer of change in his brothers, he told Judah and the others, "I'm going to keep Benjamin here to be my slave, and the rest of you all can go back home and take all the food you want." And then Judah made one of the most beautiful speeches, I think, that anyone ever made. Let's turn over to Genesis 44—I think it starts with verse 30.

CLASS MEMBER:

³⁰ Now therefore when I come to thy servant my father, and the lad be not with us; seeing that his life is bound up in the lad's life;
³¹ It shall come to pass, when he seeth that the lad is not with us, that he will die: and thy servants shall bring down the gray hairs of thy servant our father with sorrow to the grave.
³² For thy servant became surety for the lad unto my father, saying, If I bring him not unto thee, then I shall bear the blame to my father for ever.
³³ Now therefore, I pray thee, let thy servant abide instead of the lad a bondman to my lord; and let the lad go up with his brethren.
³⁴ For how shall I go up to my father, and the lad be not with me? lest peradventure I see the evil that shall come on my father.

PRESIDENT JIMMY CARTER:

I don't think there's any evidence in this speech, which is one of the most eloquent in the Bible, that Judah had the slightest tendency toward selfishness or protecting himself. He was concerned about his brother Benjamin of course, but he was more concerned, I think, about his father who was distant.

Now, he had betrayed his father in the past. Bad man. He had condoned placing Joseph in the pit. Bad man. He had been willing to sell Joseph into slavery for 20 pieces of silver. A bad man. He had perhaps delayed in coming back to get Simeon out of jail. Bad man.

But his life was transformed because of the environment of his family, the staunchness of Jacob and the influence of God. And not knowing that this was Joseph, his brother, he offered in effect his life. And he specifically said, "I will be your slave the rest of my life if you'll just let Benjamin go home to our father."

And Joseph was so overwhelmed with emotion, love and with a sense of relief, so he could forgive his worthy brothers that he wept, cried on Benjamin's neck, loved all his brothers. And this was almost the end of a beautiful story.

We didn't go into the point where he sent them back with Benjamin and his cup, but he tested his brothers very well, and they came back wanting to all be slaves. But the point that the lesson makes to us is two or threefold.

One is it's a mistake for us to judge others because of a report that we get about what they are. This is sometimes a subterfuge for covering up our own inadequacies, our own sinfulness, our own weakness because as we condemn others in the comparison, it makes us better.

One way to elevate oneself is to submerge or to lower the reputation of others. And one of the Ten Commandments prevents us in God's words from the condemnation of others or the gossip or the lies about one another.

But we have a tendency even when we're not personally involved with someone to castigate them. And Jesus had the superlative quality of being able to see the good in people that were scorned, who were outcast.

[*A class member asks whether the United States is responsible for addressing famine as Joseph did.*]

PRESIDENT JIMMY CARTER:

It is, and we are doing that as a matter of fact right now. We're not only setting up a grain reserve in our own country, but we're also working with other nations who produce wheat and corn, soybeans and so forth to set up an international grain reserve. That grain would be kept in the individual countries, but it would be available for international exchange to the countries that all particularly destitute because of a drought of some other things. Yes, it's good for our country, good for our farmers, provides a more stable price for all of us and also can help to alleviate suffering when people are hungry. Good point. Thank you.

So one thing is we ought not to condemn because it is a selfish thing. It violates directly the word of God. And secondly, we ought to see that in a spirit of common suffering, like hunger or danger, and in a spirit of the awareness of God's will [that] sinners can improve. Joseph improved, Reuben improved, Jacob improved, Esau improved as they went through their lives because of a beneficent influence of God and their willingness to be subservient to God.

And this is the essence of Christianity, that we can, all us sinners, be forgiven. And since Christ lived and died for us, our sins can be washed away just as though we hadn't even committed them.

Rosalynn and I are struggling through the Old Testament now, reading a chapter every night. And it's tedious because chapter after chapter after chapter is these little, tiny meticulous directions from God to the Israelites on how to offer a sacrifice and how many bulls to kill and how many calves to kill, how many goats to kill, how many sheep to kill, how many doves to kill and what to do with the blood.

And we know that this was done to propitiate sin and to redeem the chosen people to God in spite of their sinfulness, which was constant. And then Jesus came and gave his life as a sacrifice for us. And all we've got to do is believe in him, acknowledge our sinfulness, believe in him and we're forgiven.

But this tremendous blessing that comes to us in our lives is anticipated by the life of many in the Old Testament. Today, Judah is an example. You can be redeemed from past sinfulness through an intimate relationship with God and in the reconciliation and the strength that is derived from an association with others.

I don't think there's any doubt that these brothers helped each other to get the courage to commit a horrible sin. And in the final act of our own day's lesson, they jointly strengthened one another in turning away from that sin and eventually admitted it all to Jacob. They told Jacob what happened.

And as you know, they went back home and got Jacob, brought him to Egypt and Joseph said, "What you did, my brothers, was not done of yourselves. It was in effect the plan of God because [since] I came to Egypt, we've been able to keep many people from dying of hunger and this gives us a chance to preserve the chosen people for two or three or 400 years as slaves."

But God's ultimate purpose was to save this race of people from whom sprang Jesus Christ. And Joseph said, "God did this." That was the ultimate forgiveness, I think, for his brothers. Can't you imagine how all those brothers felt when Joseph said, "I not only forgive you, but it's just as though you didn't even commit the sin," because God's hand was in it.

And it ultimately turned out to perpetuate the chosen people who God wants to protect. ... And this is in effect what Jesus has done for us. We're not only forgiven by God, but through Christ, it's just as though we didn't even commit the sins at all.

That doesn't mean that Joseph was telling his brothers, "Sin again. You know, I've set an example now, whatever you do is wrong, you'll be forgiven," nor does it give a Christian a chance to say, "Because Christ died for me on the cross, my sins will be forgiven. I don't have to be too careful about what I commit" because we know that our sins are laid on Jesus' heart as though he committed them himself.

So there is a premonition here of the teachings of Christ about growth of a human mind and a human spirit. And in the process, of course, a concern about others.

And the last point I want to make is the difficulty of saying, "I was wrong." That's a prerequisite to forgiveness and that's a hard thing for a successful, proud Baptist Sunday School attender, church member, to do, to say, "I'm a sinner. I was wrong. I fall short of God's expectations, and I acknowledge it freely. I ask God's forgiveness."

So this is a very good lesson, I think, to show that in Judah's life, a man who's ordinarily condemned and scorned, he proved to us the essence of what our own life should exemplify. Judah sinned; we sin. Judah turned to God; that's what we do. Judah was forgiven; that's the hope that we have. He was strengthened through communion with his fellow family and human beings; that's the essence of ours, of our life.

I think it's a good lesson, and Judah is a relatively unknown biblical character. But even in those episodes where we skim over and remember just Jacob and Joseph, Judah played a very strong role. And that's the case with us, too.

Even though we may not be famous, we may not shake the earth, we in our own way, in God's kingdom, as was the case with Judah, can play a major role. God looks with love on each of us, and each life can be important in his kingdom.

FACING LIFE'S TENSIONS
SEPTEMBER 24, 1978
PHILIPPIANS 4:1-23

UNKNOWN SPEAKER:

For the past two weeks, a member of this class has been involved in some negotiations. And I'm sure you all appreciated seeing the three men principally involved in those negotiations on television. The smiles on their faces indicated that some accomplishment had been made.

Let's not forget that in the days to come, that there are still things to be done, and keep these accomplishments in mind and in our prayers as we go along through the coming weeks. …

It gives me great pleasure at this time to introduce to you the teacher of our class this morning, the President of the United States. [*Applause*]

PRESIDENT JIMMY CARTER:

Thank you very much. … Well, it's always nice to come back from a two-week vacation at Camp David.

I think some of the most unpleasant moments of my life occurred during the last two weeks and, of course, also some of the most pleasant. One of the great things about the meeting was that I was meeting with two leaders who were deeply devout and religious men. Who spent a great portion of their time at Camp David in prayer. Who believe that they and I worship the same God.

President [Anwar] Sadat refers often to his guidance from God Almighty. The fact that he and [Israeli Prime Minister Menachem] Begin are both descended from Abraham, that they're brothers not only in religious beliefs, but also by blood, was one of the things that I believe gave us a kind of a clear, unshakable purpose, because we all believed that God wanted us to work toward peace. It was one of the few things on which we agreed at first.

President Sadat, in our private meeting, brought up the hope that after a peace treaty is signed—and I predict it will be signed, without undue delay—that we might meet on Mount Sinai. And Begin immediately agreed that that would be a wonderful gesture, to combine three different kinds of people, three different races, three different religions, and a public demonstration of a commitment to peace among all people.

I don't know if it'll work out that way, but after the Sinai is restored to Egypt, Sadat will build on the top of that mountain an Arab mosque and a Jewish synagogue and a Christian church, which I think would be a wonderful gesture.

This morning we're talking about a very important thing in the lives of modern people and also ancient people. We tend to think that tension, concern, worry, burdens, are unique to a fast-changing modern world.

But as we read Paul's letter to the Philippians, fourth chapter, in that brief book, we see how he dealt with this problem of worry and the divisions that comes among those whom he loved because of the pressures of their own lives.

There's no doubt that they lived in fear because they were Christians in that early day, when it was not an acceptable thing to do. They were, in effect, religious revolutionaries, challenged from all sides, perhaps even meeting in secret on occasion.

And Paul recognized then that one of the causes of the buildup in a person's life of uncontrollable fear and tension was rapid change.

We all tend to want to maintain the status quo. When our lives are uprooted to move to another community, there's an expression of concern that wells up in us no matter how delightful the prospect for the new home might be. It might be that one got a substantial promotion and was transferred. And in spite of that, we tend to inventory the blessings of our present house and our neighbors and our church and our children in school and our friends. So just change of a location is bad.

Changing times are also cause of great concern. You've all read books recently about not only are times changing, but the rate of change is greater in our own lives than ever before—I think that's certainly true.

In the little book that I wrote before I became president, I pointed out that ... my life on the farm as a boy was much closer to farming in the time of Christ than it was similar to the farming of today. In just a 30- or 40-year period, you had more change than you had in the previous 2,000 years. And that causes us to be upset.

Doubt about the future—uncertainty, what's going to come next —is also a matter of great concern. And of course, we know that financial problems afflict us all.

There's no one in here who isn't blessed profoundly by God in material things. We are not starving. Our children are not dying, profusely at birth or within a few months. We don't sleep on the streets in human and animal filth, and millions of people in the world do.

But still, we worry about whether we make $7,000 a year or $70,000 a year, when many people live on $70 a year.

So we tend to be concerned because we compare ourselves with our neighbors, instead of comparing ourselves in absolute terms to what would be an adequate existence.

I think you can gather from what I'm saying that we tend to create problems for ourselves. We tend to search for something to worry about.

And I certainly don't deny that at times our worries are justified, when one of the people that we love is threatened with death or we are divided from someone we love by anger or by incompatibility. There's certainly legitimate reasons to be concerned. I don't deny that at all.

Although this morning we're talking about Paul and the Philippians, I'd like to start by quoting from the Sermon on the Mount. [W]ould you turn to Matthew 6, and read the 25th through 34th verses?

Jesus himself was quite aware of this need for security and peace of mind, and this is one of the most beautiful passages of all. Matthew 6:25–34.

CLASS MEMBER:

[25] Therefore I say unto you, Take no thought for your life, what ye shall eat, or what ye shall drink; nor yet for your body, what ye shall put on. Is not the life more than meat, and the body than raiment? [26] Behold the fowls of the air: for they sow not, neither do they reap, nor gather into barns; yet your heavenly Father feedeth them. Are ye not much better than they? [27] Which of you by taking thought can add one cubit unto his stature? [28] And why take ye thought for raiment? Consider the lilies of the field, how they grow; they toil not, neither do they spin: [29] And yet I say unto you, That even Solomon in all his glory was not arrayed like one of these. [30] Wherefore, if God so clothe the grass of the field, which to day is, and to morrow is cast into the oven, shall he not much more clothe you, O ye of little faith? [31] Therefore take no thought, saying, What shall we eat? or, What shall we drink? or, Wherewithal shall we be clothed? [32] (For after all these things do the gentiles seek:) for your heavenly Father knoweth that ye have need of all these things. [33] But seek ye first the kingdom of God, and his righteousness; and all these things shall be added unto you. [34] Take therefore no thought for the morrow: for the morrow shall take thought for the things of itself. Sufficient unto the day is the evil thereof.

PRESIDENT JIMMY CARTER:

We could go back in the Old Testament and find other passages that are equally as reassuring. The 23rd Psalm is one that we think of often. And I think it's good for us to compare our own lives with biblical figures whom we look upon as being imminently successful and popular and with the life that's totally fulfilling.

Rosalynn and I read a chapter every night in the Bible. We're reading 2 Samuel right at this moment about the decline of King Saul and the emergence of Shepherd King David. And you look on David as a great and noble and successful, happy man who killed a giant and who became king, who helped to build a cathedral to his son. [*sic*] But if you study the life of David. it was one of great temptation, great sin, great sorrow, great fear. When his benefactor, Saul, continued to try to kill him, Jonathan saved him.

You think about Joseph being ascendant, right, under the ruler of Egypt, handing out food for starving people all over the Middle Eastern area and how proud he was of his dreams, his closeness to God. But it caused him to be the subject of intense jealousy—thrown in a pit, threatened with death, sold into slavery, cast into prison.

I think you remember the life of Moses, who was looked upon as a savior to the people of Israel, and how he was filled with doubt and concerned that he was not adequate for the job.

But throughout all those people's lives, there's one sustaining factor and that is their intense and unshakable belief in God, their dependence upon prayer. And I think it's good to remind ourselves also that God's peace, which we're going to talk about in a minute through Paul's words, does not mean an absence of conflict, an absence of trouble, or an absence of suffering. But the peace comes with the ability to absorb or to assimilate fear and doubt and suffering, troubles, conflict, because there's something much more important on which we can always depend.

Why don't we start now by reading in Philippians, one or two verses at a time in the fourth chapter, everyone. And perhaps someone would read the first verse.

CLASS MEMBER:

[1] Therefore, my brethren dearly beloved and longed for, my joy and crown, so stand fast in the Lord, my dearly beloved.

PRESIDENT JIMMY CARTER:

This is interpreted by some biblical scholars as a summary of the whole message of Paul to the Philippians. And I'm not going to dwell on each verse at length. But the essence of it is that he says stand fast in the Lord, and then he has an interesting phrase in there that I had to study a little while this morning: "my joy and crown." What does Paul mean when he says my joy and crown?

The joy and crown is the final culmination of a tremendous achievement. And Paul, when he says my joy and crown, he says this is the most important accolade or recognition of my entire existence. ...

This little, tiny, embryonic church in Philippi that we would probably write off now as being fairly inconsequential—there weren't many people there—Paul looks upon as a culminating achievement of his whole life. Because within that tiny church, there was a breath of life through Christ by Paul. And he looked upon his evangelistic achievement, his winning people to believe in Christ, as by far the crowning achievement of his whole life. And the fact that that church existed, Paul said, this is my joy and my crown—when my life has ended, this is what I want to leave as a culmination of all my effort. I'm not sure that we look on the word of God, a belief in Christ, in such an exalted way.

I don't know what you would like to have inscribed on your tomb, or is it an epitaph? Would you like to have inscribed how many people on earth you led to Christ? Or to how many you revealed your inmost thoughts about your own relationship with Jesus? Would that be the thing that you'd like to have on your tomb? And if so, would your remaining family be embarrassed? But the point is, that this great man, Paul, that was his joy and his crown.

When we launch our lives, it needs to have some purpose. We need to be willing to sacrifice. I know that you remember the goodbye wish of the Spartan mothers when their sons went off to battle. They said come back carrying your shield or—what?

CLASS MEMBER:

Or on it.

PRESIDENT JIMMY CARTER:

Or on it. Either come back carrying your shield, having acquitted yourself well in your battle purposes, or come back on your shield, having died doing your best.

And that kind of commitment is what Paul is telling the Philippians to remember, "Stand fast in the Lord." That's an exalted sort of thing, isn't it? Kind of an ideal. Not exactly specific, nothing really tangible about it. Kind of an ephemeral thought that transcends mundane human existence.

But let's read the second and third verse, someone. Do you think Paul's going from the sublime to the ridiculous? He's talking about his own joy and crown, having established and helped to maintain the very church of Christ. And in the next two verses he said, "Here are two women arguing with each other, in your church, Euodias and Syntyche." He said, "My yoke fellows." What does that mean? A yoke fellow?

When you hook two oxen to the same cart they are yoke fellows. They work not only in harmony but in partnership, as equals. He says, "My yoke fellow, do something to reveal to these disputants, these Christian adversaries, how they might reconcile themselves." So Paul is not going from the sublime to the ridiculous; he says that "Through the Lord, these women might be reconciled" is kind of a mundane, practical part of Christianity as well.

[It's] not just the dreams, and the ideals, and the beautiful words, and the ultimate thought about what I'm going to do after I get to heaven. But there's a practical aspect to Christianity, too, that Paul very clearly recognized, and we see all through his life how these practical aspects weighed on him. And he even went back up a little bit and said their names and one other are inscribed in the book of life.

As God gives the lilies beauty, as God detects every fallen bird, he also cares about every human being. So it's not a mundane thing, because a person's life is an exalted thing as well. Let's read now the fourth through the seventh verses.

CLASS MEMBER:

[4] Rejoice in the Lord always: and again I say, Rejoice.
[5] Let your moderation be known unto all men. The Lord is at hand.
[6] Be careful for nothing; but in every thing by prayer and supplication with thanksgiving let your requests be made known unto God.
[7] And the peace of God, which passeth all understanding, shall keep your hearts and minds through Christ Jesus.

PRESIDENT JIMMY CARTER:

Very good. What's the first thing that Paul tells them to do? Rejoice. Joy, right? Rejoicing, joy. What's the last thing he comments on in the last verse?

Peace. So in the fourth, fifth, sixth, and seventh verses he goes all the way from joy to peace. That's what Paul was thinking about as he wrote this final letter to the Philippian church. Where was Paul?

CLASS MEMBER:

In Rome.

PRESIDENT JIMMY CARTER:

Where was he in Rome?

CLASS MEMBER:

In prison.

PRESIDENT JIMMY CARTER:

Right. And what was he thinking about? Joy. Peace. What was a prospect in Paul's life? Release from prison, freedom?

Execution. Death. But Paul's message was not "Come here and save me. Lament with me. Mourn my death. Share my burdens with me"—the kind of letter that I might be tempted to write to a group of friends. But it was "Rejoice." Read the fifth verse again.

CLASS MEMBER:

⁵ Let your moderation be known unto all men. The Lord is at hand.

PRESIDENT JIMMY CARTER:

That's right. What did Paul mean by, "Let your moderation be known unto all men"?

CLASS MEMBER:

Gentleness.

PRESIDENT JIMMY CARTER:

Gentleness. Compatibility with one another. Equanimity in the face of trial and temptation and fear. Why? So let it be known where? To God? Why?

As witnesses, right? What we do as Christians, even more perhaps than we realize, is observed very closely by others. And I think this has been said millions of times, it's more what we do than what we say. And when Christians are torn apart with jealousy or incompatibility, or even fear or despair, it's a living proof that Christ's message is not exemplified by us.

How could someone wring his hands and mourn over a transient circumstance in his life and believe in Christ? How can we split apart a Christian community or turn against someone that we've sworn to love for life and still exemplify in the finest sense the teachings of Christ?

The Bible sets very high standards for us. But Paul says that the standards are not too high, says you'll never be tempted, you'll never have a burden on you that's not manageable with God as a yoke fellow, as a partner, as a friend, as a supporter, sustainer, teacher. Read the sixth verse again.

CLASS MEMBER:

[6] Be careful for nothing; but in every thing by prayer and supplication with thanksgiving, let your requests be made known unto God.

PRESIDENT JIMMY CARTER:

"Be careful with nothing." That means full of care. And he said turn to God in prayer. What are some of the things that we derive from prayer? What are some of the component parts of prayer?

Thanks. Thanks, communication, right. An absence of loneliness. When you're by yourself, you can communicate with God riding in an automobile, wherever.

CLASS MEMBERS:

Adoration. Worship. Dedication. Inspiration. Praise. Confession.

PRESIDENT JIMMY CARTER:

Confession. Very good. I was hoping somebody would say confession. Request for peace, petition. God, give me these things or help me do these things. So Paul is saying that if these problems are too great, turn to God in prayer. The seventh verse is a beautiful verse.

CLASS MEMBER:

[7] And the peace of God, which surpasseth all understanding, shall keep your hearts and minds through Christ Jesus.

PRESIDENT JIMMY CARTER:

This is an interesting verse. It's got a lot in it. The peace of God. How great is the peace of God?

All encompassing. What Paul is saying here is that the peace of God is so great that human beings cannot describe it in words and cannot envision it in our minds. It's more than we could ever expect. ... the peace that surpasseth understanding means it's transcendent.

And we don't have enough faith sometimes to say, "Well, can I really get this peace in the face of all my problems and all my worries, all my doubts and tribulations?" But Paul is saying that you can.

We read a lot of books that you get peace through positive thinking and camaraderie and a forceful presence among others. And books written on this subject sell millions and millions of copies. And you tend to get the impression that if I can do some certain things, think positively, reach out my hand to friends, that I can get this inner peace. I earn it by doing things. It's the same as the concept of earning salvation through good works. Where do we get this peace from?

It's a gift. It's a free gift. You don't earn the peace by being a goody-goody person or being quiescent in the face of challenge. You don't just succumb and lie on the ground and say, "I'm going to be peaceful." You meet challenges dynamically, and you don't get peace even by being dynamic and aggressive and forceful and combative. You get peace free. Because God loves us.

And that's something we ought to remember as well. And when we think there's no way in the world that I could possibly be peaceful in my mind, no way, Christ, David, Paul, God through the Bible says, "My peace is transcendent. My peace is more than you can understand. My peace is free if you have faith in me."

All of us have times of stress and doubt. I know I do many times. And I turn to God to pray often.

Our lesson skips over verse eight, but I couldn't bring myself to skip it. It's one of my favorites.

CLASS MEMBER:

[8] Finally, brethren, whatsoever things are true, whatsoever things are honest, whatsoever things are just, whatsoever things are pure, whatsoever things are lovely, whatsoever things are of good report; if there be any virtue, and if there be any praise, think on these things.

PRESIDENT JIMMY CARTER:

The reason it was omitted, I'm sure, is that the author of this Sunday School book wanted to concentrate on the tensions and what we can get from prayer. But I think that what Paul said in the midst of this series of verses was that you have an obligation also. As you get this free gift of God through peace, through prayer, you have an obligation to exemplify the teachings of Christ. What's good and decent and honest and true and compassionate and loving, do these things.

Paul then gets back to his own life, and I think we might read. ... Let's read verses 11 and 12.

CLASS MEMBER:

[11] Not that I speak in respect of want: for I have learned, in whatsoever state I am, therewith to be content.
[12] I know both how to be abased, and I know how to abound: every

where and in all things I am instructed both to be full and to be hungry, both to abound and to suffer need.

PRESIDENT JIMMY CARTER:

This is a remarkable testimony of Paul, and it exemplifies, I think, what we've been trying to say all morning. Paul is telling the people in the church at Philippi that my life's been filled with suffering; I've been abased, abused, beaten, imprisoned, impoverished.

Paul had some affliction that he refers to several times in his letters. We don't know quite what it was. I don't think anybody really knows what the overriding suffering or cross was that Paul had to bear.

But what he's saying is that his peace of mind is not dependent on material things. I don't guess he had anything. ...

Of all the churches he had to establish and to maintain and to teach, he never asked ... for any salary, and he never received any gifts. He says, I think, in the 15th verse that the Philippian church was the only church that'd ever sent him anything. And it was a spasmodic sort of giving program they had, not a cooperative program or anything for Paul. Every now and then they'd send him some gifts. Sometimes they'd got lost on the way. Sometimes they were delayed in getting there, but he appreciated them very much.

Paul never did criticize, by the way, preachers who did accept a salary, but he had a profession of his own. And his commitment was to work with his own hands and earn his own keep and let his work for Christ be a bonus in his life so that it would prevent squabbling among the churches and also prevent dissension between Paul and the members of those churches. There was enough dissension.

As you read through the New Testament, you see that there was always some incipient quarrel or struggle for power or authority or prestige among the leaders of those churches. It was not a harmonious Christian community scattered all through the Asia Minor region. So Paul wanted to remove one source, at least, of dissension, and that was how much pay he got, how many hours he worked, how many days he spent in this church compared to the other.

I can see the deacons now, sitting around in the church at Corinth arguing about whether they should continue his salary while he was in prison in Rome since he wasn't actively visiting the people in the hospital nearby.

So Paul removed that. He said, "What I do for you is for Christ, and you don't pay me anything." And it's strange that they didn't send him gifts, other than [the] people at Philippi. Maybe that's why he cared so much for them. Read the 13th verse.

CLASS MEMBER:

[13] I can do all things through Christ which strengtheneth me.

PRESIDENT JIMMY CARTER:

Very good. It's almost impossible to realize what a strong man Paul was. One of the greatest philosophers of all time, certainly one of the greatest theologians of all time, a great writer, composer, a man who could inspire other people. And in his day, he was not appreciated at all. He didn't enjoy walking down the street in Rome and hearing the crowd's roar.

So far as I know, he was never enwrapped with hundreds and hundreds of thousands of people who eagerly listened for the words that fell from his lips. He wrote these little crummy letters and sent them to one person in a tiny church. I don't have any way to know if Paul ever envisioned his letters being read 1,900, 2,000 years later, but he didn't do it for recognition.

And you say, "How could he do it?" And he said, "I can do everything. I can do anything." How? "Through Christ who strengtheneth me."

Paul said it. Do we say it? Do we have that degree of confidence? Not in ourselves, but in ourselves plus Christ that would let us face any challenge?

How much greater could our own lives have been, or could they still be, if we had that kind of inner peace and confidence that Christ and I together can do anything?

Because our goals sometimes are lowered, lowered, lowered, lowered so that we can be sure that we don't fail. Because in our weakness, one of the things that we fear most is, what? Failure. We cannot afford to face failure.

And we read in the newspapers about those who try great things and flop, and we don't often admire them for their great attempts at high achievement. We laugh at them when they fall. And had they never striven for greatness or exalted achievement, they wouldn't have been embarrassed.

And all of us have that tendency to want to be careful, not to get out on the limb and endanger our stature. It's better to be a safe, mediocre nonentity than to be a highly publicized failure.

And that's one of the reasons that the Christian church is not moving any more rapidly than it is.

The most exalted goal of the Southern Baptist Convention is to increase, I think, by two percent a year.

Anyone in his right mind would know that one Christian with Christ could win one convert in a year. Is there anyone that would doubt that statement? Is there anyone that would doubt in this class that if you really set your mind to it among your own circle of friends, perhaps in your own family, you couldn't convince one person that what you know about Christ is true?

And if everybody would do that in the Southern Baptist Convention next year, instead of having a 14 million–person church plus two percent, we'd have 28 million Southern Baptists and Christians, more importantly.

So the point is that what Paul is saying, don't be timid in your lives. Reach for greatness. If you have doubt in yourself, which is inevitable, get your partner.

It's Christ. And the timidity goes away, and the inspiration comes in and the strength comes in and the peace of mind comes in. The confidence comes in. The awareness and sensitivity of other people's yearnings comes in. Your life's expanded, your heart's expanded, new friends, new awareness of what God's given us.

All that comes in with one simple concept that Paul is trying to tell the Philippians about in the fourth chapter and has been available to us all our lives that we kind of tend to skim over.

We profess to be Christians with faith in Christ, but where's the proof of it? Does any life in this room demonstrate that we believe what Paul [said] in the 13th verse?

I doubt it. It's such a simple thing.

But of course, everything that Christ said was simple, wasn't it? And the simplicity of it is what hurts. I can do all things through Christ who strengthens me. You can't tear the thing apart. You can't say, "I can almost do things maybe through Christ or somebody else if I'm strong enough."

But the way Paul says it is just bare bones, and Christ said God is love. Simple three words, and we tend to think about the love part.

And sometimes in the campaign, when I mentioned the word "love," there were all kinds of cartoons and cynical news analysis of how could I be so naive as to talk about love existing in the hearts of American people? And how can you talk about a nation that cares about love?

But the simplicity of what Christ taught and what he was is something that we tend to avoid because we like to have it complex enough to create a door through which we can escape from facing up to the opportunity and demands of Christ.

And if we can get it confused, we can rationalize our own failure. "Maybe he was talking about people in Israel 1,900 years ago; he wasn't talking about me. The modern times are much more complicated. Christ could not possibly have understood the complexities of my own life. How can he know how much I've suffered?"

Paul, Joseph, Moses, David suffered a lot, but none of them suffered as much as Christ. Look at Jesus' life. The Son of God who suffered so much that he asked his father in heaven to take his sufferings away. "God, take this cup from me. God, don't make me die."

But then he said, "Thy will be done."

The purity and simplicity of it is what is so impressive, and Paul had a clear view of the significance of Christ's life. Had he not had this view and had the disciples of Christ not seen clearly the simple things, the church would never have survived.

And now the precious burden of responsibility that was in Paul's hands is in whose hands? Ours.

It's kind of embarrassing, isn't it? To know that we've inherited from Paul this precious possession of responsibility for Christ. And how many millions of people don't know about him? And don't know about inner peace, don't know about gifts of God, don't know about sacrifice?

And it's in our hands to do what Paul did. It's really embarrassing to have to compare ourselves to Paul, and we won't discuss it further, but read just the 19th verse.

CLASS MEMBER:

[19] But my God shall supply all your need according to his riches in glory by Christ Jesus.

PRESIDENT JIMMY CARTER:

God will supply all your needs from his unlimited riches in glory through Christ Jesus. That's a good promise. That's a good campaign slogan, isn't it? It's so good that a lot of people don't believe it, but we know it's true.

FORGIVENESS: A TWO-WAY STREET

DECEMBER 10, 1978

MATTHEW 18:21-35 & 5:43-44, EPHESIANS 4:12, LUKE 23:24

FRED GREGG:

Now, last Sunday I felt like a hypocrite because I'd prayed all week that the President would call me and would want to teach the Sunday School class, and he didn't.

I wasn't sure exactly how I felt about prayer being answered. But if you'll recall as we got into the lesson that it said that God doesn't always answer our prayers as quickly as we'd like. He wants to make sure we're sincere.

So, I didn't let up. And I kept praying. And last night at nine [o'clock], I got that phone call. The President said, "If you don't mind, I would like to teach tomorrow."

I said, "Oh, I couldn't be happier." He said, "If you're prepared, you go right ahead."

And I brought with me my rough notes this morning just to prove to him that I wasn't ready and prepared to teach. I still believe in prayer. But every time that I get this privilege to introduce the President to teach the class, I have greater respect, deeper admiration for this man.

And I still get those cold chills when I say, "President Carter, the class is now yours."

[*Some shuffling of lectern and microphones*]

PRESIDENT JIMMY CARTER:

Are you finally ready to let me take it? I didn't know for a long time what I was going to teach about this morning, but I've been trying for so many weeks to induce Fred Gregg to let me teach that I had really gotten quite aggravated with him. And I didn't know if I'd ever get over it. I thought this morning I'd take as my subject forgiveness. [*Class laughs.*]

It's really always with some degree of trepidation that I take over from Fred because he does such a superb job. But on occasion, I do like to form a renewed partnership with him and share some of his tremendous responsibility to this class.

A friend of mine came to the White House this week and spent the night with us. And we went up to the Metropolitan to hear the opera *Aida*. He brought to me a new book that's just been published, *The 100: A Ranking of the Most Influential People in History* [by Michael H. Hart]. It's quite a remarkable book. I don't agree with its basic premises completely, but I've started reading it, and as I've gotten into it, I've seen some of [Hart's] arguments, as I say, with which I don't always agree.

He shares the great contribution of the establishment of the Christian church between Christ and Paul. And he tries to assess the new and the innovative teachings that Christ brought uniquely.

What was it from the point of view of a layman—I don't think he's a Christian—that Christ contributed to ethics or to human standards of behavior in his teachings? What would come to your mind as you try to say, "Well, what was it that Christ presented to the world of human consciousness that was new?" What would be one of the things that would come to your mind?

CLASS MEMBER:

Forgiveness.

PRESIDENT JIMMY CARTER:

Forgiveness? I think, though, that just forgiveness had been a part of human thinking for a long time.

CLASS MEMBER:

Love of enemies.

PRESIDENT JIMMY CARTER:

Love of enemies. Have you read the book?

CLASS MEMBER:

Treating others as you would yourself.

PRESIDENT JIMMY CARTER:

Treating others as you would yourself.

That's a common thought, that Christ presented the first concept of the Golden Rule, but really it's not true, because when you go back, even Confucius, I think, said, "Do not treat others as you would not have them treat you." That's so close, even in the Hebrew teaching and sometimes the Golden Rule.

But the forgiveness of enemies is a new and profound concept that Christ uniquely brought to world consciousness.

And of course, there are other things, like if you are struck on one cheek, turn the other cheek. If you're made to go a mile, go two miles. If someone demands of you his coat, give him [your] cloak.

Also, the point that Christ made was that just what's fair or decent or demanded of you by law or equity is not enough.

Read Matthew 5:43 and 44. Anybody?

CLASS MEMBER:

43 You have heard that it was said, "You shall love your neighbor and hate your enemy."
44 But I say to you, love your enemies and pray for those who persecute you.

PRESIDENT JIMMY CARTER:

Good. Is there any legal demand on a human being to love an enemy?

There is none. There's no reasonable, logical reason for a person to love one's enemy, but Christ said, "Love your enemy."

Someone else read Ephesians 4:32.

CLASS MEMBER:

[32] And be kind to one another, tenderhearted, forgiving each other, just as God in Christ also has forgiven you.

PRESIDENT JIMMY CARTER:

That's what we're going to talk about today. Read it one more time.

CLASS MEMBER:

[32] And be kind to one another, tenderhearted, forgiving each other, just as God in Christ also has forgiven you.

PRESIDENT JIMMY CARTER:

All right. This is Paul describing to would-be Christians—to Christians of that era and to us—what Christ wants us to do. Be tenderhearted, forgiving one another as God through Christ forgives us.

It's hard for us to love unless we have the security of being loved. For someone who feels alone and unloved—alienated, despised—it's extremely difficult to respond to that alienation and to reach out of a chasm of loneliness to love others.

Just coincidentally, recently Rosalynn and I saw a movie, a quite old one called *East of Eden*. Does anybody remember *East of Eden*? James Dean was in it. James Dean was a young man in California, tortured because his other brother—his brother, his name was Aaron —was loved so deeply by his father. James Dean himself, who passionately loved his father, had never felt that he was loved. And he lashed out with the most bitter and intense anger. He stayed out all night and did everything he could to aggravate his father. Finally, it reached such a crisis in his own heart that his father didn't love him, that he tried to make a supreme sacrifice.

As a young man, as the war was coming along, the First World War, he borrowed money and invested it and earned a great deal to repay his father an enormous debt that his father had incurred. When James Dean went and sacrificially laid that amount of money, several thousand dollars, at his father's feet [at] a birthday party, his father rebuffed him strongly and cast him out. Eventually they were reconciled, but the point of the movie was that Cain and Abel, after the slaying took place, that the Bible says that [Cain] left and went east of Eden alone.

What I make is, it is very difficult for us, even as Christians, to love unless we have the security of love. It's very difficult for us to forgive others unless we have a sense of being forgiven. We can't wait, if we have a personal enemy, until we are sure that the other person forgives us before we are willing to forgive.

That's a very human thing to say, "Well, I'll wait. That person hurt me 20 years ago or 10 years ago or two months ago. I'll never forgive them until I'm sure that that other person makes the initiative or I'm sure they forgive me or I'm sure they will forgive me if I forgive them. I'm not going to put myself in a vulnerable position by saying I'm ready to make peace and perhaps even being rebuffed again."

Because people don't want to be embarrassed. We don't want to feel that we've been foolish or idealistic or perhaps soft or perhaps sentimental because each one of us like to have within ourselves a sense that we have a core of steel, that we are strong, independent human beings that can stand on our own feet, manage our own affairs, fight our own battles, hold our own in the esteem of the world as a person who doesn't need to kneel down to anyone else. So, we've got to have a sense either that we are already forgiven or that we will be forgiven, or at least that our forgiveness will be gratefully accepted before we are willing to forgive an enemy.

Does that sound reasonable? That's not what Christ says, right? How can we human beings who can't really love others unless we have a sense of the security of being loved, how can we initiate forgiveness when we might even be rebuffed? How can we have the security of forgiveness enough to forgive someone else?

By God. We can love other human beings who may not love us

because we know we are loved. We have the security of being loved. By whom? By God. We can have the security of initiating forgiveness to another human being, even when we might be rebuffed because we have the security of having been forgiven by whom? God.

How many times a week do you say that to God? How many times a week do you say the Lord's Prayer? At least once a week, I know, if you come to church, right? [*Chuckles*]

We say, "God forgive us as we forgive others, provided we forgive others," right? There's no problem in a Christian's life—if we analyze it and if we have an open heart—to carry out the mandates of Christ, which is to forgive others. Not on a quid pro quo basis, not on an if-you-do-this, I'll-do-that basis, but on a unilateral basis from human beings, but with the good end of a tough deal because we would much rather have God's forgiveness than to think about the small cost of forgiving a human being.

We get a world of forgiveness from God. Jesus tells us to give a little forgiveness to our fellow human beings. That's a good deal—for us. But that's not always been the premise, and it's still not the premise of even enlightened human law. In the times of Christ, it was also not the law, even the religious law.

Our lesson this morning comes from Matthew 18. Everybody turn to Matthew 18, if you have your Bibles. Let's read the first two verses of our lesson, 21 and 22. Rosalynn, would you read those?

ROSALYNN CARTER:

[21] Then came Peter to him, and said, Lord, how oft shall my brother sin against me, and I forgive him? till seven times?
[22] Jesus saith unto him, I say not unto thee, Until seven times: but, Until seventy times seven.

PRESIDENT JIMMY CARTER:

Some of the Jewish rabbis' teaching[s] said you only had to forgive somebody three times, and then what? Then you could punish them, seek retribution, attack them, hurt them, and you were completely okay, as far as the standards of that time were concerned.

Peter thought he was being very generous. He said, "Lord, how many times should I forgive someone who sins against me? Seven times?" And I guess he felt that Jesus was going to say, "Gee, you're a great man, Peter, because you have been willing to forgive people 2 1/3 times as much as is generally acceptable."

But that's not what Jesus said. What did Jesus say?

Seventy times seven. Well, now, was Jesus saying that you had to forgive people 490 times? Right. He wasn't saying, okay, you forgive him 490 times and then on the 491st time, bust him. [*Class laughs.*]

That's not what he was saying because I'm sure that somebody would've said, well, this is something that happens every day, and my wife burns the toast or something like that. I'm going to forgive her 490 times. So you got 365 days a year and then you say, now I've only got 120-something days to go.

That's not what Jesus meant. Jesus said forgive—in an unlimited way. Is forgiveness a single act? It's not restricted by a single act. Forgiveness is what? It's an attitude. It's a way of life.

Forgiveness is a way of life. Suppose God only forgave us once. I suppose he said, okay, every human being has got 50 times and then eternal damnation or 490 times or 4,900 times. This is not the teachings of God. It's not the teachings of Christ. It's not the attitude that God has taught us. It's not the attitude that we need to have toward our fellow human beings. And this is not one of those demands which is impossible to carry out.

In a way, forgiveness is a little bit more difficult than love, at least love in the acceptable or normal dimension. Because love is quite often a mutual thing, isn't it? If you meet someone that well, certainly romantic love. If you meet someone, you kind of test each other for a while, and if you feel there's a reciprocity there, then love gradually becomes more and more intense, more and more intense, until eventually you have an obsession with the other person. And that's the way most marriages are formed because people feel that we were meant for one another.

But it's really the ultimate consummation of a process where you love a little perhaps, and then you feel that the other person cares for you and it makes you greater in your own esteem and you feel at ease with the other person. You want to spend your rest of your life with them because you know you'll be loved as well as you know that your own love will be reciprocated. So it's kind of a mutual thing. There's an obvious mutual advantage in most forms of love.

That's not necessarily the case with forgiveness. There are, obviously, times when you might forgive someone and not find it reciprocated. Obviously, there are times when you love people [who don't] reciprocate. I don't want to carry the parallel too far, but I think sometimes it's more difficult to forgive than it is to love. They're closely interrelated.

Also, sometimes love is uncontrollable. I don't think anybody would disagree with that. You just can't prevent yourself loving. But forgiveness is much easier to prevent.

There is a sense in which you can sometimes not even forgive your own father or your mother or your children or your brothers, sisters or wife. Even though you love your wife, there may be something there that you can never forgive. So forgiveness is a very difficult thing.

And Christ listened to Peter's question with a great deal of interest, and then he goes on after he gives that startling answer to teach a parable that's one of the most interesting and incisive and disturbing parables, I think, in the whole Bible. We'll read it in three stages. The first one is … verses 23 through 27. Anyone with a strong voice.

CLASS MEMBER:

²³ Therefore is the kingdom of heaven likened unto a certain king, which would take account of his servants.
²⁴ And when he had begun to reckon, one was brought unto him, which owed him ten thousand talents.
²⁵ But forasmuch as he had not to pay, his lord commanded him to be sold, and his wife, and children, and all that he had, and payment to be made.
²⁶ The servant therefore fell down, and worshipped him, saying, Lord, have patience with me, and I will pay thee all.
²⁷ Then the lord of that servant was moved with compassion, and loosed him, and forgave him the debt.

PRESIDENT JIMMY CARTER:

Very good. Jesus said the kingdom of God is like this, which is kind of a strange transition from saying forgive 70 times seven. He said, the kingdom of God is like this. What is the kingdom of God? What's our own part of the kingdom of God?

The kingdom of God is really God's influence or God's spirit in the hearts of human beings. That's part of a partial definition. I'm not trying to make it conclusive. But God's presence in the heart of a human being is like this. A certain king, who obviously was very rich, decided to make an accounting among all those who served him, his slaves or his servants. He obviously had total imperial power and … a certain servant owed him how much? 10,000 talents is one translation, 10,000 talents. Does anybody have any idea how much 10,000 talents is?

Enormous amounts of money. Some, I would say, millions of dollars. But the point was … Well, let me give you one comparison. The total taxes collected, according to the Sunday School book, from what's presently the Middle Eastern states to Rome was only 800 talents a year. And this servant owed 10,000 talents, which was an almost infinite debt.

And the servant didn't have any money. He must've been a very influential and wealthy person to have ever even expended that much money. So he came on a debt that was impossible to pay back. There was no way for him to work and earn that much money. And also there must've been some skullduggery involved in the building up of a debt that great. And he said, "Lord, I owe it. I can't pay it."

And the king said, "Okay. I'm selling you into slavery and your wife and your children into slavery."

And the servant fell on his knees and said, "Please forgive me." And the king in an outburst of notable generosity said, "I forgive you. Go free."

Well, this is an interesting act of generosity. And what was the servant's response? Somebody read 28 through 30.

CLASS MEMBER:

28 But the same servant went out, and found one of his fellow servants, which owed him an hundred pence: and he laid hands on him, and took him by the throat, saying, Pay me that thou owest. 29 And his fellow servant fell down at his feet, and besought him, saying, Have patience with me, and I will pay thee all.

30 And he would not: but went and cast him into prison, till he should pay the debt.

PRESIDENT JIMMY CARTER:

How 'bout that? That's really something, isn't it? It wasn't a month later, was it? He walked right out of the king's chamber, you might say, where he'd been forgiven and saw another servant who owed him about one third of a year's wages is the estimate.

And he said, "Pay me what you owe me. And the other guy fell at his feet—very strong parallel. He grasped him around the throat and said, "If you don't pay me, you go to jail." He couldn't pay him, and he put him in jail. Let's see what else happened. Read the 31st through 34th, someone.

CLASS MEMBER:

31 So when his fellow servants saw what was done, they were very sorry, and came and told unto their lord all that was done.
32 Then his lord, after that he had called him, said unto him, O thou wicked servant, I forgave thee all that debt, because thou desiredst me:
33 Shouldest not thou also have had compassion on thy fellow servant, even as I had pity on thee?
34 And his lord was wroth, and delivered him to the tormentors, till he should pay all that was due unto him.

PRESIDENT JIMMY CARTER:

The other servants really were the ones who first condemned the first servant. They reported to the king what had happened, and the king, we presume, let the second servant out of jail. He certainly had the power to do so, and he was a forgiving king.

But to the first servant, he did what? He carried out his original sentence so far as we know. I wouldn't want to draw an exact parallel between this parable and the actions of God. And Jesus was not trying to say that the king was God. Jesus is not saying that if we are forgiven and fail to forgive, that we are, therefore, definitely condemned.

But what Jesus is trying to do is to put us in the position of the first servant who was forgiven. Why was the first servant forgiven?

He was not forgiven because he was worthy. He hadn't earned forgiveness. He was forgiven out of the goodness of the heart of the king. By what? What's the one word?

By grace. Kind of a free gift that the servant did not deserve. And God forgives us not because of our worthiness, but because he loves us through grace. But there is another step to it. And as we say in the Lord's prayer, we ask God for his forgiveness of our debts or sins or trespasses as we forgive those who sin or have debts to us or who trespass against us.

That's a prayer that Christ asks us to pray. And as we pray it, we always are conscious of the fact that there are certain hazy sins in our lives. We very seldom specify them, even in our thoughts, but we want God to forgive us. And then we kind of cite by rote as we forgive those who trespass against us.

And we probably don't stop in either case to inventory either our sins that we want forgiven because we hate to face our sins. We just generally take an attitude, at least I do, "Lord, whatever sins I might have, I don't really want to think about them right now. I hope that you'll forgive me for all of them." Kind of like a blanket pardon.

And then we really can enumerate, if we had to, a lot easier the sins against us. If I were to ask you to list five things that you think are the most serious sins that you habitually commit and you could go off in a corner with a blank sheet of paper and write them down, that would be kind of a torturous and difficult exercise, wouldn't it? You might not even be able to. You may not be able to face the fact that there are some sins in your own life that you habitually commit that puts you far short of the standards of God.

But if I ask you to go off in a corner and name five people who have sinned against you, that would be a much easier exercise, would it not?

Well, we are Christians. We have been immersed, most of us, in the teachings of Christ with Christ's life and example since we were two or three years old.

We've heard the Bible verses—you know, God is love, and other simple but profound Bible verses—since we were infants almost.

And still we find it difficult to trust God. We think, "Well, if I'm actually put in the posture of, in my prayers at night, actually enumerating to God the sins that I've committed that day, I might remind him of some sins that maybe God might have overlooked."

But that discipline is not what God wants us to feel. What we need to do is to confront our own sins and then ask God to forgive us. That's a semblance of repentance. It's certainly a prerequisite to repentance.

I'm not a theologian. I don't know the validity of just saying, "Whatever sins I've committed, I repent." I'm not sure that that fulfills what John the Baptist meant when he said repent. I'm not sure.

My guess is that we need to confront in specific terms our sins and say, "God, I've hurt my wife"—or "God, I have cheated another human being," or "God, I have told a lie," or "I've turned away against you," or "I have put material things preeminent in my life," or "I have done this or that, that was wrong"—"and I acknowledge that I did this specific thing against John Jones, and I ask you to forgive me for it."

If we go through that discipline, and I certainly have done that on several occasions in my life, then we are prepared for the second step: to go to John Jones, no matter who was at fault, and say, "John, I did this. You may not have even known it, but I ask you to forgive me for it."

And on the Jewish holy days or in some churches like the Episcopal church, when you take Communion, at that moment of accepting the blood and body of Christ, it's mandatory that you enumerate those against you have sinned, against whom you have sinned, or enumerate those who've sinned against you and forgive them or commit yourself to reconcile with that person before you accept the blood and body of Christ. We are a little bit more careless about it, although the concept and the requirement may be there.

But the king forgave the first servant, not because of worthiness, but because of grace, love. But there was a stringent demand on that first servant to act likewise. And when that servant did not, he was condemned as he was to begin with. The king forwent 10,000 talents, or two or three million dollars back in those days before 2,000 years of inflation. So the king must have had almost unlimited resources. There again, there's a parallel with God.

God's love for us is unbounded. There's not just a certain portion of love that God's going to give us and save enough for other people. There's not just a certain portion of forgiveness that God's going to allot to us and, when we've expended our portion, that's it. God will then turn his back on us. That's not true. As was the case with the king, he forgave that servant almost an unknowable amount of debt. God does the same thing to us.

I think most of us, however, are pretty stingy with our forgiveness. There have been times in my life when I have been bitterly hurt, at least in my own subjective assessment, by others, either in my political life or sometimes in other ways. And I have harbored in my heart a resentment against those people for years. I've been kind of stingy with parceling out the limited amount of forgiveness that I have to offer.

But God, in this parable, through Christ says, "The amount of forgiveness by me toward you is unlimited." And I think with a strong insinuation that we are not limited in how much we can forgive others.

We are, as a matter of fact, not only a body of Christians who believe in this, but we're a nation which has been quite generous with former enemies. My constant problem is trade balances now with Japan and Germany, our conquered enemies.

And I don't know how many of you remember the little story of the mouse that roared that was in bankruptcy and they figured their way to get rich was to go to war with the United States, be defeated, and then they would be enormously wealthy. But our country has been generous.

So we have, in our own hearts as Christians, not only the teachings of Christ and the pattern of Christ's life, which we can emulate. But there is an acceptable kind of a social or political concept in our own country of generosity, both of which quite often transcend the degree of forgiveness that individual Christians are willing to exhibit.

Read Luke 23:34 someone.

CLASS MEMBER:

[34] Then said Jesus, Father, forgive them; for they know not what they do. And they parted his raiment, and cast lots.

PRESIDENT JIMMY CARTER:

And Jesus what? And Jesus said, "Father, forgive them for they know not what they do." When did that take place? On the cross. It's one of the last things that Christ said. If there ever was someone who had been absolutely innocent of any crime and was being punished with his own life and suffering, so desperate a degree of suffering that Christ thought God himself had abandoned Jesus, it was this instance. And Jesus didn't say God condemn them, did he? He said, "God forgive them. God forgive them." So we've got an example in Christ's life for ourselves.

Well, I would like to ask all of you to recall as we leave this class, what occurred today. Peter, like us, was one of God's chosen people. He was close to Christ. He knew Jesus loved him. We know Jesus loves us. And he was searching for a standard that he could meet.

And he thought he was being exceptionally generous when he said, "Lord, should I forgive my fellow human beings seven times when they sin against me?" Sometimes we tend to set a standard just a little bit above the requirements in our lives.

And Jesus came back and said, No, don't forgive those who hurt you seven times. Do it 70 times seven times. Don't put a time limit on it. Don't put a number limit on it. Let forgiveness be a way of life, not seven specific acts or one specific act.

And then Jesus took that question by Peter—which was designed, I'm sure, to get approbation off Peter from Jesus—and expanded it to show this is what the kingdom of God is like in our lives.

There was a sinner who had a great debt that came to his king. The king demanded retribution. The sinner's debt was so great that it was impossible to repay. And he asked forgiveness, and the king forgave him and was reconciled with him.

When that servant left the king's judgment room, there was no incompatibility between the servant and the king. And immediately the servant had a chance to exhibit what he had learned.

And in a few minutes, he proved that he did not appreciate what the king had done for him because he clutched an inferior servant by the throat, threatened to strangle him, threw him in jail. There was no exemplification in the servant's life of what he had just had demonstrated by his king. ...

The parallel is stark. We know that love and forgiveness exist in God through Christ. We've got a human example in Christ's life and teachings that we can follow. There's not a remote, cloudy, hazy concept of forgiveness. Christ forgave the Jews and the Romans on the cross for killing him, and God asked us to do the same.

I would like to ask all of you, in closing, to do this as a good exercise. Sometime today, I would like to ask all of you just to make a list of one person or two or three or maybe as many as five people from whom you are estranged in some way or with whom you have strained feelings or interrelationships.

It may be somebody back in your hometown in Georgia or Texas or California, wherever. It may be somebody in your own home. There may be somebody in Washington, D.C., or in your business, and list them down.

Skip about two or three lines. Just list the different names and then write down what they've done to hurt you. My guess is that when you write it down, you'll begin to realize how frivolous it. It's something that you've clutched in your heart perhaps for 20 years as a real sense of resentment. And then if you still feel that there's some substance to it, if you still feel that your hatred or your alienation is justified, take one step further and try to put yourself in that person's position and search in your own mird for reasons why that person may have done it, either because that person was insecure or unloved, or because they may have had a selfish interest, even, a human selfish interest. Or perhaps there's a possibility that you yourself might've been at fault, at least in a small degree, and perhaps your fault may have been exaggerated in another person's mind.

And then try to reason with yourself: Is the other person really culpable? If you then find in the third step that that person is culpable and is worthy of condemnation by you, if you can say at that point, that person really did something against me that's meaningful, and if they were really wrong, only at that point do you need to exhibit forgiveness, because up until then, there's nothing that you've got to forgive, right?

But if you find that a person has really done something bad against you that hurt you and still hurts you, by the way, and if that person was at fault and you weren't, then is the only time when you really need to exert forgiveness and then do what Christ said. Forgive the person.

I would like to go further and ask you to pick up a telephone and give the person a call or perhaps write a little note just to say, "I was thinking about you today, and I value your friendship and I hope that sometime we might be reconciled to one another."

You don't have to say, "I'm pious and I went to Sunday School this morning, and I want to be generous and Christian-like and forgive you." [*Class laughs.*]

That's not what I mean. What I want you to do is just to say, "I value your friendship very much and it's been a long time since I've heard from you, and I'd like to know how you're getting along." That's not much, is it?

I'll bet you tonight when you go to bed after you've written those little notes, that you would feel better and maybe then you might think of five other people, but I want you to pick the worst ones this time, the ones that have made your life so dismal and made you suffer so badly.

But this is what Christ means, and I hope you'll do it. I'll do it, if you will.

FRED GREGG:

Well, I want to say that I came here greatly relieved this morning that I wasn't going to have to teach, but I go away from here not knowing whether or not I'm going to be able to carry out this assignment or not. Rosalynn told me, "Go ahead and try, Fred. I will make Jimmy do his."

Aren't you glad you got out of bed and came this morning? Wasn't it good to be in the house of the Lord? Let's all stand and be dismissed.

Our Father, we thank thee for this day. We thank thee for this lesson. We thank thee for the person who brought it to us. We thank thee for his deeper conviction and his understanding of the Scriptures and his interpretation. We pray that thou will bless him as he leads our country. Be with our First Lady as she works beside him. Be with our pastor today. May this just be a glorious Lord's day in whatever's accomplished, we'll give you the praise, because we ask it in your name and for your sake. Amen.

1979

This was a big year for television. C-SPAN began covering the House of Representatives; ESPN launched as an all-sports cable network; ABC began nightly coverage of the U.S. hostages in Iran, a late-night news segment that would become *Nightline*; and President Jimmy Carter gave a nationally televised speech on July 15, best known as the "malaise" speech, although he never spoke the word.

In a little over 30 minutes, Carter focused on energy and the need for everyday citizens to pitch in on conservation and a shift from reliance on fossil fuels. He also made some prescient observations:

> What you see too often in Washington and elsewhere around the country is a system of government that seems incapable of action. You see a Congress twisted and pulled in every direction by hundreds of well-financed and powerful special interests. You see every extreme position defended to the last vote, almost to the last breath by one unyielding group or another. You often see a balanced and a fair approach that demands sacrifice, a little sacrifice from everyone, abandoned like an orphan without support and without friends.

Carter spoke from the White House at 10 p.m. Eastern time, Sunday, July 15. Twelve hours earlier, he and Rosalynn were in

Sunday School at First Baptist and attended the worship service with their daughter, Amy.

It was one of 16 Sundays that President Carter worshipped at First Baptist in 1979. He taught Sunday School four times, including April 29, when the class welcomed a Baptist pastor from Kyiv, who, along with four other Soviet detainees, had arrived in the United States less than 48 hours earlier in a swap for two Soviet spies.

The presence of the Russian pastor at First Baptist was covered by the religion editor for *The Washington Post*, but the story was not even a blip on the radar of news coverage in 1979.

The bigger headlines went to the partial meltdown of the Three Mile Island nuclear reactor in Pennsylvania, the signing of the SALT II nuclear treaty with the Soviet Union, and the installation of new leaders in several countries, including Margaret Thatcher as prime minister in Great Britain, Saddam Hussein as president of Iraq and the Ayatollah Khomeini as supreme leader of Iran.

Of course, multiple headlines—on news articles and editorials—focused on the President's perceived bemoaning of a national "malaise" in his July speech. In many places in the speech, including his wrap-up, Carter's text reads like one of his Sunday School lessons:

> In closing, let me say this: I will do my best, but I will not do it alone. Let your voice be heard. Whenever you have a chance, say something good about our country. With God's help and for the sake of our Nation, it is time for us to join hands in America. Let us commit ourselves together to a rebirth of the American spirit. Working together with our common faith we cannot fail.

LIFE IN THE SPIRIT
MARCH 4, 1979
ROMANS 7-8

FRED GREGG:

So I'm not going to take up any more time except to say last Sunday the President asked for a teacher's quarterly and his was locked up, and I had to give him mine, which is kindly tattered and torn. This morning I said, "Would you like to have yours or would you like to have one that was tried and tested?"

He handed me mine and said, "I believe I'll give you this one back. It's proved inadequate."

So with that, it gives me a great deal of pleasure to turn the class over to President Carter.

PRESIDENT JIMMY CARTER:

I learned last night that I could be here this morning, and I called Fred and asked him for permission to teach. After thinking it over for a while, he gave me permission.

It's hard to detect delays measured in microseconds, but that's about how long he delayed before he ... [*Class laughs; Carter chuckles.*]

I stayed up pretty late last night. Prime Minister [Menachem] Begin was over for supper, and afterwards we had a long talk. We did not make any progress, but I got up early this morning and at least had a chance to prepare the lesson and I will do the best I can with it. Since I was not able to teach last Sunday, I thought I would go back and add a little to what was taught. And I'd like for you to help me, if you would turn to Romans 7.

The essence of [the] lesson last Sunday was that doing right is a struggle. It was a very depressing assessment of Paul's dealings with the law and ended, as you know, with an aspect of despair.

I'll just skip about it. When I call the verses, if you'd raise your hand, I'll just point to you, and you can read it very quickly and then I'll come in.

CLASS MEMBERS:

[9] For I was alive without the law once: but when the commandment came, sin revived, and I died.

[11] For sin, taking occasion by the commandment, deceived me, and by it slew me.

[14] For we know that the law is spiritual: but I am carnal, sold under sin.

[15] For that which I do I allow not: for what I would, that do I not; but what I hate, that do I.

[18] For I know that in me (that is, in my flesh,) dwelleth no good thing: for to will is present with me; but how to perform that which is good I find not.

[23] But I see another law in my members, warring against the law of my mind, and bringing me into captivity to the law of sin which is in my members.

PRESIDENT JIMMY CARTER:

"There's another law that dwells in my members, bringing me in into captivity to the law of sin."

Well, you see, in running down these verses, this is a trend, a tone or aspect or concern or fear that Paul expresses in man's relationship with the law. "For sin deceived me and slew me. When the commandment came, I died. I am carnal, filthy, fleshly, sold under sin. What I hate, that's what I do. I know that in me dwelleth no good thing, another law in my members bringing me into captivity to the law of sin" and so forth. If you read the seventh chapter, you'll find that these are just excerpts that follow that trend.

Throughout the earlier part of Romans, there is an additional, sometimes even more vivid concept of the concern that Paul was trying to express in some degree of anguish or torture.

Romans 3:23 is well known by all those who go out and witness: "For all have sinned, and come short of the glory of God." Everybody knows Romans 6:23: "for the wages of sin" is what?

CLASS MEMBER:

Death.

PRESIDENT JIMMY CARTER:

Death. All have sinned and the wages of sin is death. I'm glad that Romans didn't stop with the end of the seventh chapter. I think that the whole final expression of anguish is expressed in the 24th verse. Would somebody read the 24th verse?

CLASS MEMBER:

[24] O wretched man that I am! who shall deliver me from the body of this death?

PRESIDENT JIMMY CARTER:

That's really the way Paul wound it up.

I think the first verse of the eighth chapter is one of the most beautiful in the whole chapter. It's one of my very favorites of all because in the most vivid possible way, Paul dramatically changes what he has been expressing: torture, anguish, despair, alienation, helplessness, a dependence on the part of a human being in one's own strength alone, a total absence of joy or expectation or hope.

One thing that Fred didn't mention last week because it would be going into this lesson, was that there's something missing in the law that Paul studied and knew and revered, and Jesus said, "There would never be anything changed about it. Not one jot nor tittle would be changed in the law." What was that missing in the law that Paul discusses in chapter seven?

There's no forgiveness there. There's no redemption there. There's no escape from the condemnation that's justified for sin. Everybody sins. What you deserve for sin is wages, death.

And under the law, as Paul knew it, there was no salvation, just condemnation. And then comes Romans 8:1, and that's when we leave Fred's lesson and take up my lesson, and I want you to observe very carefully now, the difference between the two lessons. ... Fred, would you read it for us?

FRED GREGG:

[1] There is therefore now no condemnation to them which are in Christ Jesus, who walk not after the flesh, but after the spirit.

PRESIDENT JIMMY CARTER:

Now, we know that if you have a problem somewhere in your body, say you have an ear infection and you want to treat it. And you have an injection by a doctor or something, the doctor's probably not going to take a needle and stick it in your ear, right? He's probably going to put it, what, in your arm or somewhere that I won't mention, somewhere else.

And you might say, "Well, how could it possibly get from an arm to an ear?" And the obvious answer is because the ear and the arm are in one body. There's an intimate relationship. The blood circulates from one place to another. If I had an earache and even my wife had an injection in her arm, it wouldn't help my earache because there's a separation there. But with the intimacy of a single body, then healing can be transferred from an injection in one's arm to a curing element in one's ear.

Christ is the propitiation for our sin, and Paul goes on to describe the interrelationship—the spirit of Christ, the Spirit of God, the Spirit, Christ, God—as one, two, three, four, five different fragmented elements of the deity. Paul believed in monotheism, that there's one God. We believe there's one God.

The intimacy of a Christian living in Christ means that there is no separation, no alienation, no space that can't be transcended in the healing power of God. It's a difficult concept to envision, but it exists, nevertheless.

We don't have the strength to cure ourselves as human beings from the sin that we commit against God when we violate the law, the law of the Old Testament, the law of the New Testament, the law of God. We cannot cure ourselves or heal ourselves or get forgiveness, but God through Christ can heal us if we are in Christ.

In Colossians 1:27, it mentions Christ in you. Paul says, those who are in Christ. In Colossians, his letter to the Colossians, he says, "Christ is in you." What's one description of the intimacy within which Christians live with Christ that Jesus himself used as an example? Anybody? Do you remember one very figurative thing that he used? Do you remember the expression about a vine?

I'm the vine, you're the branches. In the body, I'm the arm, you're the ear. It's all one body. He goes on to describe the whole body. What can the right hand do without the left? What can the mouth do without the tongue? What can the ears do without the eyes?

[T]here's an intimacy within the Christian fellowship that exists not just between us and Christ but among ourselves if we live within Christ. In Romans 6:3, Paul even refers to baptism as what? What is baptism as expressed by Paul in that verse? He says, we in baptism are immersed in Christ. We are buried in Christ. We are raised to salvation. We actually are surrounded by the Spirit, the knowledge, the love, the forgiveness, the intercession, the concern of Christ.

How would you define Spirit? You notice all the way through the eighth chapter of Romans that Paul refers to different kinds of ways to say "the Spirit." Sometimes he just says "Spirit." Sometimes he says "the Spirit of God." Sometimes he says "the Spirit of Christ." What would you say?

CLASS MEMBER:

The best definition I've ever heard, the power and presence of God in the world.

PRESIDENT JIMMY CARTER:

Very good. Does anyone have a better way to say it than that? I was going to say the presence of God. The Spirit is the presence of God. God, let the Spirit be in my heart. Let your presence be in my heart, and Christ says, "When I go to join my Father, the Spirit, the comforter will be with you." The Spirit is the presence of God. Read the third verse of the eighth chapter, anyone.

CLASS MEMBER:

[3] For what the law could not do, in that it was weak through the flesh, God sending his own Son in the likeness of sinful flesh, and for sin, condemned sin in the flesh:

CLASS MEMBER:

On your point about the union of Christ. Can I read John 17:21, the prayer?

He prayed in order that they all, meaning the disciples, "they all might be one exactly as you are in me, and I in you, that these may be one in us in order that the world may believe that thou has sent me." There isn't any greater intimacy than that. We're as close to Christ as Christ is close to God.

PRESIDENT JIMMY CARTER:

Yes. That's a very good verse, and it illustrates the point very clearly. When we find it difficult to imagine ourselves as sinful, unworthy creatures being in a pure Christ or Christ being in us, then we go to the words of Christ and he says, "It's the same as I am in God and God is in me." We are made blameless, free of condemnation if we are in Christ, if we recognize our sinfulness, seek forgiveness through Christ.

As the third verse says, God was able to do what the law itself could not do. Through Christ, we are able to find forgiveness, to escape condemnation, to be reconciled with God, to be made clean.

Christ lived among us. He knew what sin was. He understood temptation. He avoided sin himself. He loved those who lived around him. He loved those who lived later, including us. He accepted our own sin, gave his life for us, and if we believe, cleanses us.

There is therefore now no condemnation for those who live in Christ. No matter how sinful we might be, no matter how dirty or filthy we might be, no matter how alienated we might be, no matter how much we may have condemned ourselves, no matter how much we may have been condemned by others.

Sometimes we condemn ourselves unjustly. Sometimes, perhaps more often, others condemn us unjustly or we condemn others unjustly. God condemns us also, always justly.

I recognize my own sin. My wife recognizes my sins as well. We recognize each other's sins. God recognizes our sins and forgives us. Then should we forgive each other? Then should we be able to forgive ourselves? That's not easy to do, is it?

Jesus said, "Judge not that you be not judged." Let God judge. Let God punish. But I think we in the fellowship of Christ, seeing and knowing and believing that a Christian can be absolutely cleansed with no condemnation remaining, through a relationship with Christ, we sometimes recognize that in words. We don't deny it.We accept it as an abstract idea because we hear it in church and we trust the Bible, at least while we read it. But then it's almost impossible for us after a day or a week or a month or a year or a life-time to forgive each other, even a fellow Christian. We know that that person has prayed and perhaps even in our own direct knowl-edge, we know that they're forgiven by God and still we can't forgive them.

And I think in the first verse of this chapter, when it says, "There is therefore now no condemnation," it doesn't just mean that God doesn't condemn him anymore. It means that we have a responsi-bility not to carry the condemnation of others permanently in our heart. God forgives us and accepts us and cleanses us through grace.But grace is not a license to steal. It doesn't mean that knowing that we can be forgiven, that the law is not important. The law spells out what we shall and shall not do. And we have a tendency as human beings to take that part of the law that's least onerous to us and to place the emphasis on it.

Christ, I think every Christian feels, was and is part of humanity. It's hard for me to envision God as being part of humanity. It's such an exalted concept, and the Spirit to me is a very hazy concept. But when I think about Christ, I think about his feet being dusty, and I think about him being tired, and I think about blood running down his face.

When we think about lost people or endangered people in a common, everyday sense, we think about bravery and courage and rescue. Right? If you think about a little kid falling through the ice, you instantly have kind of a concept: I think I could be a hero if I was there because I would stretch out and pull the kid off the ice, and I might be endangered myself.

But the essence of a rescue is what? Proximity, right? You got to be there. You got to be involved in it. You got to be attached to the person who is in danger. You can't do it from remote control. You can't think a person out of danger. You can't say, "Gee, I wish that person was safe."

There has to be an intimacy and a joining of two or more people into one in order for a rescue operation to take place in a time of danger. And that's a unique characteristic of our relationship with Christ. There's a proximity there.

There's a realization there that in some way when we're tempted to steal or to lie or to condemn or to lust or to murder, that Christ kind of understands what we are experiencing. We don't imply that he's done it himself, but we kind of feel Jesus understands what's going on in my life. And that's an integral part of what Paul is describing to us as the answer to the difficult questions he raised.

And I went back and selected the phrases from the seventh chapter that were dismal in nature. He gave us hints all through the seventh chapter that something better was going to come. And in the eighth chapter, here comes the something that's better.

Let me make another point before I move on. What are the worst kinds of sin? Well, as I said a little earlier, we generally think the worst kinds of sins are the ones that don't apply to ourselves too directly. If you asked a lot of people in my home church in Plains, what's the worst sin, they would probably say, "Drinking Tennessee sour mash whiskey," perhaps, that that's a root of all evil, or at least one of the major roots of all evil.

And others might say, "Well, the killing of a fellow human being." And another one might say different things. But really the sins that seemed to preoccupy Christ most when he was teaching us about sin were not sins of the flesh. It was not necessarily greed or avarice or usury or even adultery. What kind of sins seemed to concern Christ's mind?

Bitterness, hatred, alienation, pride. Pride, self-righteousness, prejudice. If I haven't analyzed how many words have [been] devoted to each one of the sins in the New Testament, I'm sure some scholars have. But I would think that self-righteousness or pride would be right up at the top among the things that seem to concern Christ most because self-righteousness and pride imply self-reliance in the absence of God.

And you go right back to what Paul was talking about in the seventh chapter. I can deal with myself. I can take care of my own needs. And I have heard several people when I was witnessing to them for Christ say, "I keep the Ten Commandments."

I visited a woman once on a Baptist mission trip, and when I read the verse, "All have sinned and come short of the glory of God," she asked me and my fellow witness to leave her house. She said she had not sinned, and I don't think she was trying to be false about it.

Probably she had taken [stock of] her own life, and she knew she was basically a good person. She knew what her motivations were, and she felt completely self-reliant in handling the problems and vicissitudes of life, dealing with the temptations adequately. If she did sin, as we all do, she could very quickly find a rationalization for it.

And that's the kind of alienation from God that concerned Christ apparently most. That's my general impression of what he talked about most.

Let's skip over this so we won't run out of time and read the 12th verse of the eighth chapter. Anyone?

CLASS MEMBER:

[12] Therefore, brethren, we are debtors, not to the flesh, to live after the flesh.

PRESIDENT JIMMY CARTER:

Okay. What does that mean, saying we are debtors?

CLASS MEMBER:

We have a responsibility. We're morally obligated.

PRESIDENT JIMMY CARTER:

Something to pay. We owe somebody something, right? You don't owe your old sinful nature anything. Where is your debt?

CLASS MEMBER:

To the Holy Spirit.

PRESIDENT JIMMY CARTER:

To the Holy Spirit. Your debt is to the entity that has given you something valuable. If you want a new automobile, you go and purchase one. The dealer has given you an automobile. You have a debt of several thousand dollars to repay.

God has a debt to pay us when we sin. What was the debt? Death. The wages is a debt. If you work two hours at $4 an hour, then the employer owes you a debt, $8. The wages is $8 because you did something.

If you sin, you have a debt owed to you, death. God said through Christ, I forgive your sins. Not because you're good, not because you're better than others, not because you've redeemed yourself, not because you've rationalized away your separation from God, but [it's] free because God loves you. That's what grace means: free, a free gift of God.

So we are debtors when that occurs. Salvation is God's free gift and also a demand. Being in debt to God, God demands that in our hearts, in our minds, we acknowledge an obligation because of the love of Christ. It is a tangible thing. We love Christ. We realize, when we think that our sinfulness falls on the shoulders or on the brow of Christ, whom we love.

If every time I committed a sin Amy had to take the punishment and I had to witness the punishment, I would be much more careful not to sin. If I had to come home every night and go in my little girl's room and watch her suffer the legitimate punishment for all the lies I may have told that day or the people I might have hurt directly or inadvertently, I would be very careful the next day to avoid sin.

Do we love Christ less than we love our Amys? Well, as a matter of fact, we tend to depersonalize it. We tend to separate ourselves from that intimacy with Christ that's so valuable to us when it works the other way.

When we are destitute or alone or in need or are suffering or facing an abject future, we reach out for God, and we reach out for Christ. We want him to be part of our lives. But when it comes the other way, we tend to think, oh, Jesus is just a spirit. God's just a spirit. I'll pass over it right now. It's kind of like a bank account. When I need Christ later, when I need God later, I'll call. And God loves me so much, he'll answer. But Paul is trying to tell the Romans that when this blessing comes to you, when a prayer is answered, that you become a debtor to God. ... Why don't you read the 13th verse [of Romans Chapter 8]?

CLASS MEMBER:

[13] For if ye live after the flesh, ye shall die: but if ye through the Spirit do mortify the deeds of the body, ye shall live.

PRESIDENT JIMMY CARTER:

What does that say to you, just in kind of common language? What does that verse say to you? Are we helpless victims? Are we kind of a quiescent mass of flesh and blood that stands dormant, and the sin comes and washes us away like a piece of flotsam at sea?

We are not helpless victims. In expressing our debt to God, we also have the courage and the will within us to withstand temptation. We don't have to yield to every temptation and then later say, "Well God, please forgive me for all those temptations that came my way."

In one place Paul said that you would never have a temptation that with God you wouldn't be strong enough to withstand. And the essence of that obviously is that when we have a very attractive temptation, we have a second one come along simultaneously: Let's don't get God involved in this. Just for this next 10, 15, 20 minutes, let's leave Jesus out of it.

But if we resolve in our hearts that we have a debt to God because of our blessings, then that ought to become more and more and more an unthinking act on our part to say, "Christ, be with me. God be with me. Holy Spirit, be with me. Fill my heart."

And then the temptation that seemed to be so attractive … won't be too attractive anymore [according to God's promise]. I mean, it won't even look like it's attractive anymore. You'll start saying, "Well, that extra thousand dollars that I might get if I cheat on this business deal isn't nearly as attractive as I thought it was."

That's what this verse 13 says in kind of a torturous way. My own concept of it after I thought about it this morning was that it meant that we are not just helpless victims that sin sweeps over because we are so weak. Because, though we might be weak, with Christ, through Christ, in Christ, we are very, very strong.

As human beings, we are helpless victims, right? We are kind of helpless victims by ourselves. And that's what Paul said all during the seventh chapter: When I want to do something right, I can't even do something right. When I know something's wrong, it's exactly what I do.

And that was Paul. It wasn't one of us average folks. That was Paul. And it obviously applied to him, applies to us. But with Christ we're different. Let's turn over to the 26th verse, eighth chapter.

CLASS MEMBER:

[8] Likewise, the Spirit helps us in our weakness for we do not know how to pray as we ought. But the Spirit Himself intercedes for us with sighings too great for words.

PRESIDENT JIMMY CARTER:

That's good. And in the King James Version, it says, "With groanings which cannot be uttered." "Likewise, the Spirit also helpeth our infirmities" is the King James Version. In the teacher's book it said the word "help" was a Greek dual word, which meant "with" and "over against." It's kind of a help [that] means you form kind of a partnership to do something together.

And one illustration is when I lived on the farm, for instance, and we had to carry a heavy, say, a black pot full of boiling water to where we were scalding pigs. Those of you who've lived on the farm know what I'm talking about—it was too heavy for one person to carry. And you couldn't grab a hold of it because the handles were too hot. So we'd get a pole and run through the hay wire on both handles. And then you get somebody on each end of the pole, and you could walk or stagger over to where you wanted the hot water, take it off the fire, and put it down. And it would be a fairly safe thing.

It was the most valuable kind of partnership that there was. And if one person walked with his right foot when the other one walked with his left foot, the pole wasn't very long, that hot water would be splashing everywhere. And the ultimate catastrophe would be if one of the people dropped his end of the pole because you'd have 20 gallons of scalding water taking the bottom part of your legs off.

But the point is that the word "help" has a much more vivid meaning when it's significant. In the average daily life around an office, the word "help" doesn't have much meaning. Come and help me pick these books up off the floor, or help me move this chair, or would you help me hook up this television set? The word "help" there kind of gets lost in the shuffle, doesn't it?

But can you just think in your own mind sometimes when the word "help" really means something. Somebody that screams "help" if a life's in danger, then that rescue operation becomes very, very significant. And the word takes on a new meaning. And that's what they're talking about here in the 26th verse.

"Likewise, the Spirit also helpeth our infirmities." That's almost in an ultimate case. When we are in danger of losing our own soul and suffering eternal condemnation or damnation, the Spirit, which is the presence of God, helps us to overcome our infirmities. The vividness of the word needs to kind of come through. Otherwise, it's kind of a dormant, meaningless sentence.

"For we know not what we should pray for." We don't even know what we should pray for. When we know what we want to pray for, sometimes we can't express it. It's in those times of confusion and despair and alienation and loneliness that an emotion ... wells up in us, almost threatening to destroy our lives, is so hard to express.

Sometimes within a family circle between a husband and a wife, there are gropings for one another, when you really wish you could tell someone else what you feel, and it's just not an easy way to express it. When Robert Browning and his wife would write poems back and forth, they were absolutely beautiful expressions of ultimate love. And they were perhaps the best who could ever express love to one another in words.

But most of us don't have that command of words, and we don't have two or three days to sit down and laboriously put words together in an exact way that are meaningful and beautiful and well coordinated. So the absence of words to express your love for your own wife or your sweetheart or your children is one that we recognize because there's no way to tell how much you love someone.

And when you're in anguish and need God, it's very difficult if you pray and try to form words, to find English language words or expressions that can express that ultimate desire for forgiveness and reconciliation that's there.

And what this verse says is that the Spirit will help you pray. Don't worry about being spiritually illiterate or spiritually inarticulate. If you have a yearning in your heart that's sincere, it will reach God even if you can't put it in words that sound very good to yourself. Let's read the 27th verse.

CLASS MEMBER:

[27] And he who searches hearts knows what is the mind of the Spirit because the Spirit intercedes for the saints according to the will of God.

PRESIDENT JIMMY CARTER:

The Spirit intercedes for the saints as [Paul] says, in accordance with the will of God. God knows us. Unfortunately, sometimes, God knows us. We don't hide anything from him. We don't hide the bad things from him.

And when you put your finger on somebody, they'll say, "I know that God understands my ugly thoughts. I know that God knows that I did this wrong yesterday." But we have a tendency to be overly condemnatory because God also knows the good parts of our life. He also understands the gropings and the loneliness and the self-condemnation. And that's kind of a reassuring thing, isn't it?

Somebody said that prayer is the divine within us, appealing to the God above us. In every human being—a despised person, a sinful person who's condemned by fellow human beings, a retarded child—there's an element of the divine. I'm not even sure that if there's different amounts of the divine within different people. I wouldn't want to claim that there is.

But in the first story of the Bible, it says God created man in his own image and put within us an element of the divine that can atrophy and wither away and become insignificant, or it can be nurtured and grow and be vital and vigorous and dominate our lives. And if we want that to happen, then the something of God within our human body can be very significant.

Well, let's kind of summarize. The peace of mind, the peace of heart, the peace of soul that we yearn for exists in Christ, through Christ. In the hurly-burly life of the day, in the self-deprecation, the despair, the loneliness of a life, there is a peace waiting for us through Christ.

Secondly, we are not slaves to sin with Christ. We are strong enough, vigorous enough, intelligent enough, resolute enough with God through Christ to withstand sin. Christians, knowing Christ, have a direct avenue to divine power. We recognize the power of God.

Tomorrow morning I'm going to get up at 7:15 and watch a closed-circuit telecast from NASA through a little outstation in Australia, of the first live close-up pictures of Jupiter. And scientists more and more are beginning to believe in what's called the big bang theory, that the world indeed was created, that it's not oscillating back and forth or a steady state. And they can't explain it in the absence of God. And that's a tremendous unrealizable power.

And Christians, through Christ, have access to that divine power.

Paul, as you know, has equivocated here back and forth about flesh and spirit and mind. And what we're looking for is a totality of a person's existence. We ought not to get bogged down in saying, "Well, my flesh is weak, and I'll separate myself from any responsibility for it, but my mind and my heart are pure." The totality of our being is what we are responsible for.

And the last thing is: God understands us. The overriding concern of human beings is our own life. And the fact that we inevitably face death—we all know it—shows that in God's sight, the human life, the human body, the temporal fleshly life is relatively insignificant. It's transient.

But the Spirit—the relationship with God, the relationship with Christ—is permanent. But we put most of our emphasis on the fleshly part. And that's what Paul is trying to tell us to escape from. And in closing—I've run a little bit over—I would like for you all just to read with no comment verse 15 in the Living Bible.

CLASS MEMBER:

[15] And so we should not be like cringing, fearful slaves, but we should behave like God's very own children, adopted into the bosom of his family, and calling to him, "Father, Father."

A CRY FOR JUSTICE
APRIL 29, 1979
1 KINGS 21:2-20

The class opens with unidentified speakers making introductions and offering prayers to welcome Georgi Vins, a Baptist pastor from Kyiv who had just been released from Soviet custody along with four other Russian prisoners.

UNKNOWN SPEAKER:

Holy Father, how can we thank you enough for all the ways you have led us? For this moment in history when our hearts take hope again and we renew our commitment to Christ and to his gospel for the marvelous, liberating power that is in him, for the bonds of fellowship that bind us one to another. We ask blessings upon the Vins family, upon all who are still in prison. You have called us to release the captives, and you have enabled us to do that, so we say thanks be unto God. Bless our President as he opens the word of life to us. Through Christ our Lord, Amen.

PRESIDENT JIMMY CARTER:

I've just been told that four days ago, Pastor Vins was in a cattle car being transported within Siberia as an exile in his own country because of his belief in Christ and because of his own personal courage in expressing that belief in the strongest and most forceful way, in spite of the intense pressure and punishment placed on him and his family by the Soviet officials.

There could hardly be a better lesson than what I've already said. Coincidentally, perhaps, or because of the works of God in some strange and mysterious way, our lesson today is precisely a lesson about our visitor. His life in the Soviet Union, his altercation with state officials, his intense courage, his punishment, and I guess it is a coincidence, but I'm not quite sure.

April the 29th, 1979, and in our Sunday School text, the title of our subject is "A Cry for Justice." And the lesson comes from 1 Kings, the 21st chapter. And if you would open your Bibles there, we will follow along for a while discussing Ahab, Jezebel, Naboth and the prophet Elijah. And then later we will talk about the lesson that we can derive from this text as we discuss these personal verses.

And I would particularly want you this morning not to think about the time of Ahab, not to think about even the Soviet Union, but to think about the United States, the Washington, D.C., community and, preferably, my life and your life and our actions in the eyes of God.

I think I will designate Ed Sonnenschein as our Bible reader this morning and ask him if he would read the first verse, which is the second verse, really, in 1 Kings 21. And then I'll let Ed do the reading because he has such a clear voice, and I want everybody to hear the text. Ed, would you just read … well, read two, three, and four.

ED SONNENSCHEIN:

2 And after this, Ahab said to Naboth, "Give me your vineyard that I may have it for a vegetable garden because it is near my house, and I will give you a better vineyard for it. Or if it seems good to you, I will give you its value in money."
3 But Naboth said to Ahab, "The Lord forbid that I should give you the inheritance of my fathers."
4 And Ahab went into his house vexed and sullen because of what Naboth the Jezreelite had said to him. For he had said, "I will not give you the inheritance of my fathers." And he lay down on his bed and turned away his face and would eat no food.

PRESIDENT JIMMY CARTER:

Why did Naboth refuse to give up his land?

CLASS MEMBER:

Generations.

PRESIDENT JIMMY CARTER:

It had been in the family for generations. It was an inheritance or a heritage that was very precious to him, right? What else? [T]here was a Hebrew law, the law of whom God passed down to the Israelites, through Moses, that said what?

You couldn't sell land. And as you know, there was a reason for it. … You had to pass it along to your children.

Part of the strength of God's chosen people and their societal structure was that they be intact, that they strengthen one another, that they not be divided, that there be a clear teaching of God's word, and that it be passed down from generation to generation.

And for land, which was a basis for their presence, their ability to sustain themselves through earnings, their temporal or human work. And for the cohesiveness of the community itself—and for the teaching of the word of God—it was important that the tribes not be completely intermixed or that land be sold to an alien who might come in with superior wealth or influence and take away this part of the inheritance.

It was a very strict law. Suppose a family got destitute and had nothing left and needed to sell the property, then what could be done? It could be sold under those circumstances, preferably within the tribe. But there was a special year. Does anyone recall what it was?

Yeah, the Jubilee year. Who knows what the Jubilee year was?

It was the 50th year. There were seven times seven, and that's 49, and then the next year was the Jubilee year. And if you had sold your land during that 49- or 50-year period, at the end of that time, title reverted back where it was before, and slaves were freed and debts were considered to be resolved. There was a cleaning of the books every 50th year.

But the point was that part of the cleaning of the books was a transfer of title to the land, even though it had been paid for, back to the original owner. So God's law was very clear in this instance. And God, of course, monitored—through prophets, through teachings, through his chosen people—the enforcement of this law and others.

When did God say, Where are you? Does anybody recall God asking someone that? Where are you?

CLASS MEMBER:

In the Garden?

PRESIDENT JIMMY CARTER:

Yes, in the Garden of Eden. He asked Adam, right? ... There was another question asked: Where is your brother? Who remembers where that was asked?

He asked Cain, "Where is your brother?" And there was a response given: "Am I my brother's keeper?" And all through the Bible, there are questions that God asks human beings that required them to give an embarrassing answer or to search their own souls for an answer, in the presence not only of God, but in the presence of the people.

And even in Jesus' time, we have some very difficult questions asked by God and by people, but one of the most important ones was: Who is my neighbor? Who is my neighbor?

And those four questions kind of form the pattern of God's relationship with human beings, as we study this lesson and as we think about its application in our own lives.

We tend to rationalize our own behavior. One of the easiest ways to rationalize it is to say, "Well, that doesn't apply to me. That was very embarrassing to Cain, and how could anybody be so foolish as to ask Jesus, who is my neighbor?"

But sometimes we should be required to answer the question and to realize that we don't ask it with as heartfelt an inquiry as we should. Who is my neighbor? Is, or has been, Pastor Vins our neighbor? He lives almost halfway around the world.

And there are many Christians and there are also many non-Christians around the world, who, compared to us and [our] material wealth and freedom and happiness, suffer severely. Are they just a transient kind of disturbing thought? Or a realization, every now and then, when we read about a horrible deprivation of rights? Or are they a constant concern of ours every time we kneel to pray or every time we assess our own blessings?

My guess is that they're a transient concern. But God says, Christ says, in the Prodigal Son, in the Good Samaritan, and in many other parables, and directly, that our neighbors are those throughout the world and about whom we should constantly be concerned.

It's difficult for us, in a free society, to obey God because, in effect, in our country, we are encouraged under the law to obey God: "one nation under God." We know that the founding fathers of our country, we know that those who wrote our laws, we know those who wrote the Bill of Rights, who wrote the Constitution, implied or directly stated that we should live our lives under the laws of God.

So we not only have God's law to support us toward righteousness and love, but we also have man's law. Patriotism, for us, is an inclination toward God. It's easy for us when you look at it, but it's not easy, as proven by our own sinfulness, our own shortcomings, our own insensitivity, our own selfishness.

How much more difficult would it be for us, living in a society, knowing God's law, but having every tiny incremental part of man's law trying to seduce us from God, convincing us in the schools, the kindergartens, the television, the radio, the news media, statements of respected officials that it's sinful, in effect, to obey God? How much easier would it be then for us to turn against God's laws? Much easier.

This is a problem that Ahab imposed upon Naboth. Ahab was a strange man. I won't go into his character this morning, but you read about Ahab, where he came from, what he did, his effusive endorsement of God on one occasion, his selfishness and weakness on another, his abject admission of his sin, his repentance.

He, indeed, goes from one extreme to another. He's kind of a weak man, avaricious, though, as we say and always have said in South Georgia in the farming areas, he doesn't want all the land; he just wants the land that joins him. And they have had great power, great wealth.

Jezreel, really, was his winter palace. It's where he went to relax and kind of enjoy himself, and there was no doubt about his authority. And he had a queen, Jezebel, who enhanced Ahab's image of authority because she was so ruthless. She had no commitment to God's law.

In fact, she considered God's law to be an obstacle to the proper recognition of the rights of her husband and the authorities. God's law was something to be destroyed. God's law was something to be proven ineffective.

And when her Baal-worshipping priests were killed in the lesson last Sunday, she was extremely bitter and undoubtedly looking for a way to come back and to prove that God's laws were impotent.

And in this awesomeness, not only of the power of Ahab and the fear that people suffered under him and his queen, was exacerbated by the fact that Naboth was an immediate neighbor living right under the observation of the king. And for the king to call him in and say, "Look, I want this little piece of land of yours for a vegetable garden or herb garden. I'm not going to steal it from you. I don't want you to give it to me. I'll buy it, give you an adequate price for it or I'll give you even better land in exchange for it."

It's a pretty good deal. Naboth could very well have said, "That's good. Although it is a violation of God's law, surely, God won't mind because this is a king who ostensibly is endorsed by God, because the elders have laid their hands on him, and he's even talked to God's great prophet."

Naboth could very well have rationalized the transfer of that land in contravention to God's law, but he decided not to. And he said, "May God curse me if I give up this land, your majesty. I would be cursed by God if I gave up this land."

It was a very courageous thing to do. And I have no doubt that, although Ahab went back to his quarters, laid down on the bed, turned his head against the wall, and pouted and grieved, I have no doubt that, when Naboth got back home, he was extremely fearful.

And I'm sure, as he discussed it with his own family, he recognized that dark consequences might result from his adamant refusal to obey what seemed to be a reasonable request of the king, but that's what happened.

And then here comes Jezebel into the bedroom and saw Ahab lying there, grieving. She said, "What are you grieving about?" He said, "Oh, I wanted [the] land next to me, and I asked Naboth for it, and he wouldn't even give it to me." And he possibly even had tears in his eyes. And she said, "What kind of king are you?"

Jezebel had an attitude toward freedom or equality or basic human rights that was genuinely despicable. She had no thought that Naboth's rights should be preserved. They were of no concern to her. As a matter of fact, they further aggravated her. How could this commoner violate the rights of her husband, who was a king, even particularly when her husband had given him a fair deal?

So the reaction against Naboth was very severe. And Jezebel, recognizing the weakness of her husband, said, "Don't worry about it. Get up and have a good meal and enjoy yourself and be happy again. I'll get the land for you."

Ahab was sworn to uphold the law. He was the personification of God's law in his own country. That was a duty of the king, as supported by the entire church organization as well as a secular organization, … to uphold God's laws.

Because almost invariably down through history, the basic elements of law have been predicated upon religious law, not only in the Judeo-Christian ethic, but within other similar ethics as well. And so Ahab knew that by right, he had no claim on that land. Had he detected the slightest, even devious, way under the law that he could have taken the land, he would certainly have already taken it.

And when Jezebel said, "Don't worry, I'll get you the land," Ahab didn't say, "How will you do it?" And so far as I know, Ahab never asked Jezebel any questions. What did Jezebel do?

Let's let Ed read the seventh through the 10th verses, and we'll all follow along in case there might possibly be one of you that didn't study your lesson.

ED SONNENSCHEIN:

[7] And Jezebel his wife said unto him, Dost thou now govern the kingdom of Israel? arise, and eat bread, and let thine heart be merry: I will give thee the vineyard of Naboth the Jezreelite.
[8] So she wrote letters in Ahab's name, and sealed them with his seal, and sent the letters unto the elders and to the nobles that were in his city, dwelling with Naboth.

[9] And she wrote in the letters, saying, Proclaim a fast, and set Naboth on high among the people:

[10] And set two men, sons of Belial, before him, to bear witness against him, saying, Thou didst blaspheme God and the king. And then carry him out, and stone him, that he may die.

PRESIDENT JIMMY CARTER:

Jezebel saw quite clearly that one of the ways to establish what I will call uncontested temporal power was to destroy religion. There was obviously a conflict between what she and Ahab saw as justice, based on the enhancement of their own rights of the powerful on the one hand, and justice in the eyes of God on the other. And the only way when that conflict arises for those in political power to deal with it, is to denigrate or to actually destroy or to distort the religious teachings.

So Jezebel, as I said earlier, was, in effect, killing two birds with one stone. She also made a mistake as it turned out, ultimately. By considering the consequences of her act, she knew that in the eyes of the Jewish leaders, if not in the eyes of God—I don't know what her attitude was towards God—that her actions would not be judged proper. And she knew that there was one very important witness against her who had already demonstrated superb courage. And who was that? Naboth.

So what could she do? This is not completely alien from our own experience in this generation. She decided to silence Naboth. There was no Siberia in Israel, so she decided that Naboth would have to be destroyed.

And as Ed has just read to us, she wrote a letter, signed Ahab's name, put Ahab's seal on it—illegally, of course—and directed to her friends among the church elders, a letter that was patently illegal. ... There was a trial, ostensibly based on law and justice, but subverted because there was no truth. Deliberate lies were contrived under the guise of justice.

The law was a very good law. The so-called constitution of Ahab's nation was a very good constitution. Basic human rights were protected. The right to own property, the right to move, the right to speak, the right to worship were protected in the law. It's a good law.

You couldn't execute a person based on the testimony of one witness because it might be false. You could only find someone guilty of a serious crime on either the uncontested testimony of two or more witnesses, or if there was a contest, then the elder sitting in judgment would decide. But the whole system of justice was subverted by the state officials to get rid of a voice that spoke for God.

And Jezebel apparently was very successful because the two men did come in and testify that Naboth committed blasphemy, that he cursed God, and also that Naboth cursed his own king. Naboth was convicted, and he was stoned to death. And the Bible in 2 Samuel tells us something that's quite obvious—his entire family was also eliminated. It would not have been enough to eliminate Naboth and leave his wife and his sons alive.

So his whole family was exterminated, apparently very rapidly, because even the next day, Ahab, who was then very happy, was out in his new land, planning where he would grow his vegetables and herbs. And I'm sure, as he looked out of the window of the palace in Jezreel, he could see his new property, and a feeling of self-satisfaction swept over him because he had achieved his goal.

A dissident voice was quieted, a potential enemy, or testifier, would never be heard of again.

It's very difficult to find laws, even contrived by men, which are not apparently fair. They are always written in the guise of justice. No leader or group of leaders would ever write a constitution saying, "I will deprive my people of human rights." That would be unacceptable.

So the laws are written with loopholes. They're very difficult to discern. Or they are written with a degree of vagueness that permits flexibility on the part of the officials when it's to their advantage to be flexible.

There was another element of the trial that's significant: It had to be done in secret and, in addition to that, the news media had to be controlled. [*He chuckles.*] Jezebel could not have afforded to let the truth be known. Can you imagine the headlines? "Two liars testify against Naboth" or "Israeli justice subverted" or "Innocent man executed" or editorials calling for a further inquiry into the facts. That's inconceivable.

So in order to subvert man's law, there has to be secrecy and a deprivation of the rights of those governed to know the truth. And it was accomplished.

Why do you think the witnesses were willing to testify against Naboth falsely? What are some of the motivations that Jezebel created or of which she took advantage? Can you think of one?

CLASS MEMBER:

Gaining favor with the king.

PRESIDENT JIMMY CARTER:

That's right, to gain favor with the king for possible future benefits. And I don't have any doubt that Jezebel arranged in ways that are not described in the Bible to reward those who went along with her in the violation of the law. Because had they been detected, there would've been severe consequences. And so there were undoubtedly some sorts of either privilege bribes or monetary bribes to those who cooperated in this deprivation of rights. Can you think of another reason?

CLASS MEMBER:

They were men of low moral character.

PRESIDENT CARTER:

That's right. They were men of low moral character to begin with. There was no conscience constraints on them, right? [And] they were afraid, right? They were afraid to violate the interests of Ahab, and although Ahab didn't tell them what to do, they thought Ahab told them because his seal was on the letter, or they didn't much care. They may have been more fearful of Jezebel than they were [of] Ahab.

And there was another very subtle one that's difficult to detect. What was it that Jezebel told them to do with Naboth? First, she told them to take Naboth and do something else with him: put him on a pedestal. Why do you think she wanted to put him on a pedestal? Anybody? To draw attention, yes. But when you put somebody on a pedestal, you kind of exalt them in the eyes of their fellow human beings.

It was deceptive, or he may have deserved it. He may have been a very righteous man. We don't know about that. But why do you think Jezebel wanted to exalt Naboth before the trial in effect?

She may have been just laying a rationalization for herself if anybody questioned. "Well, I told them to put him on a pedestal. I wasn't trying to hurt that guy. I didn't know he was guilty. I was trying to put him on a pedestal." But there's another reason that appeals to one of the human traits that are in the hearts of everyone here. What is that?

CLASS MEMBER:

Jealousy.

PRESIDENT JIMMY CARTER:

Jealousy. There was Naboth, a farmer. All of a sudden, the king exalted him. He was sitting on a pedestal above all of them, and there's a natural inclination to want to cut him down. So when he was found guilty, and most of his neighbors probably knew that he was a righteous man, they had never heard him blaspheme against God, they had never heard him be treasonous against his own king, but, by golly, it served him right. How could he possibly think he was better than they were?

I'd say jealousy, fear and various forms of bribery. The circumvention of the truth, the control of the knowledge, those elements went into this trial, elements still applicable in our time and day in some places in the world.

Well, God is not in this episode condemning government, because we've seen in previous lessons that God said, "Honor those who lead you. Honor temporal governments." Because there can't be any realization of God's hopes, there can't be any protection of basic rights of human beings, in an anarchy when the power of the most mighty prevails over those who may be weak or timid or without influence. You've got to have some structure of society to protect one another.

But that temporal or man's government has got to be based on truth. It's got to be based on justice. There have been times in our own country when we have not quite been willing to face up to this question, and I'm almost hesitant to bring it up because the press is here, and I don't want to be misinterpreted. But one of our most famous sayings is, "My country, right or wrong."

I doubt that God would approve that statement, "My country, right or wrong." And the first time we ever had to face it, in my lifetime, was in the Vietnam War. At first there was a general adoption of that: "My country, I hope it's right, but my country, right or wrong. If my president says, 'Bomb Cambodia,' if my president says, '500,000 lives or 50,000 lives shall be expended,' so be it."

But the longer we were involved in the Vietnam War, the more we realized that our country's government may not always be right, and if not, it ought to be changed. It didn't mean that we were unpatriotic, but it meant that American citizens have not only a right but a duty to constantly inquire into the righteousness of our nation's action. That is not treason and that is not in violation of God's law, and it has not always been easy in our own country to do so.

I'm a Southerner, as you know, and I remember the horror with which many white people observed Martin Luther King Jr. walking down the street without a permit. He was violating the law. And among many of us, he was condemned because of it. To violate the law in order to be proving a point is a difficult question.

But when the point can be made that the law itself is unjust or the administration of the law itself is unjust, then in God's eyes, a human being has a right to question that law and sometimes to take the consequences even in a free society or democracy.

What's the salvation for this question? We're just about out of time. The best we can hope for in a society, under optimum circumstances, is to approach, what? What does a society strive to achieve? A government, what does it strive to achieve?

Justice. Justice is the highest ideal that a government can hope to reach. Justice based on freedom, justice based on truth, but justice is the highest possible achievement of a free society based on truth.

What is the highest ideal that a human being might achieve?

Love. Love's the word I want. A government, a nation can provide freedom. A government, a nation can provide justice. A person can provide freedom, truth, justice, and love.

And God's relationship to us is one based on love. So inherently, a human being who comprises a tiny part of a nation can have a higher ideal and can have a higher achievement than a nation during those moments, perhaps transient, perhaps relatively permanent, when we are close to God and when we represent what Jesus Christ is and what Christ said God is.

What did Jesus say that God is? One word: "love." It's one of the first memory verses all of us learned, "God is love." So a human being, the monitor of government, the monitor of a society, basing one's own influence on the highest possible ideal, which is God's love, can help to maintain a standard that will elevate society to a higher standard itself.

Pure justice, pure truth, based on individual freedom, and the cumulative influence of courageous human beings can correct defects in government and can correct defects in a family or a community or a society.

Well, I don't want you to leave here thinking that Ahab and Jezebel got away with it, because God spoke to Elijah, and he said, "Elijah, you go down yonder and look in Naboth's field and you'll find a sinful king rubbing his hands with glee, condemned in my sight, where Naboth's blood flowed on the street as a result of the cuts of stones. You tell Ahab the dogs are going to lick his blood in the same place."

Ahab was sinful. Jezebel was sinful. The people who stayed silent were sinful in the face of justice—Naboth's neighbors, the Jewish council of elders, who held a trial, those who threw the first stones, which had to be those who testified against him. It's sinful to be silent in the face of injustice.

And I would like to remind you and be reminded myself that the people of God who know Christ must represent the cause of justice on behalf of the oppressed everywhere.

FRED GREGG:

Thank you, Mr. President, for that wonderful and inspiring lesson. And our time is out. I would like to ask us all to stand for a closing prayer.

Once again, we appreciate our visitors being with us. We welcome them back. Pastor Vins, you honor us by your presence, and you have contributed much to the atmosphere of this moment, and we appreciate your being with us. Now shall we just close in prayer.

We thank you, dear God, for the opportunity to gather together and to pursue heavenly thoughts and the challenges that lie ahead of us. We ask thy blessing upon each of us in the ways in which we especially need you, upon our nation and upon our leaders and upon all those serving thee this day. In Christ's name, Amen.

ONE GOSPEL FOR ALL PEOPLE

AUGUST 5, 1979

ACTS 15:1-35

PRESIDENT JIMMY CARTER:

I'm going to need a lot of help this morning. Fairly late last night, I had a 15-minute argument with the titular teacher for whom we always substitute, and I finally won the argument and he agreed to let me teach.

All of you who have Bibles or a Sunday School book, turn to Acts 15. This is going to be a lesson with maximum participation, I hope. I have enjoyed the last three or four Sundays, listening to [others] teach. …. The thrust of all these lessons recently has been one of interest, but also one of some concern and doubt and uncertainty about the early struggles of the Christian church.

It was not a sure thing. At that time, there was a need to forge a basis for the spread of the Christian gospel. And there were fits and starts, successes and failures, [and] the most intense communal feeling of brotherhood and sisterhood as they shared threats to their own lives. At the same time, [there were] the most vivid demonstrations of dispute, argument, division, separation.

There was a desire on the part of the early churches to be autonomous, to express their own will, to make their own decisions, to probe for the truth based on Jesus' teachings without being subservient to the views that were evolved in other places.

There were different kinds of leaders who sprang forth. We read a little about them. We know a lot about some of them—Barnabas, John Mark, Apollos, Paul, James.

And the very brief explanation that we have about the early church, Paul's letters plus Acts—and to some degree Romans—just gives us a glimpse every now and then of what went on in this kind of a Christian turmoil.

Distances were fairly great. I think from Damascus to Jerusalem were maybe 300 miles, I didn't measure on the map, but from Antioch to Jerusalem was even further. And it took a long time to get there.

We studied a couple Sundays ago that I think there were 11 or 12 years between visits by Paul to Jerusalem. We tend to have an impression that everything was very close together in that border area that encompassed Paul's journeys, but those journeys were a lifetime of Christian work for Paul.

So the isolation of the churches, their internal struggles, the need to bind them together with a common faith and a common basis for spreading the Christian gospel throughout the world were in conflict.

And at the same time, when we study these early churches, we want to learn how their struggles apply to our own.

Do we still have within the Christian community the kinds of characteristics that I've just described? Closeness, division, commonality, disparity, love, sometimes even hatred, a binding together, a separation one from another, a reaching out in the name of Christ, an exclusion in the name of human pride and selfishness?

It's obvious that their troubles are our troubles. Their achievements are our achievements. Their experiences can be the source of our own lessons and learning.

So this morning we'll see kind of a typical episode, although a very important episode, from which we ourselves as modern-day Christians can learn. And the lesson would be fruitless if we looked at it just as a study of ancient history.

My own time and yours would be wasted if we didn't try to search individually, not collectively, but individually in our own hearts what can I get out of this lesson that would make me be a better Christian, a more effective disciple of Christ, to modify my own thoughts, my own yearnings, my own actions, to be more subservient to the teachings of Christ and to let my life be patterned after the example Christ set.

If we don't strive for that goal in this lesson this morning, there's nothing I can say that can make any difference, that would be of significance.

We've got two churches, first of all. What would you say would be the difference between the church at Antioch and the church at Jerusalem? Anyone just ... we'll spend a little time on this because it's very important.

CLASS MEMBER:

Gentiles.

PRESIDENT JIMMY CARTER:

Okay. There were a lot more gentiles in Antioch, although I think they had both gentiles and Jews there.

And in Jerusalem, what?

Mostly Jews, probably some gentiles. So it's accurate to say that the church at Antioch were primarily gentiles who had become Christians and the church at Jerusalem were mainly Jews who had become Christians.

Don't forget that now, because it's very important when we start going from Antioch down to Jerusalem to remember that they were not having the debates and the arguments and the discussions in a Jewish synagogue absent Christ. They were having the discussions in a Christian church. Okay? That's one difference. What's another difference?

FRED GREGG:

One big difference to me in this lesson was the church in Antioch was on fire. They were reaching out.

PRESIDENT JIMMY CARTER:

Absolutely. And what about the church in Jerusalem, Fred?

FRED GREGG:

They wanted to keep it right among their own group, but they were willing to let gentiles become member[s] of the church under conditions like "I have a tendency to accept people on my terms."

PRESIDENT JIMMY CARTER:

That is the most important difference, and that's the basis for this whole episode. The church in Antioch, as Fred said, was on fire with evangelical fervor. They were reaching out to tell people about Christ, the fact that Jesus lived, that Jesus was a savior, that God's grace was all encompassing, that men and women who sinned could be forgiven, and there was a broad definition of a Christian. When somebody came and said, "I believe in Jesus Christ. I would like to be forgiven of my sins. I have faith," the people in Antioch said what? Welcome brother or welcome sister.

What was the definition, in the Antioch church, of a Christian? A person who what?

CLASS MEMBER:

Accepts Christ.

PRESIDENT JIMMY CARTER:

Who has faith in Christ.

What was the other parts of the definition? What were the other things that you had to be, to be a Christian? The first one was you had to have faith in Christ. What others?

CLASS MEMBER:

He died for us.

PRESIDENT JIMMY CARTER:

That's right.

But if you have faith that Christ died for us, that he is the Son of

God, what other definitions did you have to fulfill to be a Christian in the church at Antioch?

None. That's the point. That's the point.

A person is a Christian who is saved, through grace, by faith. Through grace.

You don't have to trade for it. You don't have to work for it. You don't have to meet certain standards. You don't have to be a Jew. You don't have to be 18 years old. You don't have to be a man. You don't have to be white. You don't have to be an American.

You have to be a person who has faith in Jesus Christ, period. And the thing that makes that definition so difficult, even for us to accept, is we cannot believe that God is so generous.

There must be something else. How could God have so much grace that he would take a sinner like that person over there, a drunk or an unwed mother, and let them be a Christian? How could God be so openhearted? There must be something more to it than that. Look at me, I'm not a drunk. My children were born in wedlock. Therefore, God must want that person at least to meet the standards that I maintain, right?

So it was a startling thing for even the early Christians to depart from a whole long list like Deuteronomy and Leviticus, of all the things you had to do, almost indecipherable, to be accepted in the heart of the church, the synagogue. To go from that to one simple definition, "I love Christ, I believe in him, I have faith in him," and to believe that that was enough for God to accept a person.

In Jerusalem, it was a little bit different. The Jerusalem church was still a little bit exclusive. It wasn't quite so easy to be accepted in the church in Jerusalem. With some, I'm sure they mirrored accurately the most enlightened attitude to the church in Antioch because in every church there are differences among members. But in general, the church in Jerusalem was somewhat exclusive. Could a Roman soldier who had been persecuting the people of Israel for decades come off the street and say, "I have faith in Jesus Christ," and be a member of the church in Jerusalem? It was difficult, wasn't it? In Antioch, they probably would've accepted that soldier without any question. In [the] Jerusalem church, even a Christian church, it was a little more difficult.

There was some narrow definition of what is a Christian in Jerusalem, and they were hearing about Antioch. There may have been some jealousy, I don't know, because the church in Antioch was exploding all over. I mean, not just in Antioch, people were going out of Antioch and forming new churches and recruiting new Christians and saving new people and transforming communities.

So there was certainly some jealousy there. And I imagine they said, "Well, their standards are too low. They're just taking in anybody." And that was another kind of a little thing that happened that maybe added insult to injury. You remember what it was? There was a famine coming, and what happened?

Yeah, this upstart church in Antioch brought a donation to the church in Jerusalem out of the goodness of their heart. But again, you may have seen some problem created.

Well, it's hard to have a legal definition of righteousness. Jesus says, "Judge not that you be not judged," but there's a tendency on the part of all of us, including me, to define what a Christian is. Who is worthy to join me in a Christian church? We can't resist it.

And ordinarily, our definition of a Christian fits myself. "What I am as a Christian must be what God wants all Christians to be." It's human nature. But it's an aspect of human nature that we must resist. Not quiescently, but actively. Because if we just drift, we are inclined to be exclusive.

I grew up in the South, and in my own town of Plains, it is still difficult for white church members to reach out genuinely to a Black. The South is not alone. In this attitude of prejudice, who were the Judaizers? This is not a word that's a reflection on Jews.

What was a Judaizer? And what was the Judaizer's definition of a Christian?

CLASS MEMBER:

Wouldn't it be that you had to almost accept the Jewish tradition?

PRESIDENT JIMMY CARTER:

You had to be a Jew first. The Judaizers said that in order for you to be a Christian, you first had to become a Jew. And only Jews—and of course we know that Jesus was a Jew—only Jews could become Christians.

So if you had a Hellenist or a Roman, in order for that person to become a Christian, they first had to become a Jew. Circumcision was part of it. The adoption of the laws of Moses was another. Certain eating habits was another. The way of honoring the Sabbath was another.

Okay, now we're coming down to our lesson today. If you all have your Bibles, we'll read a couple of verses first. …

CLASS MEMBER:

¹ And certain men which came down from Judea taught the brethren, and said, Except ye be circumcised after the manner of Moses, ye cannot be saved.
² When therefore Paul and Barnabas had no small dissension and disputation with them, they determined that Paul and Barnabas, and certain other of them, should go up to Jerusalem unto the apostles and elders about this question.

PRESIDENT JIMMY CARTER:

Okay. Where was Judea? Said they came down from Judea. Where was that? Jerusalem. From Jerusalem. Now, that's an interesting word. It said they came "down" from Jerusalem.

Actually, Antioch is several hundred miles north of Jerusalem. So where do you think the Bible got the word "down"?

CLASS MEMBER:

Mountainous.

PRESIDENT JIMMY CARTER:

Maybe it's mountainous. I don't know exactly what the elevation of Antioch would be, but I'm not sure.

FRED GREGG:

Source of authority.

PRESIDENT JIMMY CARTER:

Right, the source of authority, I think.

Although there were ostensibly no distinctions between Antioch and Jerusalem and the other churches, they were all autonomous. All the way through, even when Paul was speaking or Peter was speaking, they said, "Let's go up to Jerusalem," and the Judaists came down from Judea to Antioch, although it was north. It may have been a difference in elevation. I don't think it's the elevation they're talking about.

There was a recognition on the part of all the Christian churches that the focal point, the mother church in other words, was in Jerusalem. And these Judaizers came there and told the happy people in Antioch, "Look, you're wrong. You have to be circumcised to be saved." And what was the response among the people in Antioch?

CLASS MEMBER:

A heated debate.

PRESIDENT JIMMY CARTER:

There was a heated debate. I mean, there was a heated debate. What do you think they may have said?

FRED GREGG:

Crazy idea.

PRESIDENT JIMMY CARTER:

That's right. That's right. That's right. "Look, Mike, you're crazy. I'm already saved," right? And this was such a divisive issue. And although they did not obviously convince the people in Antioch, Paul and Barnabas saw it as so important that they decided to go to Jerusalem. Why was it so important?

It was law versus grace, yes. That's exactly the argument. Now, why was that argument so important that, although the Antioch people did not accept it at all, Paul and Barnabas decided to go to Jerusalem?

CLASS MEMBER:

If the church in Jerusalem had won out, it could have had the tendency eventually to exclude all the gentiles.

PRESIDENT JIMMY CARTER:

That's right. This debate could have struck at the heart of the evangelical movement on which a church in Antioch was embarked and which was the root of the belief in Christ for that generation and for our own. And had the church in Jerusalem prevailed, it would've severely curtailed the missionary effort that was centered around Paul, Peter, Barnabas and others.

It also created a problem in harmony. There come times in history when a great crusade is just beginning or when a great threat exists, and if the people who are embarked on that crusade or the people who are threatened are not united, they almost inevitably will suffer defeat.

Because in the initiation of a great crusade or in the threat to a group, quite often the issue is very narrowly decided. World War II: We could have been defeated. The balance of our nation's existence hung very narrowly. Could have gone either way. Had Einstein stayed in Germany, had the Nazis developed the atomic bomb, had the Midway battle gone differently and so forth, had there been no substitute for natural rubber, a lot of things could have happened, and our nation could have gone under.

And the key issue which often determines the outcome of this kind of struggle is which side is the most unified, which side works with a common purpose, which side is willing to put aside petty differences and combine efforts rather than having their own limited strength wasted away with internal dissension.

And Paul and Barnabas and Peter and James and others could see very clearly that this struggling church. where the evangelists were directly threatened, might be killed in its embryonic state.

Herod had already found, as you know, I think in the 12th chapter of Acts—I'm not sure which chapter—that it was very popular among the Jerusalem Jews to persecute the Christians. When he put Peter in prison, that was a popular thing. And the Bible says, Herod found this to be a very popular act. That's when Peter escaped from prison with God's help.

By the way, do you remember who the first person was that he wanted to notify? That Peter wanted to notify? James, the brother of Jesus. He was the head of Jerusalem church. But the fact is that this was a threat to the existence of the church, so Paul and Barnabas said, "Let's go to Jerusalem." And then let's read what happened. Well, let's just read the third verse. Rosalynn, you have the third verse?

ROSALYNN CARTER:

[3] And being brought on their way by the church, they passed through Phenice and Samaria, declaring the conversion of the gentiles: and they caused great joy unto all the brethren.

PRESIDENT JIMMY CARTER:

Right, they left Antioch. I don't have a big map here, but they came down through what's now Lebanon and Northern Israel, Phoenicia and Samaria.

And all along the way, they stopped and told the little churches, the little groups of Christians, what great response they had had in Antioch and in Asia Minor. And those little isolated, fearful Christians in Phoenicia and Samaria were overjoyed.

It's a good little aside to show you the feeling that existed in the Christian community when they discovered that there was some success in the missionary effort. And how were they received?

Read the fourth verse. Okay? Please read. Anybody has the fourth verse?

CLASS MEMBER:

[4] And when they were come to Jerusalem, they were received of the church, and of the apostles and elders, and they declared all things that God had done with them.

PRESIDENT JIMMY CARTER:

They were welcomed. Now, I think this is important because I don't want to create the impression that all the way there were these differences in philosophical attitude, evangelistic fervor and definitions of Christians. I don't want you to get the impression that it was Jerusalem versus Antioch because the ties that bound them together were much stronger than the differences that threatened to divide them permanently.

They were not seeking a way to destroy the church. The Christians in Jerusalem ought not to be castigated or condemned. They were not seeking to divide the church. They were looking for a way to avoid division. And the fifth verse describes the opposition. Somebody, anybody read.

CLASS MEMBER:

5 But there rose up certain of the sect of the Pharisees which believed, saying, That it was needful to circumcise them, and to command them to keep the law of Moses.

PRESIDENT JIMMY CARTER:

Right, there was a certain group that rose up and said that it was necessary to be circumcised in order to be a Christian. So that group existed in the Jerusalem Christian church. And I guess out of that small group, this delegation had gone to Antioch.

And the sixth verse describes a kind of a private meeting. It's not clear there. The rest of this debate occurred before the multitude, but the sixth verse describes a private meeting. Would anybody read the sixth verse?

CLASS MEMBER:

6 And the apostles and elders came together for to consider of this matter.

PRESIDENT JIMMY CARTER:

Right, just the apostles and elders. Now, in another part, you'll see that when Peter and Paul and Barnabas spoke, and James, it was before the multitude, but apparently they went off by themselves, just the apostles and the elders, to decide how should this difficulty be resolved. Who was the first one that had a chance to speak?

Peter. Why? ...Why didn't they call on Paul? If we compared, if we had three people back in the back room, Barnabas and Paul and Peter, I don't know whom we would call on to explain the theology of that early day. I mean, if you were looking for a theologian, you'd probably call on Paul, right? ...

I think perhaps the most important of all is that they knew that Jesus himself had chosen Peter, and they knew that Peter had been filled with the Holy Spirit, right, at Pentecost. And thousands of people listening to the fervent witness or testimony of Peter had accepted Christ, so his credentials were there.

There wasn't any doubt about Peter and his faithfulness to Christ and his ability to witness successfully. Also, he had been on the other side of the question. That's a very interesting point. Turn to Galatians 2. ... Read 11, 12 and 13. It's in the New Testament. [*Carter laughs.*]

CLASS MEMBER:

[11] But when Peter was come to Antioch, I withstood him to the face, because he was to be blamed.
[12] For before that certain men came from James, he did eat with the gentiles: but when they were come, he withdrew and separated himself, fearing them which were of the circumcision.
[13] And the other Jews dissembled likewise with him; insomuch that Barnabas also was carried away with their dissimulation.

PRESIDENT JIMMY CARTER:

Peter had a hard time. ... He was at once one of the strongest people and one of the most wishy-washy people. Peter was the guy that went to Cornelius, right? We're going to get to that in a minute. And he was the first one that knew that God accepted the gentiles.

But even after that, he came where Paul was. Paul was kind of a neophyte then. And although Peter had made a habit of eating with the gentiles and associated with them and so forth, after his experience with Cornelius, when James raised a question—is it right to share food, for instance, with the gentiles?—Peter quit eating with his old gentile friends.

He kind of backed off. And I guess in his own mind he felt, well, maybe gentiles are not equal. And Paul jumped on him and said, "You have betrayed what you formerly believed and taught."

So that's another reason, perhaps, that James called on Peter to speak first, because Peter had been on both sides of the issue. It had obviously affected Peter very deeply, this question of, are gentiles equal in the eyes of God or do Jews have a preferred position in the eyes of God as Christians? That was a difficult issue that Peter had already had to face. Let's see what Peter had to say now. Read the seventh through the 11th [verses of Acts 15], someone.

CLASS MEMBER:

7 And after there had been much debate, Peter rose and said to them, Brethren, you know that in the early days God made choice among you, that by my mouth the gentiles should hear the word of the gospel and believe.
8 And God, who knows the heart, bore witness to them, giving them the Holy Spirit just as He did to us,
9 And He made no distinction between us and them, but cleansed their hearts by faith.
10 Now therefore, why do you make trial of God by putting a yoke upon the neck of the disciples which neither our fathers nor we have been able to bear?
11 But we believe that we shall be saved through the grace of our Lord Jesus, just as they will.

PRESIDENT JIMMY CARTER:

That's really something. ... Peter had told many people, I'm sure, about his aversion to gentiles, about his vision. When God told Peter, "Go to Cornelius' house, lower the sheet," and he saw that some things were there that Peter thought were unclean and God said, "Go." And Peter went into Cornelius' house and, as an expert, recognized that the Holy Spirit was there.

Peter knew what it was like to be in the presence of the Holy Spirit, right? And in Cornelius' house the Holy Spirit was there, in a gentile's house. And Peter saw it and saw the change in Cornelius' life, knew that as an uncircumcised gentile, Cornelius and all his household became Christians, and knew that God accepted these uncircumcised gentiles as Christians, as his children through Christ, and saw their faith. So there was no doubt in Peter's mind that this had happened in the case of Cornelius.

And then Peter said, "Why do we put this yoke? Why do we put these other problems on the shoulders of the new Christians that are just trying to be born, that are trying to spread the word of Christ? They've got enough problems already." And then he turned that last verse around in the strangest way, because ... why? You tell me. Why is that last verse so significant?

CLASS MEMBER:

It's the reverse of everything they had heard prior to that.

PRESIDENT JIMMY CARTER:

Sure. The Jerusalem Christians were sitting there saying, "We are so good. Do you think that God would possibly let the gentiles be saved like we are saved?" And what did Peter say?

He said, "Isn't it great that God would let us big-shot Jerusalem Christians be saved just the way he lets those gentiles be saved?" It's kind of an interesting, and I presume deliberate, reverse that may have added a little bit of humility to the discussion in the Christian church in Jerusalem.

Okay, we've talked about Peter. Now, how do you think the Jerusalem Christians considered Paul? We put Paul almost at the top, second only to Christ. I'm not trying to set an order of priority and I don't want you to hold me to that, but in general, we look on Paul, we study Paul, we revere Paul. ... He hadn't been around much had he?

CLASS MEMBER:

That's why he's second to Barnabas.

PRESIDENT JIMMY CARTER:

Second to Barnabas. It was obvious that Paul was chosen to be a servant or an aide or a vice chairman or whatever, associate pastor to Barnabas. And even in this chapter, Acts 15, when it said who spoke, I believe it says Barnabas and Paul, not Paul and Barnabas. And that's significant, because they did not look on Paul yet as the forthright leader of the evangelical movement in this generation. So Paul was not all that much of a big shot.

And I would guess that Barnabas, in comparison to James and Peter, was not either. It's interesting. We'll see what happens to them. And we won't read the whole thing, but let's just read the 12th verse.

CLASS MEMBER:

[12] There was no further discussion, and everyone now listened as Barnabas and Paul told about the miracles God had done through them among the gentiles.

PRESIDENT JIMMY CARTER:

Very good. That was about the summation of what the Bible says about Paul and Barnabas. They listened to them, and they told about the signs and the wonders and the occurrences and the achievements that they themselves had seen, and the people listened. And then when James responded, right after Paul and Barnabas had spoken, to whom did James respond? Peter. …

We won't read all of James' comments, but let's just read three or four verses. First of all, the 13th and 14th verses.

CLASS MEMBER:

[13] And after they had held their peace, James answered, saying, Men and brethren, hearken unto me:

[14] Simeon hath declared how God at the first did visit the gentiles, to take out of them a people for his name.

PRESIDENT JIMMY CARTER:

Okay. There's a strange word in this 13th and 14th verse. Anybody know what it is?

Well, it's actually Simeon, I think. ... It's easy to get Peter confused. He didn't even call him Simon, like Simon Peter; didn't call him Cephas. He didn't call him Peter. He called him Simeon. ... James, I think, was trying to show a very Jewish orientation of his thoughts. In other words, he's trying to keep as much as he can in an attitude of a leading Jew. A Christian, yes, but a Jew.

And he doesn't even refer to Peter by the name that Jesus used, either Simon or Peter or Cephas, but went back to the more ... I don't know how to describe it, more ancient Hebraic word, Simeon.

When the Christian church is in trouble, or being challenged, or being divided or weakened, what's the best resource we can tap for the healing process? Anybody?

CLASS MEMBERS:

The authority of the Scriptures. The people within that church. The power of prayer. Faith. A good leader.

PRESIDENT JIMMY CARTER:

A good leader. That's what I was trying to get at. All those other answers are very fine, but you have to have a leader, right? All right. Who are the leaders?

CLASS MEMBERS:

James? Paul?

PRESIDENT JIMMY CARTER:

You don't have to be Paul to be a leader. You don't have to be a president or Sunday School teacher to be a leader.

CLASS MEMBER:

People being led by the Holy Spirit.

PRESIDENT JIMMY CARTER:

That's right. Every one of you should assume the posture of Peter. The root of the weakness of the Christian church, one of them, is the reluctance on the part of us average Christians to assume the responsibility that Christ placed on our shoulders.

You have a circle of friends—5, 50, 500. How valuable are those 50 people in God's eyes compared to the 50 people that I might list as my closest friends? Just as precious, right? Okay.

How many of those 50 closest friends of yours know without any doubt that you are a Christian and know from your own voice that they can be saved through grace by faith? Well, you, in effect, are Peter and Paul and Barnabas and James. You're the voice of Christ.

And so am I. And for us to stand 2,000 years away and look back down through history and say, "Wasn't Peter great? He went to Cornelius' house, he witnessed about Christ," when I don't know if your next-door neighbor has been visited by you on behalf of Christ. People won't walk 50 feet to invite someone to come to church or to sit down with them and say, "Let me tell you about Christ."

And it's difficult to do. I've done it hundreds of times, because my church in Plains believes in it, and we're almost forced to do it. We all go on Christian missions, and nobody can come into the Plains community without being visited almost immediately by a member of our church. But that doesn't mean that the Plains church is better than this one.

But the fact is that the source of the spread of the Christian gospel is not powerful preachers exclusively. We are inspired by a Peter or a Billy Graham or a John Wesley or a Lottie Moon.

But their voice would be nonexistent in its effect almost, were it not for others whose names never did show up in the Bible and never will show up in Baptist history books, who simply go from house to house and say, "I believe in Christ. This is why."

Suppose you fail? Suppose you get kicked out of the house? Suppose they won't let you in the front door? Don't worry about it. Don't worry about it. Let that be God's responsibility.

It's hard to get in that frame of mind. I was in Korea not too long ago, and at the embassy we had about 20 of the Christian leaders in Korea, Protestant and Catholic, the most effective evangelical group in Korea. Does anybody know what denomination? You may not believe it. Presbyterians. They got started earlier, and they are the envy, in a nice way, of the Catholics and the Baptists and the Methodists and everybody else.

The Presbyterians really have done great. And they are adding in Korea now, 500,000 new Christians every year, 500,000 a year net growth. They can't build churches fast enough. And we had the welcoming ceremony in an ex-airport, a former airport site, where Billy Graham had a revival.

One of the leaders of the revival was a guy named Billy Kim. He's been to the United States often. And they had blocked off places on their airport all the way down where 50,000 people could assemble to hear Billy Graham. And you know how many of those blocks were filled with people? 20.

A million solid people came there to hear Billy Graham preach Christ's gospel. And Rosalynn and I went to church in a new Baptist church that had been built in that same area since Billy Graham was over there, and Billy Kim rode in the car with us. And you could not believe the fervor with which that pastor preached. I mean, it just took you back to the old-time revivals when it was in its most spirit-filled moment.

It was really something. And afterwards, we had to wait a few minutes so the traffic could clear out, went down below and they gave me a Bible, unfortunately written in Korean. And the pastor said, "I was kind of caught up with this sermon, too." He said, "Would you do me a favor?" I said, "Yeah, I will." He says, "When you meet with President Park [Chung Hee], would you witness to him about our Christian faith?" And I said, "Okay."

So as we rode from the Blue House, which is the same as our White House, back to the airport, nobody was in the car except me and President Park and an interpreter and the security guard. And I told him about our faith, and he was very interested.

And I said, "I'm sorry we don't have more time together. Would you let one of our Christian friends come and talk to you about it more? And he said, "Yes."

And I said, "Do you have a preference?" And he said, "Well, I know Billy Kim." And I said, "I'll tell Billy Kim to come and see you." He said, "No." He said, "I will invite Billy Kim to come and see me." I said, "Great."

So I wrote Billy Kim a little note and wrote the pastor a little note and wrote President Park a little note. And I don't know what will come of it, but so be it. It's in God's hands. But this is a kind of little incident that can happen between two presidents, but that's no more important in the eyes of God than you and your next-door neighbor. And that's what these testimonies meant.

This was a profoundly important convocation of Christians in the year, what, 48, 49 A.D. But this was perhaps a turning point in the church because it opened up an avenue of continued witnessing that we still have today and which, unfortunately in the eyes of God, we don't use very much. Well, let's read very quickly the 19th, 20th and 21st verses, and then we'll go.

CLASS MEMBER:

[19] And so my judgment is that we should not insist that gentiles who turn to God must obey our Jewish laws,
[20] Except that we should write to them to refrain from eating meat sacrificed to idols, from all fornication, and also from eating unbled meat of strangled animals.
[21] For these things have been preached against in Jewish synagogues in every city on every Sabbath for many generations.

PRESIDENT JIMMY CARTER:

Okay. This is hard to understand because he's talking about fornication, he's talking about eating blood, he's talking about different kinds of proper acts.

The point is, we ought not to deify freedom. We ought not to say if we have a faith in Christ, we can do anything, no matter whether it hurts our neighbors or separates the church or causes divisions or causes arguments or not.

What James is saying is, "OK, faith is enough for salvation, but you still oughtn't to do anything that would divide the church or alienate people who might come to Christ."

So they gave a blanket of approval, a document of approval through a letter to the people in Antioch. "Go ahead and witness and accept people who are not circumcised into the church but do everything you can to obey the laws of God and man and keep unified the struggling Christians."

It's a good lesson. Historically, it's interesting. It describes not only the kind of people involved, but also the kind of churches involved. It kind of puts together the autonomy of the church, which is very precious to Baptists, but also the fact that we need to work in unity through a cooperative program to the support of missionaries.

And it says also that you don't have to be a Peter or a Paul to be an important evangelist for Christ. It's a good lesson, and I thank you very much.

FRED GREGG:

Let's all stand and be dismissed. Our Father, we thank thee for this day. We thank thee for thy messenger. We pray thou will bless him as he leads and guides our country. We pray for our First Lady as she serves with him. We pray for all world leaders. We pray for the one who fills our pulpit today. May this be a glorious Lord's day, and thy name be glorified. Amen.

THE COST OF CONCERN

SEPTEMBER 9, 1979

ACTS 21-23

PRESIDENT JIMMY CARTER:

One of the good things about this class is the cosmopolitan nature of it. We have people here from all over, not only our own nation, but, literally, throughout the world. And I think it gives us a perspective and a breadth of experience. It's certainly beneficial to everyone who attends.

I notice when I ask questions or when Fred or others, Ed Sonnenschein, ask questions of the class, there's always an instant response and the answers are diverse and from the heart. And there's no embarrassment in this class about participating, as a lesson is studied, and that's very helpful to any teacher.

We're going to study today from Acts, the 21st, 22nd, 23rd chapters, about one of the most important experiences in Paul's life and perhaps in the life of Christianity. It's a lesson that illustrates some important points, not only for that day and age, but also for our own lives and for the modern church.

As you know, we've been studying Acts for a number of weeks now, and the evolution of the Christian church following the death of Christ is one of excitement and challenge, one of hope and one of despair, one of close communal or community living, love, and one of division, one of success and failure. There was such a breadth of factors involved in the early church's life that it's truly almost like a mystery novel and a history lesson and an adventure story and tremendous biographies are all tied in together.

And this morning is a diverse kind of experience for us. One of the lessons I think is directly from the title, "The Cost of Concern." We can always relate to people in a business sale—the sale of insurance, the sale of seed, the purchase of items from farmers, the merchandising of our own services—if there's something to bind us together with them.

If I meet someone in Washington and they say just, "I'm from the South," it's a kind of first step toward saying, "Well, where are you from?" And they say, "Well, I'm from Alabama." And I always say, "Well, my next-door neighbor." If they say from Georgia, I say, "What town?" And if they say Sandersville or wherever, I say, "I've been there a lot of times."

And you instantly have an entrée into that person's life. And there's really kind of a building of mutual trust just because somebody happened to live 140 miles away from you in the same state or in one of the four or five regions of our nation. And if you coincidentally went to the same college, that's an even tighter tie that builds mutual trust. And if you can search around among the folks you know in Sandersville and find somebody that's a mutual acquaintance, that's really a step forward, too.

This is an important attribute of human life, the finding of a common ground on which to communicate better.

If you've had trouble that's the same, that's really an instant, human time. If you're both alcoholics and you've struggled successfully to stop drinking, there's such a breadth of common experience and common suffering that instantaneously you are almost intimate friends.

Or I'm sure if veterans of the Vietnam War who've suffered a permanent physical disfigurement or lost a limb or had a severe setback and they've overcome it, that would be an equally important tie.

But I think you can see that the most important things that combine people together are a shared, deep experience. And perhaps the deepest experiences of all are the ones where people have suffered in the same way.

Paul was destined, as we know, to be perhaps the greatest Christian witness of all time. He's witnessing to us today and to thousands and thousands, even millions of Christians, all over the world today. Paul is witnessing to us—one man. And part of his ability to witness is that he suffered.

I don't even claim he suffered willingly. I think Paul would much rather have not suffered, but he was warned before he went to Jerusalem, "You ought not to go." Among his own friends, they said, "Paul, don't go." In one place, it said the Spirit led one of the other Christians to say, "Don't go."

And his girth or his belt was taken from him, and a demonstration was held, saying, "The person who wears his belt will be bound, not just around your waist to hold your clothes together or to carry your goods, but you'll be bound with chains."

And those who accompanied Paul said, "Please don't go to Jerusalem. You'll suffer. You might be bound with chains." And Paul said, what did Paul say?

He said, "I'm not only willing to be bound with chains, but I'm willing to give my life for Christ."

So Paul went to Jerusalem. I don't know how convinced Paul was that he would suffer. That's not very clear. But there was a well-known fact, which was known by all the Christians in that early time, that there was a sharp division in Jerusalem. Jerusalem was kind of an anvil where differences between the Orthodox worshippers in the Jewish church and their beliefs were contrasted with and hammered out against the new Christian beliefs, also among Jews.

And this division was so sharp that there was a recognized danger there. It's hard to know how much fear Paul felt or how much he could anticipate what would happen.

He was carrying gifts. He was well received. When he got there, James and others were glad to see him. What was the status of the Christian church in Jerusalem when Paul arrived? What would be your assessment of its size and strength and spirit? Anybody?

CLASS MEMBER:

It was huge.

PRESIDENT JIMMY CARTER:

Huge. Yeah. How do you know it was huge? How do you know? Just an impression.

FRED GREGG:

In Acts 21:30, it said, "Brother Paul, you can see how many thousands of Jews have become believers."

PRESIDENT JIMMY CARTER:

That's right. Some translations say myriads. So it was thousands or maybe 10,000, I don't know, but certainly thousands of Christian believers lived in Jerusalem under a very strong leader, James, and others. There was a solid church. And I think that's one of the reasons that Paul and the other disciples, the other Christian leaders, were willing to go in there because there seemed to be kind of a haven for them within the existing Christian church.

Paul could have been very secure when he got there. He could have been a quiet, dormant, safe, admired, non-witnessing Christian, the kind of description that I'm sure would not apply to any of us. Safe, secure, admired, self-satisfied, non-witnessing Christian. And I'm sure he could have gone through Jerusalem, left his gifts, been thanked, been honored, back home, no Acts 21, 22, and 23. But that's not what Paul chose.

The Christians were still under attack in Jerusalem. They were criticized in Jerusalem by their Jewish brethren, who had not accepted Christ's teachings or, if they had, who deeply believed that there had to be an interrelationship between Jewish customs and Jewish religious worshipping techniques or habits and the acceptance of Christianity. And they wanted to kind of alleviate this tension.

So what did they ask Paul to do, to kind of show that he wasn't such a bad guy and that Christians in general ought to be more readily accepted? What did they ask Paul to do?

It was a very old ceremony whereby if a person wanted to be purified in a special way and set aside for religious service, they would go to the temple and offer fairly expensive gifts to God, sacrifices, and be set aside for more fervent worship of God. They were Christians, but they were doing it within the synagogue and as Jews.

And so James and the others said, "Paul, why don't you go with them and participate in the ceremony?" They even asked Paul, and he agreed to pay for the cost of the ceremony. So he went. And then we come to our lesson. In fact, I hope all of you open your Bibles to Acts 21, and we'll read a few verses here this morning. I'm going to scrape up one extra verse and ask Fred, would you start by reading Acts 21:27 through 33?

FRED GREGG:

27 And when the seven days were almost ended, the Jews which were of Asia, when they saw him in the temple, stirred up all the people, and laid hands on him,
28 Crying out, Men of Israel, help: This is the man, that teacheth all men every where against the people, and the law, and this place: and further brought Greeks also into the temple, and hath polluted this holy place.
29 (For they had seen before with him in the city Trophimus an Ephesian, whom they supposed that Paul had brought into the temple.)
30 And all the city was moved, and the people ran together: and they took Paul, and drew him out of the temple: and forthwith the doors were shut.
31 And as they went about to kill him, tidings came unto the chief captain of the band, that all Jerusalem was in an uproar.
32 Who immediately took soldiers and centurions, and ran down unto them: and when they saw the chief captain and the soldiers, they left beating of Paul.
33 Then the chief captain came near, and took him, and commanded him to be bound with two chains; and demanded who he was, and what he had done.

PRESIDENT JIMMY CARTER:

Was the story that the Asian Jews told about Paul accurate? When they saw Paul in the temple and they started shouting, "Grab this man. Let's do something about him. Get him out of the temple." Was the story that they told about him accurate? Was it the truth?

It was kind of half true, wasn't it? It was partially true because this was a man who was preaching a new gospel, right? But they also said that he was taking gentiles into the temple and defiling it. That part was not true. And why did they say that? What was the basis for the lie?

Because he had been walking up the street with a gentile from Ephesus, an Ephesian. So part was true, part was not true. A half-truth, which is almost always the case. In order for something to be believable, that for a mob or to condemn a person's character, you need a little element of truth in it, and then some more lies that can't be acceptable. In this case, the truth part and the lie part were both difficult for the Jews to accept. The fact that the man was preaching a new gospel and the lie that he had taken gentiles into the temple were both a basis for deep concern.

So what did they do with Paul? They protected the character of the synagogue by doing what? They pushed him out of the temple and shut the door, a very religious act. So that what could happen? So that Paul could be killed just outside the temple door.

This past week I had at the White House, Rosalynn and I, representatives from religious faiths throughout the world, 45 different nations dedicated to peace. They've had a convocation at Princeton University primarily, but they came by the White House to see me. And I think four years ago, they met in Belgium. And four years before that in Tokyo. This is the third meeting.

It was intriguing because they had about 50 people from Japan and 30, 40 people from Canada and had large number from India, from Great Britain, from West Germany. But they also had a group from the People's Republic of China and a group from the Soviet Union and about 40 other nations.

And one of the things we talked about there was the bloodshed that has occurred because of religion. And we know that in our church—in the Christian Church—since the time of Christ, tens of thousands of people have died because of holy wars and terrorism and torture in the name of Christ. Obviously not with God's approval but using the name of Christ.

I have seen in my own church in Plains, 15 years ago, brother-hood meetings when people would come in there to try to prove that

Blacks were inferior to whites using the Bible as a text. And you see now in Northern Ireland and in other places: terrorism, bloodshed, murder in the name of Christ, in the name of religion, in the name of God. And several nations around the world that I need not mention are being torn apart now because of religious wars.

The difference between the sects within the Muslim religion is the most serious political concern of many leaders in the Mideast, in Syria, in Iraq, in Saudi Arabia, already in Iran and other countries. The tension that exists because people worship God in a slightly different way within the Islam religion or within Christianity causes death.

And I particularly appreciated this international group because they're trying to probe not for the differences that exist among them —and the differences are quite severe—but they're trying to discern the common ground on which people can worship God in different ways.

Many of them unfortunately don't worship Christ like we do, but at least they have a common goal in wanting peace and harmony, brotherhood among human beings, and a chance to evolve an accommodation perhaps in the future without bloodshed. And in that process to exemplify in our own lives of teachings of Christ or the teachings of Muhammad or even the learnings of people who worship as Hindus or Buddhists: peace, contemplation, love, concern, honesty, integrity, compassion, forgiveness, humility. The characteristics need to be preserved, even when we have differences of religion.

That doesn't mean, though, that a Christian should violate the directives of Christ to preach the gospel throughout the world.

And Paul came to Jerusalem knowing that he could have not rocked the boat. He could have been very cautious. Who would've known the difference? He didn't. He was a man who believed deeply and he was a man who taught deeply, and he was taken by a Roman soldier who had command of how many troops? Anybody study the lesson and know?

CLASS MEMBER:

A thousand.

PRESIDENT JIMMY CARTER:

A thousand. Great. This Roman soldier in some Bibles is called a colonel. ... A colonel had charge of 10 centuries. And as you know, each century had [80 to] 100 hundred troops. Is there anywhere in the Bible in the New Testament, by the way, where Roman centurions are criticized or made to appear in a bad light? I don't believe so. Strangely enough, I think in every case when a reference is made to a centurion or to a Roman soldier, it's in a favorable light. I haven't figured out why. Maybe there's not a reason, maybe a coincidence.

But this Roman soldier had his troops stationed, where? Where was the concentration of his troops? Next door to the synagogue, to the temple. There were two things that the Romans demanded throughout their occupied territories. What were those two things? Anybody?

CLASS MEMBER:

Peace and taxes.

PRESIDENT JIMMY CARTER:

Peace and taxes. That's right. Those were the orders from Rome: Collect the taxes, maintain order. And that's why the Roman soldiers were concentrated or bivouacked just adjacent to the temple or the synagogue, because that's where, in the fermenting environment of Jerusalem, the altercations arose. And a few years before this, there had been tremendous violence there.

And when the Roman soldiers had come in and the Jews had tried to escape, hundreds had been crushed in a riot just escaping from the Roman soldiers. And I'm sure that this was present in mind, but when the Roman troops arrived on the scene, why did they arrest Paul, who was a fellow being beaten? He was a victim. Why did they arrest him?

He was obviously the focal point of the problem, and they weren't trying to make a judgment at that time. I think they were just trying to put an end to that riot, and they removed the person who was being abused and carried him to the headquarters.

When he got back to the headquarters, what was one of the first things he did? He was surrounded by Roman soldiers instead of surrounded by Hebrews, by Jews. So what did he do?

CLASS MEMBER:

Didn't he say he was a Roman citizen?

PRESIDENT JIMMY CARTER:

Well, that was the second thing. The first thing was he spoke in Greek, and the colonel was quite surprised to hear this Jewish leader, religious leader obviously, speak Greek. And Paul very quickly let him know that he was a Roman citizen.

What precipitated this information when he told him that he was a citizen of Rome? What had the colonel decided to do to Paul?

CLASS MEMBER:

You don't beat Roman citizens.

PRESIDENT JIMMY CARTER:

That's right. The Roman justice was not all that admirable now because the way the colonel was going to get at the truth was what? Beat him, scourge him, give him a lashing. And I know that scourging sometimes caused death. Somehow or another, the Romans were going to find out the truth.

And Paul said, "Hold on a minute." He said, "Is it legal to scourge a Roman citizen without trial?" And the power of Rome was so great, and their discipline was so great that immediately the colonel realized that he might be in very serious danger to his whole career. I'm not sure how strong his status was. Paul was a Roman citizen, why? By what?

CLASS MEMBER:

By birth.

PRESIDENT JIMMY CARTER:

By birth. His father was a Roman citizen. This colonel was a Roman citizen, how?

CLASS MEMBER:

He bought it.

PRESIDENT JIMMY CARTER:

He bought Roman citizenship. We don't know the circumstances. So he was on shaky ground to start with. It was an admixture of two different kinds of background, which is what we experience every day in our lives. But they both recognized certain duties: Paul, as a Roman citizen, but also as a Christian, as a Jew. The Roman colonel as an officer in the military, obviously very competent, a Roman citizen, probably ambitious.

I don't know why he would save up enough money to buy Roman citizenship, but he had done so, and he had reached a high level. And they confronted one another. They both recognized that duty. Then Paul said, "Well, I would like to make a request of you." What was that request?

He said, "I want to talk to my people." Paul was a man of caution, too, and I think Paul was a consummate politician. I say that to help my own reputation a little bit, but he was. He was 100 percent Jew when he was in the temple going through the purification rights. He was 100 percent Christian Jew when he met with James and delivered the gifts to the Christian church. He became for a few moments 100 percent Roman citizen when he was about to be scourged. And then the overwhelming truth in Paul's life, which ought to be the overwhelming truth in our life, came forward, and he said what? "I want to go speak to these people, to my people."

And I don't know why the lesson text omits this next part, but it's a beautiful presentation by Paul of why he was a Christian. He stood very cautiously where? On the balcony, on the steps. He didn't go down among the people who had been beating him up. He stood aloof, surrounded by Roman soldiers, but he spoke as a devout Christian witness and he told them, "Look, I've been educated right here among you. I admired the same leaders in the Sanhedrin that you admired. My education is the same as these knowledgeable Jewish leaders who preach in the synagogue. I'm one of you, and I persecuted Christians just like you were trying to persecute me.

"And I was on the way to Damascus," he said, and he described a blinding flash of light and the voice that said, "Paul, why do you persecute me?" He stayed blind. He was carried into Damascus blind. The scales were removed from his eyes. He became a Christian and he was going along pretty well until he finally used one word. What was that?

CLASS MEMBER:

Gentiles.

PRESIDENT JIMMY CARTER:

Gentiles. He said, "I began to witness among the gentiles." And at that point, the crowd had been deathly quiet up until then, but when he said he was witnessing among the gentiles, that was just like throwing another bomb in the whole crowd, and they immediately demanded his death, and he was taken back and protected by the Romans.

Let's read a few more verses, because it's all very interesting, I think. I hope that when you get home, you'll read the 22nd chapter, one through 21, because it's a very succinct, very exciting description by Paul of what his life had become and why. But we won't have time to do that. Acts 22 now, 22, 23 and 24. Anybody read that?

CLASS MEMBER:

22 And they gave him audience unto this word, and then lifted up their voices, and said, Away with such a fellow from the earth: for it is not fit that he should live.
23 And as they cried out, and cast off their clothes, and threw dust into the air,
24 The chief captain commanded him to be brought into the castle

and bade that he should be examined by scourging; that he might
know wherefore they cried so against him.

PRESIDENT JIMMY CARTER:

Paul would be known in our time as what? Paul said the word "gentile." He would be called a gentile lover, right?

Sometimes when we try to bridge a racial gap or a social gap,
we're condemned by our peer group. As long as we're kind of homo-
geneous—all Christians, perhaps all white, all fairly prosperous, all
belonging to a respected church—there's a safety there and a mutual
admiration because all those around us represent what we are. And
the fact that everybody's staying that way is kind of a self-imposed
proof that that's the best thing to be. But let somebody become a
little aberrational, do something a little bit different, start witnessing
among the poor, or make an extraordinary gift, or take some time off
to work exclusively for Christ, and immediately, they become a little
bit suspect. That's a religious fanatic or a gentile lover.

I've got a neighbor that lives not too far from me named David
Guest. He grows very fine Duroc Jersey hogs. Good breeder and a
good farmer. We went home two, three weeks ago and found that
David and his wife had rented out their farm, sold their hogs, and
had spent a full year in Haiti working among perhaps the poorest
people on earth. And we talked to David, and I told him how much I
admired him for it, but he doesn't have quite the social status that he
used to have. I love him more because I'm not there, but I think if I
were there and David had done that, I would feel, "Well, David
should have taken care of his farm, and he's kind of making me look
bad because I'm not going to Haiti. I'm not even witnessing down
the street."

So to be exceptional—even in your worship of Christ and even in
your unselfishness and even in your forgiveness or even in your
humility or even in your fervor—will bring down condemnation on
you. And someone who's an exceptional advocate of peace can be
condemned. To be a little bit different is a source of condemnation,
and that's what Paul had to face. The next morning, Paul was
unshackled by the Romans, and what happened? What did the
Romans soldiers do with Paul the next morning?

Yes, they delivered Paul to the Jewish religious leaders, the

Sanhedrin, to be tried, to determine the charges against this man, what should be done with him. The Romans didn't want to get involved in it. They wanted to have it settled without disturbing the community. And Paul, again, very shrewd, facing a unanimously antagonistic group of trial judges, decided it would be better if they weren't unanimous. Right? So he did something very wise. What did he do? Got half of them on his side. Which half got on his side?

CLASS MEMBER:

The Pharisees.

PRESIDENT JIMMY CARTER:

The Pharisees. Why?

CLASS MEMBER:

They believed in the resurrection.

PRESIDENT JIMMY CARTER:

Paul knew they believed in the resurrection, did he not? And he knew the Sadducees didn't, right? So Paul said, "I come here before you as a Jew who believes in the resurrection." And instead of them being all the Sadducees and Pharisees on one side and Paul on the other, the Pharisees began to shout, "We see no fault in this man!" Why? Because he said, "I believe in the resurrection," and they believed in the resurrection. There was an ongoing battle, debate between the Pharisees and Sadducees. Pharisees said, "There is a resurrection." Sadducees said, "No."

There's a pattern here that's very, very close to the trial of Christ, and Paul did a good job in splitting his opposition. [T]here was such a furor raised that Paul found his haven, which was what? His physical haven, which was what? Back among the Roman soldiers. I think up until this point in the study, it's been kind of an exciting and interesting picture of Paul and his character, his shrewdness, his commitment, his various characteristics—racial, citizenship, religious characteristics. Let's read Acts 23, 11 through 15.

CLASS MEMBER:

[11] And the night following the Lord stood by him, and said, Be of good cheer, Paul: for as thou hast testified of me in Jerusalem, so must thou bear witness also at Rome.

[12] And when it was day, certain of the Jews banded together, and bound themselves under a curse, saying that they would neither eat nor drink till they had killed Paul.

[13] And they were more than forty which had made this conspiracy.

[14] And they came to the chief priests and elders, and said, We have bound ourselves under a great curse, that we will eat nothing until we have slain Paul.

[15] Now therefore ye with the council signify to the chief captain that he bring him down unto you tomorrow, as though ye would enquire something more perfectly concerning him: and we, or ever he come near, are ready to kill him.

PRESIDENT JIMMY CARTER:

Forty deeply committed, religious worshippers of God took an oath that they would neither eat nor drink until they had killed Paul. They were not members of the Sanhedrin. They were perhaps religious terrorists or fanatics who weren't even acceptable among the community.

I can't say about that for sure, but they wanted to have some imprimatur of respectability, so this 40 went to the Sanhedrin and asked for, in effect, approval of what they had promised to do.

They plotted that Paul would come back before the Sanhedrin to be tried further, that the argument between the Pharisees and Sadducees would be prevented, and that the Sanhedrin's hands could be clean. ...

[T]his was a plot that might very well have succeeded, except for what?

CLASS MEMBER:

His nephew overheard them.

PRESIDENT JIMMY CARTER:

Yes. His sister's son overheard the plot and did what? Went to Paul who was in prison, and Paul and the nephew decided that what ought to be done?

That the nephew should go to the Roman colonel and tell him about the plot. And at that point, the Roman colonel decided that it was time to get Paul out of Jerusalem and mounted a very heavy military force to escort Paul safely out of Jerusalem. I think the Roman soldiers had become convinced of the importance of Paul. It was obvious that a full-scale effort was being made to eliminate this person, and the substance of his crime or even his alleged crime was not clear.

And I would guess that the Roman soldier said, "There's more to this than meets the eye. Let's get this guy out of Jerusalem until we can assess the situation further, because the aftermath of this man's death might be very severe for us. It might rock the peaceful relationship that we want to maintain in Jerusalem." So there was a heavy deployment of foot soldiers and I think about 200 horses on one of which Paul was mounted, and they moved Paul where to?

CLASS MEMBER:

Caesarea.

PRESIDENT JIMMY CARTER:

To Caesarea on the seacoast. For the rest of the book of Acts, Paul is a prisoner. He stayed in Caesarea how long?

Two years, and he was transferred from one place to another. This was a turning point in Paul's life. He eventually went to Rome, still as a prisoner, and the suffering that was brought on Paul could have been interpreted in a way as a condemnation of his efforts and of his life. He had been warned by the Spirit and by prophets not to go to Jerusalem. He had gone. At the same time, God had told him in a vision in Jerusalem that he wanted him to go where? To Rome.

We live in a time of challenge and of trial: trial of ourselves, of our standards, of morality, our commitment to the elements of life taught by and exemplified by Christ. The Christian church is divided, searching for an alleviation of division.

Our nation is examining its own soul, the characteristics that describe an American, our relationship with other countries, the cohesion that should bind us together in a spirit of Christian fellowship. And so we have a time of testing on us, which is not unique. All down through the ages, men and women have been doubtful and uncertain about changes that were taking place around them, and we see changes taking place around us that cause us doubt and uncertainty.

And Paul, in this particular incident, which was not unique in Paul's life, certainly was doubtful and uncertain about the future because change was so rapid. One question came to me as I studied this lesson. Where was James?

Yeah, where was James? Where were those thousands of Christians? You don't hear one word about the Christians in Jerusalem in these three chapters of Acts, when one of the top Christian leaders was under physical attack. You don't hear that James came to the colonel and said, "Please release this man. He's okay."

And you don't see 500 Christians coming forward to stand in front of the Roman barracks and saying, "Let us walk with you to Caesarea to make sure nothing happens to our brother Paul." As a matter of fact, never again in the New Testament is a Jerusalem Christian church mentioned, and I'm not sure it survived.

There's no record of the Jerusalem Christians ever going outside the city limits of Jerusalem to witness for Christ or even to witness within their own city. It's as though the Christian church in Jerusalem itself died with this incident, because of timidity or cowardice, I'm not sure.

Nobody can prove it, but we ought to think about it. Did that mean that the Christian church was dead? No, because Paul lived and other Christians lived who carried out Christ's mandate to witness with words and with acts. Paul's life could have turned into nothing. There's a guy with two chains on him, either one around his neck and one on his wrist or his feet, or we don't know. He was bound with two different chains.

He lay in Caesarea, a nothing place for two years. And Paul could very well have said, "I've done my part. My life is over. I've witnessed. I've sacrificed. I've not been a coward. I've gone where other people wouldn't go, and I've spoken when other people were quiet. But God has used me now enough." He could have gone to Rome and lived in luxury, but Paul's greatest witnessing came after this incident. It was not the end of Faul, and because it was not the end of Paul and others like him, it was not the end of the Christian church. The church has been tested time and time again because of divisions within it and because of timidity of those who profess a faith in Christ.

And what applied to Paul in this time applies to us, and what applied to the church in Jerusalem at that time could very well apply to the church in which we worship if we forget the mandate of Christ, if we rest on our laurels, if we are so proud of our status in religious circles and in social circles that we forget the fervor and the courage and the ability and the commitment and the dedication, which is inherently within us.

All of us are tested in different ways. We have different responsibilities, different lifestyles, different circles of friends, different opportunities, and Christ God recognizes those differences. And we cherish the individuality that sets us apart, but this lesson shows the cost of concern for others.

Who came out worse? Paul paid a severe price because he witnessed for Christ. It was not the end of him. The Christian church in Jerusalem didn't pay a price because they stayed quiet and they stayed secure and we never heard from them again. That is a deep lesson here, and I hope we will remember it.

1980

By January 1980, President Jimmy Carter had delivered two State of the Union addresses to Congress. In each speech, he wasted little time before declaring, "The state of our Union is sound."

The President offered no such reassurance in his State of the Union address on January 23, 1980.

"The 1980s have been born in turmoil, strife, and change," he said. "This is a time of challenge to our interests and our values, and it's a time that tests our wisdom and our skills.

"At this time in Iran, 50 Americans are still held captive, innocent victims of terrorism and anarchy. Also at this moment, massive Soviet troops are attempting to subjugate the fiercely independent and deeply religious people of Afghanistan."

From that gloomy beginning, the President's year took a steep, downhill turn.

In late February, the U.S. Olympic Committee acceded to Carter's wishes and pulled U.S. athletes from the 1980 Summer Olympic Games in Moscow to protest the Soviet occupation of Afghanistan. In April, Fidel Castro opened the port of Mariel, Cuba, and thousands of Cubans began arriving daily in Florida in what became known as the Mariel boatlift. The influx was so great that Carter issued an emergency declaration on May 6, putting the housing of the migrants under the purview of the Federal Emergency Management Agency. FEMA had been created barely a year earlier under executive orders issued by Carter.

Later in May, Mount St. Helens erupted in Washington state, killing 57 people and decimating wildlife and the landscape for miles.

Despite the international and domestic challenges of 1980, Senator Ted Kennedy of Massachusetts wanted Carter's job, forcing the sitting chief executive to campaign to keep the White House. Kennedy won a few primaries but continued to dog Carter through the Democratic convention in New York. The President won the nomination to be the Democratic candidate on the November ballot against Republican and former California governor Ronald Reagan as well as Independent and former Illinois congressman John B. Anderson.

In spite of—or possibly because of—the year's events, 1980 found Carter in worship at First Baptist of Washington 13 times. He taught Sunday School three times: in March, July and, finally, on November 16, when the church moderator presented Carter with a resolution passed unanimously by the congregation a few days after he lost re-election in a landslide.

The resolution made it clear that while the members of First Baptist loved Jimmy Carter as a brother in Christ, not every member was keen on him as President of the United States. But they said it nicely.

COPING WITH PERSECUTION

MARCH 30, 1980
REVELATION 1:1, 2:8-11, 6:9-11, 11:15-18

PRESIDENT JIMMY CARTER:

I have thought about this lesson a lot. It is very difficult for a non-biblical scholar to teach from Revelation because it requires literally a lifetime of studying and prayer and meditation and discussion to understand what Revelation is and what it means to us as Christians.

In some lives, Revelation is excluded because of the complexity of it and because [of] the doubts it proposes; because of the difficulty of comprehending what the lesson is that the author—his name is John—put forward to us. In some few Christians' lives, however, Revelation is a central part because it does provide us with a very sharp distinction of the elements that comprise human existence.

I got my good dictionary last night and looked up what "apocalyptic" meant. I thought I would get some insight into what I was going to teach today, and it says, "Apocalyptic means revelation." [*Class laughs.*]

I had to go back to the Bible and back to the Sunday School lesson from there.

How many of you understand or have any thoughts about what apocalyptic writing is? What are the elements of it? What are the characteristics of it that might kind of put it in perspective? Anybody have just an idea about apocalyptic writing or the elements of Revelation that sets it aside from all the other books in the Bible?

CLASS MEMBERS:

Dreams. Numerology, numbers. Angels, demons. They're usually very pessimistic. Astrology. Prophetic. Symbols. Visions. Prophecy. Catastrophic events.

PRESIDENT JIMMY CARTER:

Catastrophic events. You see why our Sunday School teachers shuffle around, don't you ... about who's going to teach from Revelation? [*Class laughs.*]

That's right. Vision, symbols, even animal symbolism. There are a lot of things about bulls and horses and eagles and birds of strange kinds in Revelation. Does anyone know for sure who the author of Revelation is?

CLASS MEMBER:

His name was John.

PRESIDENT JIMMY CARTER:

His name was John. His name was John. We don't really know which John it is. ... It was written almost at the end of the century after Jesus was born. But a lot of people think it is that same John. I've had that impression a lot until I studied lately.

But we don't know who it is, but his name is John. Under what circumstances did John write this book of Revelation? What were the historical circumstances that prevailed in those days?

Does anyone remember the emperor's name? It's not all that important.

CLASS MEMBER:

Domitian.

PRESIDENT JIMMY CARTER:

Domitian, I think. Domitian. And he ruled from the year 81 until the year 96, right at the end of the first century after Jesus' birth. And before that, emperors had been worshipped. What was the difference about Domitian's demand compared to his predecessors'?

He wanted them to say Caesar is Lord. But in the past, the emperors had been worshipped primarily after their death. When they had died, their successors erected temples to them, and they were worshipped after their death. But Domitian insisted that he be worshipped as a God [before] his death.

This created very severe problems for believers of all faiths. There was a difference, however, between how onerous this was on the Jews compared to the Christians. Can anyone explain to me why?

As the Romans had extended their empire into Israel, for instance, they had worked out agreements with people who lived in those captured lands. The Romans were very wise in some ways. The emotional or the spiritual beliefs of the people whom they conquered were kind of left alone. They let them worship their own God.

They wanted the taxes paid on time, and they wanted absolute allegiance to Caesar. And their foreign policy, of course, and the decisions made concerning other nations were handled by Rome. But they had worked out an agreement that the Jewish faith, which was an ancient faith, would be honored, and Jews would be excluded from having to worship, for instance, either dead Caesars or, in this case, a live Caesar. The Jews were excluded from the requirement that they say Caesar is Lord.

But Christians, the Christian faith was new. It was not a recognized faith by any government. And so Christians were required by Domitian to worship to Caesar. So, what happened in this last part of the first century?

John was exiled on Patmos, and he was part of the problem. He was one of many. He was, what—a Christian, right? And in his early writings, which we'll read in just a minute, he pointed out that he was a Christian, a brother, a fellow sufferer. There arose during this time a persecution of the Christians by Rome, which had not previously existed to this degree. It was much more severe persecution than they had known before.

And there was another thing that happened, too, concerning religion as we know it today. What was that? There was a cleavage between what?

Between Judaism and Christianity. Before this, there had been kind of a partial melding of the two. Jesus was a Jew, and there were many devout Jews who became Christians. And there was an argument, as you know, between for instance, Paul and Peter, about exactly what was going to be the relationship. Did you have to be circumcised to be a Christian? But there was no severance of Judaism and Christianity as such in that there was a constant attempt, quite often successful, to proselytize among the Jews and to gain Christian converts.

And this was abruptly halted—as we know now, permanently with minor exceptions—only at this time of Domitian's imposition of these different standards on Christians and Jews. It forced them apart even more.

And from that time on, that partial melding of Judaism and Christianity in the worship of Christ, the recognition of Christ as the Messiah was permanent. John referred to that in this book of Revelation when he condemned the Jews quite severely because they did not accept Jesus as the Messiah.

It created a very uncomfortable time for the Christians, but it's not all bad. There was a prediction of catastrophe, of a cataclysmic occurrence in the future. There was an analysis of despair, and many Christians did despair.

But there was a holding out of hope for the hopeless and a very deep and penetrating analysis of the difference between a temporal life on earth—life among men—and the spiritual life, the life in heaven, the life with God. Obviously, in the teachings of Christ and his disciples and the teachings of Paul, there was a similar drawing of these distinctions between earthly, manly, bodily gratification on the one hand and heavenly, spiritual gratification on the other.

But in Revelation, there is a jumping back and forth between suffering now on Patmos as an exemplification of Christianity as being persecuted on the one hand, and an immediate present tense analysis of Christ in heaven, the lamb in heaven, and a melding not only of the past and the present, but also the present and the future.

It was kind of like dreams or visions, but "symbols" is a little more tangible word than dreams and visions. Why is symbolism a little more concrete, a little more tangible than dreams and visions in this instance?

It's something you can understand. If you know what the symbol means, you can understand the language. When we look back on it from almost 2,000 years, it's very difficult for us to understand those symbols. But those symbols were much more understandable to this John and to the other Christians who lived in that first century. They understood the symbols much better than we can understand them now looking back. They may have used those symbols in their discussions with one another in the marketplace as they walked down the street in hearing distance [cf], say, Roman soldiers.

They may very well have used these kind of symbols in their discussion as kind of a code word to bind them together like you would today in a college sorority or a college fraternity or in the Masons and so forth. There are certain symbols and certain words and certain expressions and certain handshakes that the inner group of Christians understood at that time very clearly.

So when the order went out for all except Jews and maybe a few other recognized religious worshippers to say, "Caesar is Lord," what was the Christian response?

CLASS MEMBER:

Jesus is Lord.

PRESIDENT JIMMY CARTER:

Jesus is Lord. Jesus is the only Lord. And so this meant not only that the Christians were looked upon as different and stubborn and obstinate, but it also made them look as though they were what?

CLASS MEMBER:

Rebellious.

PRESIDENT JIMMY CARTER:

Rebellious, right. Traitors. Traitors to the government. Insurrectionists. They were rebelling against their own government. They were unpatriotic. They were accused of being traitors. So there was not only a spiritual or religious condemnation of Christians, there was also an official government condemnation and a persecution of them that struck terror in the hearts of those early Christians, the members of the church, to which we still belong. And this is what John's writing about, and he's trying to tell them some very serious things.

And let's read the Bible this morning, our lesson. Ed Sonnenschein, would you come up and read? You have a good voice. I think you might just read the entire lesson and then I'll go through it as quickly as I can because I want us to understand as best we might, what John is telling us in Revelation.

ED SONNENSCHEIN:

REVELATION 1:
[9] I John, who also am your brother, and companion in tribulation, and in the kingdom and patience of Jesus Christ, was in the isle that is called Patmos, for the word of God, and for the testimony of Jesus Christ.
REVELATION 2:
[8] And unto the angel of the church in Smyrna write; These things saith the first and the last, which was dead, and is alive;
[9] I know thy works, and tribulation, and poverty, (but thou art rich) and I know the blasphemy of them which say they are Jews, and are not, but are the synagogue of Satan.
[10] Fear none of those things which thou shalt suffer: behold, the devil shall cast some of you into prison, that ye may be tried; and ye shall have tribulation ten days: be thou faithful unto death, and I will give thee a crown of life.
[11] He that hath an ear, let him hear what the Spirit saith unto the churches; He that overcometh shall not be hurt of the second death.
REVELATION 6:
[9] And when he had opened the fifth seal, I saw under the altar the souls of them that were slain for the word of God, and for the testimony which they held:
[10] And they cried with a loud voice, saying, How long, O Lord, holy and true, dost thou not judge and avenge our blood on them that dwell on the earth?

[11] And white robes were given unto every one of them; and it was said unto them, that they should rest yet for a little season, until their fellow servants also and their brethren, that should be killed as they were, should be fulfilled.

REVELATION 11

[15] And the seventh angel sounded; and there were great voices in heaven, saying, The kingdoms of this world are become the kingdoms of our Lord, and of his Christ; and he shall reign for ever and ever.

[16] And the four and twenty elders, which sat before God on their seats, fell upon their faces, and worshipped God,

[17] Saying, We give thee thanks, O Lord God Almighty, which art, and wast, and art to come; because thou hast taken to thee thy great power, and hast reigned.

[18] And the nations were angry, and thy wrath is come, and the time of the dead, that they should be judged, and that thou shouldest give reward unto thy servants the prophets, and to the saints, and them that fear thy name, small and great; and shouldest destroy them which destroy the earth.

PRESIDENT JIMMY CARTER:

Thank you. Well, we've got a lesson today in four different chapters in Revelation, and as you can see, it jumps from one scene to another very rapidly, but we'll try to go through it as briefly as we can. But I want to point out some very important elements of the message. What was the primary message that John was trying to bring to the Christians in that troubled time?

CLASS MEMBERS:

Victory is assured. Hope. Patience. The certainty of the return of Christ.

PRESIDENT JIMMY CARTER:

The certainty of the return of Christ. Very good. And what voice does John use to bring this message?

ED SONNENSCHEIN:

His own.

PRESIDENT JIMMY CARTER:

His own, first of all. He said, "I'm John, I'm living on Patmos. I'm a brother of yours. I'm a fellow Christian. I'm being persecuted like you are." And then he shifts to Christ. The voice of Christ said to the Christians, "Do not be afraid. Do not fear."

I would say that's the main word that John was trying to get to those early, frightened Christians, discouraged Christians, who may have been filled with despair. Don't be afraid. And now we need to go into the lesson and see why should they not be afraid. They certainly had a lot to be afraid about. Their worries were well justified.

But first of all, the fact was that the message came from Christ, "Do not be afraid." And we had impressed on us in our studies of the Bible throughout our lives, and these early Christians are having impressed on them, kind of an order of priorities. What is important in a person's life? What's the most extreme punishment that we as human beings either administer to others or fear having perpetrated on us?

CLASS MEMBER:

Physical death.

PRESIDENT JIMMY CARTER:

Physical death. Physical death. The extreme punishment is death. Physical death. "He's sentenced to death" kind of sends shivers through us. And you can imagine how an accused person who's guilty of a horrible crime feels when the punishment, as the chairman of the jury reads it out or the judge states, is death. And this is actually what the early Christians faced, was physical death.

When a message comes from Christ, and we think about his life and what it meant, and then we're talking about physical death with Christ, it changes the image of death. A few minutes ago, thinking about a judge saying, "You're sentenced to death" —horrible. Sitting down, contemplating with, praying or listening to the words of Christ, what kind of image do you get of physical death? How did physical death apply to Christ? [H]e faced physical death on the cross, right? And we look on that as a ...?

CLASS MEMBER:

Victory.

PRESIDENT JIMMY CARTER:

As a victory. It's a strange mixture, though, of horrible suffering, because our heart goes out and we sometimes even weep when we sing those hymns and hear a description of Christ's death on the cross with blood coming off his head and nails driven through his hands and the torture that he suffered from thirst and his feeling of being abandoned by God. It is a heart-wrenching vision that we have of the one that we love so much, Jesus Christ.

But then we look upon that physical death, as Christians, as a great victory, as a necessary step to prove that physical death is not the end, and that we boost it up to a paramount consideration when, in the eyes of God, it is not a paramount consideration.

My favorite poet is Dylan Thomas. I first got to know him when I was reading an anthology of poems one time in the back office of my old warehouse down in Plains when I didn't have any customers coming by. And I was reading a poem by him. I think it was the only one in the whole thick book by him, the refusal to mourn the death by fire of a child in London. And the last line is: "[A]fter the first death there is no other." And I read that poem and I started to go to the next poem and it kind of stuck in my mind, and I went back and read the whole poem again. It's extremely difficult to understand the poem. That was the only line in it that I could understand on the first reading through. "After the first death," he said, "there is no other." I don't know Dylan Thomas' religious faith, but that's kind of [stuck] in my mind.

And I think what we have to remember, and what John was trying to get across to the early Christians, was that punishment by other human beings can only cause us physical death at its utmost, and no action by another human being can separate us from Christ, from God, which is the ultimate consideration in the life of a human being.

There are two deaths, according to John's teaching. One of those deaths is a physical death. The other is what?

CLASS MEMBER:

Spiritual.

PRESIDENT JIMMY CARTER:

It's a permanent death, a spiritual death, which is defined as what?

CLASS MEMBER:

Separation.

PRESIDENT JIMMY CARTER:

Permanent separation from God, permanent alienation from God, permanent condemnation. And the first death pales into insignificance when compared with the triumph of living through eternity in the presence of God.

With all our sins and all our mistakes and all our failures and all our weaknesses, when God says, "You're forgiven. Christ has accepted the punishment for your sins. Live forever with me," that life far transcends a suffering of a physical death or an imprisonment.

So, in effect, John's message was, "Cheer up. The worst is yet to come." [*Class laughs.*]

He did not predict that they would be removed or relieved of their suffering or of their punishment, of their persecution. He said, "Cheer up. The worst is yet to come." Or he could have said, "The worst is yet to come, but cheer up."

John is not only giving them a factual description of what the present circumstances are, but he is also trying to put things into an order of priority and telling them you've got good reason to worry about the actions of the Romans. But there are things much more important than that.

There is another element of suffering. All of us suffer and have suffered in varying degrees. We cannot be removed from suffering or anxiety or fear or uncertainty about the future, but that's part of life. And there again, there is something good to come from suffering. What is that?

CLASS MEMBERS:

Patience. Humility. Understanding. Long suffering. Strength. Character.

PRESIDENT JIMMY CARTER:

Character. But I want to go one step further.

CLASS MEMBER:

Spiritual growth.

PRESIDENT JIMMY CARTER:

Spiritual growth. That's exactly right. As you suffer and as you're punished, and as you get more patience and as you see you're not the only one suffering, and as you get humility because you know you can't control your life and all its elements, then the inclination for a person is to turn to things more important.

[T]o the extent that we can learn from human experience, that we cannot get the ultimate joy, the ultimate pleasure, the ultimate achievement out of human things and bodily things and self-gratification, we have learned a very good lesson because then we can say to ourselves, "What is important?"

I would guess some of the most unhappy people on earth are the ones who are multibillionaires and some of the happiest people on earth are those who don't have fame or great fortune. And some may not even have health. I think there are some people who have lost their limbs or who are permanently in a rolling chair or in the bed who still could be happy and gratified and fulfilled. So even however you might want to define what good things relate to the bodily existence or the earthly existence, you couldn't ever equate those with peace or with self-assurance or with humility or with love. Or sharing with others, concern about others.

And if you would go off by yourself without even remembering this lesson and list the things that are very important, I think ultimately you would get down to things like truth, decency, honesty, compassion, love, generosity, faith, sharing. And you can't put a price tag on any of those things, can you?

But if you just had a snap judgment, what would you like to have? Big car, a lot of vacations, a lot of travel. The snap judgments cost a lot of money, and they derive primarily from the esteem that you want to have in the eyes of other human beings. But if you just think a few minutes, you quickly come to the fact that those are not the most important things in life. And John's trying to tell these early Christians—and us—about that fact.

Christ said that eternal life with him would be a crown of victory. And I would guess that the crown of victory would be even sweeter for those who fought the hardest, for those who gave up the most for Christ, maybe for those who suffered the most, if they suffered in the cause of Christ; if they stood on their beliefs when it was difficult; if they didn't yield to temptation; if they told the truth when it hurt—I would guess that the victory would even be sweeter for them and that Christ would even love them more. But he loves us all, as you know.

Well, the same thing applies to nations. Arnold Toynbee, as you know, has written a long thesis about the rise and fall of nations or societies and what's his basic premise? Anybody?

CLASS MEMBER:

It comes from within.

PRESIDENT JIMMY CARTER:

The strength of a nation or a society comes from within. And what's the kind of a cycle of nations down through history?

CLASS MEMBER:

Rise and fall.

PRESIDENT JIMMY CARTER:

Rise and fall. When do they rise?

CLASS MEMBER:

When they're young.

PRESIDENT JIMMY CARTER:

When they're young, but also what else? When they're facing challenges, right? When it's a dynamic, struggling, hard-driving, inspired, reaching for greatness and overcoming difficulties. And when does the decline journey come to a great nation, a great society?

CLASS MEMBERS:

When they lose their values. Greed. Riches. Morals.

PRESIDENT JIMMY CARTER:

Morals, compromise. I was trying to get to complacency. When a great society or great nation becomes complacent and says, "We've got it made," then you start internal squabbling, emphasis on material things, greed, avarice, persecution of others, arrogance. And that's when the decline starts.

And in Toynbee's long list—he's got a one-volume history, but he's got I think 19 volumes in all—but he analyzed every major society that's ever grown, sometimes not having very many natural resources, sometimes having good natural resources. But when they get to be powerful, they start going down, if they lose that spark of challenge.

Another word for challenge, to stretch your point a little bit, might be anxiety. Reinhold Niebuhr says that human beings live in a realm between anxiety and complacency, and we need a little anxiety in our lives. What comes out of anxiety?

CLASS MEMBERS:

Fear. Growth. Struggle.

PRESIDENT JIMMY CARTER:

Anxiety is not always a bad word by the way. I'm not trying to picture it as a bad word, but as you're a young person, say in college, you have a little bit of anxiety about what your family life's going to be in the future and how are you going to measure up against your competitors. Are you going to be a good physicist or mediocre physicist or a very poor one? Are you going to be able to expand your mind and expand your heart the rest of your lives and grow as a person, or are you going to be confined with the drudgery of work and the despair of failure?

Anxiety about the future inspires people to do better. It gives us ambition, which is not bad because if you don't have any anxiety, you become, as you know, like the Pharisee in church that said, "Lord, I thank you that I'm not like all the rest of these people." And I guess if there's one point that Christ emphasized over and over, it was self-pride, and self-pride and complacency might be equated to some degree with an absence of anxiety.

So, being anxious about the future, anxious about our status with our fellow human beings, anxious about our relationship with God is not bad. If we think we've got a perfect relationship with God, then we are suffering from one of the most severe sins condemned by Christ. That's part of the Bible.

How would you describe the Bible? What is the Bible? Anybody?

CLASS MEMBERS:

It's a constant struggle for superior spiritual growth towards God. God revealing himself to man. God speaking to man and joining him to him.

PRESIDENT JIMMY CARTER:

Okay. God, speaking to man and joining him to him.

I'm going to argue with you. I hate to do it. That was the point I wanted to make. I don't think that's right. The Bible to me is not a monologue. It's not God sitting here telling everybody, "This is a rule that you've got to go by," and so forth.

When you read the Bible, it is really a description of a dialogue, isn't it? It's man speaking back.

In the Old Testament, horrible arguments [occurred] between God and man and between the prophets speaking for God and the other people around him who are listening to them. Terrible struggles, terrible arguments.

In the New Testament, Christ dealt with and argued with and contended with sinful people. And Paul did the same thing, struggling to understand God, saying, "I don't understand this. Why do you make me do this?" Many of the prophets fought back against God and said, "I don't want to do this." Paul did.

It's hard. It is a struggle. And I think we have a tendency to struggle as well. And in the struggling, in the striving, we learn. And that's not bad. God doesn't want us to be automatons.

He could have made human beings all exactly the same with absolute subservience to a sharp, defined set of principles, so we didn't have any will of our own. But we are the ones that make a decision about our relationship with God.

And this is what message John is trying to get over to us in Revelation: Man cannot harm our relationship with God. That is determined between us and God.

And as we look at these verses that seem to be strange in Revelation, we understand a little more about what John was trying to say. When we had, for instance, the vision in heaven and the image of believers under the altar, what was that supposed to signify?

CLASS MEMBER:

The fate of the martyrs.

PRESIDENT JIMMY CARTER:

Yeah, that's right. It dealt with the fate of the martyrs. And I guess the martyrs were the ones who were under the altar, discovered under the altar in this vision in heaven in the sixth chapter—I think it was, yes—of Revelation. But why are they under the altar do you think?

Not just for protection. I think possibly because the symbolism is that they have been sacrificed. They have been sacrificed in their service to God as Christ was sacrificed on the altar.

There's a parallelism here that these favored people who were martyrs to persecution for Christ were under the altar. Not only that they were being protected by God, but also because that's where they would've been had they been sacrificed on the altar.

So these were, in effect, sacrificial lambs, and they were telling God, "How soon, man, are you going to persecute these people that sent us to a physical death?" They were impatient with God, weren't they?

And then of course, the message came back to them through Christ that what?

CLASS MEMBER:

Wait a little while longer.

PRESIDENT JIMMY CARTER:

Yeah, wait a while. Wait a while. Take your watches off. Let's don't apply temporal measuring times to the workings of God's kingdom. That's one message that was given to them. Be patient. In the cycle of a lifetime, 70 years, this is just a blink of the eye. Be patient because God said that others will come to join you. Others will come to join you.

CLASS MEMBER:

He gave them a white robe.

PRESIDENT JIMMY CARTER:

He gave them a white robe just to kind of reassure 'em, I guess. I don't know why. But the essence is "You are favored; you have been blessed." The blessing is permanent. Now, later on, when the 24 leaders knelt down in worship, does anybody have any idea about what that might signify?

CLASS MEMBER:

It could have been the 12 disciples and the 12 apostles.

PRESIDENT JIMMY CARTER:

Could have been the 12 apostles and 12 disciples. That's right. And why do these 24 powerful men in John's book on Revelation kneel down? What's the message there?

If these were the 12 disciples of Christ and the 12 major prophets of God, they were, in the spiritual kingdom, the top 24 people, weren't they? Of God's earthly kingdom, they were the top 24, weren't they? And they were kneeling down, which is a message of what?

FRED GREGG:

Worship.

PRESIDENT JIMMY CARTER:

Right. Even the most powerful things on earth are subservient to Christ, to God, right?

The thing, again, is another message coming back to us in these strange symbols and visions: that even the people that we look on as the most powerful—Moses, John, Peter, Ezra, Isaiah, that we look on with awe and reverence—kneeling down to the lamb, prostrating themselves on the ground in this image or vision that John gives to us. Even the most wonderful things that we envision here on earth, even relating to God are as nothing compared to God himself and our Lord Jesus Christ.

Almost every human being has two elements. Today we'll act as two different human beings. One is a human being that's acting and carrying on our affairs, sitting down at lunch with our wives, watching the television this afternoon, dealing with our children, studying, preparing for next week.

That's just dealing with circumstances that confront us on a daily existence. And the other life that we live is a remote life of viewing what we are. One is an acting life, and the other one is a viewing life.

We back off subconsciously, and sometimes consciously, and kind of say, "What is Fred Gregg? What is Jimmy Carter? What is my relationship with God? What is my relationship with other people? How am I performing? What are my problems? What are my anxieties? Why am I being treated this way? Why am I treating others that way?"

We kind of measure ourselves from one existence and we do things with our other existence, and that self-contemplation is carried to a beneficial extreme when we get into the depths or the heights of sensitive prayer, which doesn't happen very much, certainly not enough.

But when we can genuinely subjugate ourselves to Christ in the most sincere prayer, that's when we can see ourselves most clearly, and we can understand better what is important and what is not important. We can understand what we're doing right and what we're not doing right, and we can get some guidance about what we ought to do next to repair the damage that we've perpetrated on our own lives.

God never promised us freedom from suffering and persecution. Suffering can be a test of our faith. It can let us grow, and we get our ultimate and most important rewards or punishment where from? In the judgment of God. Not in the judgment of human beings. Sometimes they're parallel. If we murder somebody, obviously we arouse the justified condemnation of our fellow human beings and God, but the judgment that we need to consider as paramount is the judgment of God.

Well, the last thing I want to say is this: We have to realize that there's no power on earth that's strong enough to determine our place in God's kingdom. There's nothing that we can marshal in our earthly life in power or influence or wealth that will determine our place in God's kingdom. That is dependent upon our actions and our judgment in the eyes of God.

When we get into the depths of despair or have intense anxiety in our lives or are disappointed or fearful, that's when it's most important for us to turn to God where the ultimate measure of our life might be.

Charles Beard, one of the great historians, would ask in all his studies of human history, what were the things that impressed themselves most on his mind? And I thought it was interesting. He said, "Whom the gods would destroy, they first make mad with power." So the grasping for power is destructive.

Secondly, he said, "The mills of the Gods grind slowly but exceedingly small." And third, he says, "The bee fertilizes the flower that it robs." And fourth, he says, "When it's dark enough, that's when you can see the stars."

Well, I think this is a good lesson as we discern that John is giving a symbolic description, a vision of life for the early Christians and their future life with Christ in heaven. And the same message applies not only in the first century after Christ's death, but also in the 20th century with us.

FRED GREGG:

Well, I know you're glad you came here this morning. Now you visitors, this is one of the substitute teachers. So can you imagine what's in store for you when you come back, when the first team's teaching? Let's all stand and be dismissed.

Our Father, we thank thee for this day. We thank thee for this lesson we have just had the experience to worship with, and we just thank thee so much for the teacher. We pray that thou will guide and direct him as he leads our country. We pray for our First Lady as she works with him. We pray for our messenger today. May he give us the message that we stand in need most of, and may this be a glorious Lord's day, one that you will be pleased with. In thy name we ask. Amen.

FROM FAILURE TO FULFILLMENT

JULY 20, 1980
LUKE 22:31-34 & 56-69, JOHN 21:15-19

FRED GREGG:

Rosalynn, we've missed you, we really have. And Mr. President, we missed you too. And the teaching efficiency of this class has probably dropped way down, but I know you'll bring it back this morning. So it gives me a great deal of pleasure to turn the lesson over to President Carter.

PRESIDENT JIMMY CARTER:

Fred just casually left a letter lying here on the podium, I guess wanting me to see it. It's addressed to Reverend Fred Gregg. He'll do anything to let me realize that he is the teacher and I'm the substitute. It's kind of hard to replace a reverend.

Well, we haven't been here in several Sundays. We've enjoyed being in other churches, hearing other Sunday School teachers. We had the chance to go to church in Venice, Italy, and last Sunday we were in church in Sapelo Island at St. Luke's Baptist Church. The pastor kept looking at his watch and saying, "We've got to cut our service half in two this morning to let the President leave." We got there at 11 o'clock and at 12:30 we left; they continued ... they continued until 2 o'clock.

Sapelo Island is a very small island off the coast of Georgia that was originally settled back in the early 1500s by the Spaniards. And the permanent residents there [are] a relatively small group of Black citizens, who speak the kind of English that I can understand, but I guess that most of you probably couldn't understand it. But it's a delight to go down there and to be kind of isolated from the press and also to have a chance to worship with people whose belief is fundamentalist in nature—simple, as all Christians belief ought to be —devout, and where Christ is really the center of their lives. They've been through slavery times, their families on that island, and they've changed very little. Also on the island you might be interested in knowing is a marine research institute, and some of the finest marine biologists and others come there to study and to do their work.

We're continuing a part of a three-month study about Peter. Of all the disciples that we study, with which one do you feel most at ease? Peter, I think. I do. Why? Anybody?

CLASS MEMBER:

He is very human.

PRESIDENT JIMMY CARTER:

He is very human. That's right. Why do you say he is human?

He was kind of impetuous, wasn't he? He overdid things. When he was exuberantly in love with Christ, he showed it, didn't apologize for it. When he failed, he really failed abominably. And when he bragged, he bragged too much. He kind of fumbled around.

It's not difficult to feel a companionship with him, kind of a partnership in human failure and belief. But there was another disciple that failed even worse; who was that? Judas. What was the difference? The two stories were very intimately entwined. When was the most vivid demonstration of Christ dealing with both men almost simultaneously? In their failure? Does anybody recall?

CLASS MEMBER:

The Last Supper.

PRESIDENT JIMMY CARTER:

At the Last Supper, right. And Christ was crucified how long after that? Next day. The next day. This was a last day that Christ spent with his disciples before he was crucified.

Failure is something that we all have to face. Thomas Edison was probably one of the greatest inventors, maybe the greatest of all times. And once he was visited by one of his friends, and Thomas Edison took him down to the basement to show him a new invention, the electric light bulb, and he put it all together and it didn't work.

And the friend said, "Well, I really am sorry about your failure." And he said, "That was not a failure, it was a success." Why?

He found one more thing that wouldn't work, right? So he could eliminate that and go ahead and work on the things that might succeed.

One of my favorite politicians first ran for the legislature in '32, and he was defeated. There were 13 people in the race; he came in eighth. And then finally was elected to the state legislature and in '38, I believe, he ran for speaker of the house and was defeated badly. He decided to get out of state politics, and he wanted to be appointed to the federal commission of lands. And he didn't get the appointment. A few years later, in '58, he ran for the U.S. Senate and was defeated.

And he didn't give up. In 1860, he ran for president and was elected and made perhaps the greatest president this nation's ever seen. But Abraham Lincoln's life is a picture of constant, apparent failure, but ultimate victory as perhaps the greatest political figure of our time.

And when I meet with leaders in foreign countries, in Asia or in India or other places, they always revere Lincoln above anyone else who's ever served in this country.

When I went to visit the Prime Minister of India, for instance, he gave me a dual sculpture, a bust, one of Mahatma Gandhi and one of Lincoln on the same base. A very beautiful piece, but it shows the reverence with which they hold this man whose ideals never varied. It may have varied. We learn the good things about Lincoln's life, but he had constant series of failures.

This morning, we're going to be studying about Peter, a very interesting man because of his failures. And I think it's important for us to realize that Peter was one of the first followers who came to Christ when Christ began to assemble his disciples, but his faltering continued to the end of Jesus' life on earth.

And Christ had a special feeling for Peter, I think. John, when he wrote his, in effect, autobiography, always referred to himself as a disciple that Jesus loved. Peter didn't do that so obviously, but when other disciples wrote about Peter, it was always with a halfway recognition, at least, that he was a leader among them.

Christ never said, "You are my super disciple, and the others are going to be subservient to you," but I think he recognized in Peter in a strange way perhaps that Peter was indeed the leader among a group of equals. It's hard to know exactly why. What do you think might be some of the reasons? Yes.

CLASS MEMBER:

He had a strength.

PRESIDENT JIMMY CARTER:

A strength, yeah. Probably physically he was strong and had a possessing appearance, I would guess. What else?

He was passionate, impetuous. That's what it showed. Even though we described it earlier this morning as excessive sometimes, he was a guy that would move rapidly and do something that was dramatic. Anybody else?

CLASS MEMBER:

You always knew that he was forthright and said what he really meant.

PRESIDENT JIMMY CARTER:

Yeah, he spoke out. That's good. Good point. He understood Jesus, too. What's one incident that might come to your mind about Peter's understanding of Christ?

He understood that Jesus was the Christ. How do you know that?

Jesus said, "Who do people say that I am?" And some of them said he was the prophet returned and John the Baptist and so forth. And Jesus said, "Well, who do you all say I am?" And Peter spoke up and said, "You're the Christ, the Son of the Living God." And Jesus then said, "Peter," which means rock, "on you I will build my church."

We were in the Vatican not too long ago and saw that little place where Peter's body is supposed to be buried. And the symbolic part of the Catholic Church is that, on that, on Peter's grave, they built their church. But Christ saw in Peter some special things that in a way endeared Peter to Christ and apparently endeared Peter to the other disciples as well.

Perhaps they did see, as this young man over here said, that Peter embodied some of their own failings, and he showed them.

A lot of people have failures and doubts and so forth and never express them, never express their doubts. And they're so timid about not trying anything because they're afraid they might fail that they never attract any attention to themselves. They don't fail much, but they don't do much.

Well, Peter failed a lot because he tried a lot, and he showed a lot of failures because he wasn't timid. And he was a strong person in many ways and very weak, as we'll see later on this morning.

Well, I'd like to ask you another question about Peter and his relationship to Christ. How did Peter envision Christ's ministry on earth? Peter was always telling Jesus, "You can't do that. Don't do that." Or "That wouldn't be proper."

CLASS MEMBER:

Peter was still looking for a King Messiah. He was looking for a ruler, and what Christ was doing, a king or a ruler wouldn't go through. He kept telling Christ he shouldn't be telling some of the things he was telling him because that's not the way it's going to be.

PRESIDENT JIMMY CARTER:

That's right. Peter couldn't accept the fact that Christ was going to be crucified. Peter couldn't accept the fact that Christ might be tempted or hurt. Peter could not accept the fact that Jesus would not be an exalted human being, revered by those subservient to him.

Right in the middle of this Last Supper … there was a squabble among the disciples about what?

CLASS MEMBER:

Who was going to be the greatest.

PRESIDENT JIMMY CARTER:

Who was going to be the greatest, yeah. Who was going to be the greatest among the disciples. And Jesus performed an act that really was impressive to those disciples, including Peter, and to me and you today. What was that?

CLASS MEMBER:

Washing feet.

PRESIDENT JIMMY CARTER:

Yes. Slaves were a commonplace thing in the lives of wealthy citizens of that time. Slavery was accepted as a normal part of life. The Bible doesn't necessarily condemn slavery. It refers to the duties of a slave to his master and so forth.

There was one thing that a slave probably would not do. What was that, which would not have been customary? That is to get on his hands and knees and wash the feet of a master. He would go and bring food. He would make up the beds. Perhaps he would clean up the house, and he would do the subservient duties. But a personal sign of abject subservience like getting down on your hands and knees and washing somebody else's feet, I would guess in most places it would draw the line now. But Jesus didn't draw the line, did he?

And Jesus got on his hands and knees and washed the feet of those very disciples who were struggling among themselves to see who would be the greatest. How could you possibly answer that question—"Who's going to be the greatest?"—better? They didn't say, "Are we going to be greater than you, Lord?" They said, "Among us, who's going to be the greatest?"

And Jesus got down below them and washed their feet. I'm sure this surprised Peter. Peter had a tendency that we would probably not like if he served among us. Can you think of what I'm trying to say? He was boastful. He bragged. In what way did he brag this particular time, this important time?

He wanted Jesus to wash him all after he got through washing his feet. But he also made a boast that he would never forsake Christ. Somebody might, these other disciples might, but [Peter said,] "I'll never desert you, Lord. I'll never be fallible. I am so strong as a human being that no temptation can prevail over me."

In effect, he was saying, "I'm so strong in my love for you and in my own inner commitment, that I don't need God to help me withstand temptation." That, in effect, is what Peter was saying.

I think before we go too far, we ought to read the lesson. I'm sure that all of you have studied ahead of time, but perhaps just a review. Fred, would you read the first part, the part in Luke? … Just read the whole thing through.

FRED GREGG:

[31] And the Lord said, Simon, Simon behold, Satan hath desired to take you, that he may sift you as wheat.

[32] But I have prayed for thee, that thy faith fail not, and when thou art converted, strengthen thy brethren.

[33] And he said unto him, Lord, I am ready to go with thee, both into prison and to death.

[34] And he said, I tell thee, Peter, the cock shall not crow this day, before that thou shalt thrice deny that thou knowest me.

[56] But a certain maid beheld him as he sat by the fire, and earnestly looked upon him and said, This man was also with him.

[57] And he denied him, saying, Woman, I know him not.

[58] And after a little while another saw him, and said, Thou art also of them. And Peter said, Man, I am not.

[59] And about the space of one hour after another confidently affirmed, saying, Of a truth this fellow also was with him: for he is a Galilean.

^{60} And Peter said, Man, I know not what thou sayest. And immediately, while he yet spake, the cock crew.

^{61} And the Lord turned, and looked upon Peter. And Peter remembered the word of the Lord, how he had said unto him, Before the cock crow, thou shalt deny me thrice.

^{62} And Peter went out, and wept bitterly.

PRESIDENT JIMMY CARTER:

This Lord's Supper, the night before Christ was crucified, impressed on the disciples—and I think Jesus was very avid in making sure this happened—that a new stage in their development had arrived: a new stage in, quote, "discipleship," unquote. …. Jesus saw that this development in the life of his disciples was going to be a shock to them. It was obvious. They had been dependent on Christ. They had not had to stand on their own feet and make their own decisions and take their share of the condemnation that had been building up against Christ among the leaders in Israel.

They were not prepared for it, and Christ knew that. And his attempts to prepare them had not been fully successful. He had told them that he was going to leave. They said, "Don't leave. You can't do it." He had told them that he would not have an earthly kingdom. They couldn't quite accommodate that disappointment in their lives. And also, they were going to become a different kind of citizen after Christ's crucifixion. What kind? Read Luke 22:35-38.

CLASS MEMBER:

^{35} And he said to them, "When I sent you out without purse, or bag, or sandals, did you lack anything?" They said, "Nothing."

^{36} He said to them, "But now if you have a purse, take it, and also a bag, and if you have no sword, sell your mantle and buy one.

^{37} For I say unto you, that this that is written must yet be accomplished in me, And he was reckoned among the transgressors: for the things concerning me have an end.

^{38} And they said, Lord, behold, here are two swords. And he said unto them, It is enough.

PRESIDENT JIMMY CARTER:

I think that's part of the teaching of Christ, that their lives, which had been fairly, fairly tranquil, they had been through the hurly-burly of Christ's persecution, but it hadn't been focused on them. They could always say, "Well, we love Jesus and he's in the center of it and we back him, but we depend on him implicitly to make the ultimate decisions in this daily life of ours."

And Christ told them, "You're going to have to put a new mantle now. Not as a warrior, not out killing people, but you're going to have to fight back, and you're going to have to face condemnation and trial and disappointment and deprivation equal to anything that I have so far suffered in my own life." Jesus was trying to prepare his disciples for a very difficult life after his death. Yes?

CLASS MEMBER:

In verse 35 he said: When I sent you without purse, and scrip, and shoes, lacked ye anything? And they said, Nothing.

PRESIDENT JIMMY CARTER:

I believe that's exactly right. During most of his ministry, they could go out with nothing, and they could fare very well in a human way. They didn't lack for food; they didn't lack for adequate security. They didn't suffer from intense persecution or the threat of death themselves.

But after Christ died, that situation was going to change, and he was trying to prepare his disciples for a very difficult challenge ahead when they would have to make the decisions in a daily temporal way, which they had not yet had to make.

This supper was followed by what? What happened next after this supper? Jesus went to the Mount of Olives, right? Yes. He had told Peter that the devil wants you.

If a Southerner had been translating the King James Bible, he would've said the devil wants you all. Because the word in Greek is plural, "you." But Yankees haven't yet learned how to express English very clearly.

But then, when he went on to say, "I'm going to intercede with my prayers," he was talking about "you" singular. Four times in that one verse he said, "I'm going to pray for you that the devil will not take over your life." And that you will not, what? It's a very interesting thing. That you will not what?

In one of the translations … it says that you will not utterly fail, that you will not completely fail. And that you'll be able to come back and therefore do what? Strengthen the others, right?

So, here again, Christ is saying you're going to set a bad example, but I'm going to hope that the devil does not prevail completely in your life because I want you to come back for yourself, but also to sustain and to support and to convert others. Jesus then saw that after Peter's trial and temptation that he had a good chance to come back. …

Christ's prayer for Peter cannot be the ultimate judgment about what will happen. Within Peter had to be the decision to stand with Christ or not. To yield completely to the devil or not.

Peter, as are we, was a free spirit. And Christ loved him and supported him and tried to predict what was going to happen, which was a very great boost to Peter. But didn't help, because Peter still did exactly what Christ knew he would do with his failure. But knowing that Christ loved him, Peter made a decision ultimately to be a great witness, a great disciple, a great beneficial effect on our lives. Peter made a decision. It's the same in our life.

We are the ones who have the ultimate choice to follow Christ or not. To stand with Christ or not. To try to resist temptation on our own without God or to recognize our human fallibility and turn to God.

After Peter was asked by Christ at the Mount of Olives to perform a duty after he had sworn that he would never let Jesus down, what happened?

Christ went off alone to pray in danger, knowing that his life was almost at an end. He told his disciples, what? Stay awake, guard for me. Don't let anybody bother me. I want to go and talk to God. And immediately what happened?

CLASS MEMBER:

They fell asleep.

PRESIDENT JIMMY CARTER:

Peter went to sleep, and the others there, too. And then Jesus came back and woke them up and said, "Look, I tell you to watch out for me. Please be alert." And went back to pray again. Back to sleep.

Peter went to sleep, and the others had, too. And then Jesus came back and woke 'em up and said, "Look, I tell you to watch out for me. Please be alert." And went back to prayer again, back to sleep.

It's a vivid demonstration of just repeated failure. And then Christ was arrested. Peter snatched the sword and cut off the servant's ear, which I guess did show that he was willing to go to prison for Jesus. His impetuous nature showed that he had courage in that time of trying and testing because he could have stood back because the soldiers were there. And the temple priests and leaders were there. They saw Peter, I guess, get the sword and cut the guy's ear off. He could have faded into the background. He didn't do it.

And then they went on to the courtyard for Jesus to be brought before the Sanhedrin. John apparently made arrangements for Peter to come inside the courtyard, and when he sat by the fire, the maiden who saw Peter said, "Aren't you one of them?" Apparently, according to John ... we won't take time to look it up in the Bible, but apparently according to John, she was the one that had opened the door to the courtyard to let them come in. She saw Jesus and John together. John was with Jesus.

And John said, "Why don't you let this man come in too?" So Peter sneaked in and sat over by the fire, and you all know the story. Three times he denied Christ, denied he even knew him.

And one of the versions says the last time when Peter denied knowing Jesus, that Jesus looked at Peter and Peter looked at him. That's in Luke.

All four Gospels described this event of Peter's betrayal of Christ. They approach it a little bit differently, one from another. After the cock crowed and Jesus looked at Peter, what did he do?

He wept.

He went out and wept bitterly. And the Bible refers to a conversion. The word "converted" is used. What does that mean? Does that mean that Peter had lost his faith and was born again as a Christian? I think not. My own belief is that it means that he repented and turned away from the sin that he had just committed. And in his bitterness, in his bitter weeping, he was forgiven.

This is a story that could end there. And as far as Peter goes, I think three of the Gospel writers only mention Peter very briefly on Easter morning.

But John wrote another book, another chapter, the 21st chapter of John, which we'll look at now. What is significant about John's Gospel that makes the 21st chapter meaningful to us?

I think one of the great things about this is to prove the honesty of the New Testament. John is just writing what Peter got in the ... I would say pulpit. But that he was writing what Peter preached himself how he had done this to Christ and how Christ had forgiven him and how Christ would forgive [anyone] as a result.

It makes it possible for us, with all of our failures, to identify that we have that love and that love's strong; that we will fail, but that love will always bring back us back. That's the same love that caused him to go out and weep, otherwise he could have shrugged it off and gone like Judas did. That love that was so deep caused him to weep, caused him to be able to tell that story in true reality that would relate to people and cause people to make their decision for Christ.

I think Fred's put his finger on the significance of this event. It's hard for us as Baptists to understand about predestination and things being preordained and what part God plays directly in the ordering of human events. That's a matter for debate and discussion. It can go on and has gone on ever since people knew about God.

But if the story about Peter here was different, none of you would've said earlier that you relate closest to Peter. If Peter had gone out and the maiden had come up to him and Peter said, "Yes, I know him. I'm one of his disciples. Do what you want to with me;" and if Peter had stayed alert when Jesus was praying on the Mount of Olives and all the other disciples had slept; if Peter had never made any of these mistakes, we would probably discount Peter as meaningful in our own lives if he took on the aura of perfection. In other words, almost a mirror image of Christ himself.

This is a dramatic, intense human. Even a kind of humorous way to show that Peter was fallible like we are. He went to sleep on watch and bragged that he would never do something and immediately did just the opposite.

What Fred says is very true that John describing these events in an unvarnished way, not trying to make the disciples or himself look heroic or perfect or better than other people is the significance of the Bible stories. The Bible is filled with human beings who fail. When? When do they fail?

Yeah, when they try for something, but also when they try without God, right? Peter didn't get down on his knees, at least as far as we know, between the time of the Lord's Supper and the court-yard and say, "God, please don't let me betray my Lord." He thought he was so strong that Jesus would be mistaken. ...

I jotted down the list, in one of the books I read, of the seven sins. Anger, envy, gluttony, lust, covetousness, pride, and sloth. Which one of those is most written about in the New Testament? And which one did Jesus teach most about? Covetousness, envy, anger, gluttony, lust, pride, sloth?

Pride. Pride by far. Pride. And pride has a much broader meaning than just being proud of yourself.

It means thinking you're better than someone else, thinking you're self-sufficient which takes on a very sinister meaning. Self-sufficiency has a kind of a macho sound, but self-sufficiency means also the rejection of God. The rejection of the need for God is a very serious human trait or attitude. And in effect, this is what Peter was doing in this lesson. He told Jesus, "Don't worry about me. I am strong enough to resist any temptation that would separate me from my Christ."

Let's read very quickly, John 21:15 through 19. Rosalynn, would you read that?

ROSALYNN CARTER:

[15] So when they had dined, Jesus saith to Simon Peter, Simon, son of Jonas, lovest thou me more than these? He saith unto him, Yea, Lord; thou knowest that I love thee. He saith unto him, Feed my lambs.

[16] He saith to him again the second time, Simon, son of Jonas, lovest thou me? He saith unto him, Yea, Lord; thou knowest that I love thee. He saith unto him, Feed my sheep.

[17] He saith unto him the third time, Simon, son of Jonas, lovest thou me? Peter was grieved because he said unto him the third time, Lovest thou me? And he said unto him, Lord, thou knowest all

things; thou knowest that I love thee. Jesus saith unto him, Feed my sheep.

¹⁸ Verily, verily, I say unto thee, When thou wast young, thou girdest thyself, and walkedst whither thou wouldest: but when thou shalt be old, thou shalt stretch forth thy hands, and another shall gird thee, and carry thee whither thou wouldest not.

¹⁹ This spake he, signifying by what death he should glorify God. And when he had spoken this, he saith unto him, Follow me.

PRESIDENT JIMMY CARTER:

Very good. I'm glad that John wrote this 21st chapter. John wrote his Gospel after the others had been written, and John was able to look back possibly knowing how Peter died.

The very early historians say that Peter was crucified in Rome with his head down because he didn't think he was worthy to be crucified in the same fashion as Christ. We don't know that for certain, but this was written within 100 or 200 years after Christ died.

Well, where were the disciples when ... this event, by the way, took place after Christ's resurrection ... when the disciples had gone back to their home, and what had they decided to do?

They were fishing. ... Peter says, "I'm going fishing." And six of the others says, "We want to go with you."

Why do you think they were fishing instead of preaching? This was their previous occupation before they met Christ. I've only got just two or three minutes. Let's look at that a minute. First question, why do you think Peter denied Christ in the courtyard?

CLASS MEMBERS:

Pride and fear. Satan. He was by himself. He didn't have the Holy Spirit. ...

PRESIDENT JIMMY CARTER:

I think Peter lost faith. I don't think he was physically afraid. That may have been part of it. But my belief is that Peter saw Jesus arrested. He saw him debased. He saw him abused. He saw him helpless. None of the people that touched Jesus were stricken dead by God.

So why die for a lost cause? I mean, as long as Jesus was succeeding—healing the blind people, raising people from the dead, thousands of people coming to hear him preach, making little pieces of bread into enough to feed a multitude—that was a winning team.

Well, all that time, everything looked rosy. But once Jesus got arrested, he didn't stay on. He said, "I don't even know that man. I never was with him in Galilee" He succumbed to a profound disillusionment and disappointment because he found himself separated from Christ, and he lost his faith temporarily.

I think he got his faith back when the cock crowed and he remembered that Jesus, who he thought was incompetent even to protect himself, had predicted what was going to happen. And when Jesus looked at him, he was remind[ing] Peter: this is exactly what my Lord said was going to happen.

So then he went out and cried bitterly, which shows that he had a change of heart. He was absolutely heartbroken. "I have betrayed the Son of God," he said. But a few minutes before he was saying, "He's not the Son of God." …

[T]here was a prior arrangement by Jesus that he would meet with his disciples afterwards. They may have been carrying out Jesus' orders. We don't know how explicit or clear those orders were. He may have told them, "Immediately after my crucifixion, be quiet for a while until I can come back and until the Holy Spirit comes." We don't know what Jesus had told them.

I don't believe that the disciples had failed completely to follow Christ just because they went fishing. When Christ appeared on the beach, somebody said, "There's a man there." John says, "Jesus." Peter jumped in the water and swam ashore.

He couldn't wait to get to the shore. And as Jesus ate a fish, [which] would show that he was not just a spirit or a ghost but a human being who was hungry, he cross-examined Peter again. How many times did he ask him did he love him?

Three times.

He denied him three times, let him say it three times. And Jesus was using the word "agape." But Peter continued to respond, "phileo," which means "I love you," but it's not an absolute tender, unbounded love. And then John goes on to say that Peter became a great man as we know that as well.

Well, the point is, our life—every life here—is very closely patterned after Peter's. We have innate pride; we have doubts at times. We are tempted and succumb. When we are separated from God, we will fail. When Christ is part of us or the Holy Spirit's in our heart, we will not fail to meet temptation successfully. After we fail and repent, God will forgive us as he did Peter. And that's a building process for a greater discipleship.

And as Peter devoted the rest of his life to the service of Christ so effectively that here, almost 2,000 years later, we still are inspired by and reassured by the life of Peter and his ultimate great success.

That's a lesson for us, too. Through Christ with God, we will not fail. Without Christ, our achievements, which may seem great to us, are insignificant. I think it's a beautiful lesson about a disciple that I'm very glad was human like us.

FRED GREGG:

Well, isn't that great? Let's all stand and be dismissed. Aren't you glad you came here this morning?

Our Father, we thank you thee this day. We thank thee for the privilege to come to Bible study, and we thank thee so much for the lesson we've heard this morning. We pray for our President as he leads our country. We pray for our First Lady; she serves with him. Be with Dr. [Clarence] Cranford in the morning worship service. And may this be a glorious Lord's day and, whatever's accomplished, we'll give you the praise because we're asking in your name and for your sake. Amen.

GRACE FOR SINNERS

NOVEMBER 16, 1980
LUKE 5:1-32, 1 JOHN 4:8

FRED GREGG:

Before we begin the lesson this morning, we're delighted to have with us our moderator, and I'm going to ask Mr. McNear if he would come forward this time for a presentation.

FRANK ED MCNEAR:

Thank you, Mr. Gregg. Mr. President, Mrs. Carter, members and guests of the Couples Class.

Last Wednesday evening at our quarterly business meeting, the membership of our church passed unanimously a resolution drafted by Dr. Robert G. Jones, who is a professor of religion at the George Washington University and the teacher of the Adult Two department of our Sunday Church School. That message is entitled, "A Message of Love and Support for President and Mrs. Jimmy Carter." And I'd like to read it for you at this time:

> Almost four years ago you became with us, fellow members of the Body of Christ in this place. Although none of us could begin to realize the awesome burden of your public office as we all joined in a continuing fellowship of prayer for you and for our nation's first

family, for you and for members of our congregation. This love and care continues even now.

We have wanted to share with you the resources of faith and devotion to a cause which transcends all political parties, the kingdom of our Lord, and of his Christ. Being good Baptists we have been aware that our freedom to differ politically has not destroyed that fundamental Christian commitment that we all share. To our diverse congregation, you have brought an appreciation for the presence of fellow Christians who have given themselves to political leadership in this nation.

Now, none of us can imagine the feelings in your heart after the election, but still all of us—devoted citizens of many political persuasions—understand the meaning of the commandment, that we will "bear one another's burdens and so fulfill the law of Christ."

Therefore, we wish to say to you simply and directly, that our love and prayerful support continue with you. Even those who may have differed from you in matters political shall treasure the association with you in these years together and pledge continually to work with you in the spread of the gospel of our Lord Jesus Christ.

We pray for you—and for ourselves—that we may attain the peace which passes understanding and the joy which can lighten every day in Christ our Lord.

Your friends and partners in the gospel, the members of the First Baptist Church of the City of Washington D.C.

Mr. President, I'd like to present the original to you at this time.

PRESIDENT JIMMY CARTER:

Thank you very much. Thank you so much.

FRED GREGG:

Thank you, Frank Ed.

Well, you know the Lord moves in mysterious ways, and he says that he hears our prayers, but he doesn't tell us when he's going to hear them. And I learned that the past week that my prayers, it takes five days for them to get answered.

On Monday night, Dr. [Clarence] Cranford and his wife and

about six other couples met at my house, November the 3rd, for a very special prayer meeting. And we asked the Lord to really do something for us. And, you know, it was Saturday before he did anything. He didn't help me out a bit on Tuesday, November the fourth [Election Day].

But when I got up on my house on Saturday to check the paint on one of the windows and the ladder slid out from under me and I fell on my back about 12 feet and hit right on top of that ladder on an asphalt driveway, surely he must have been riding with me.

Now, all of my dear friends have called and have given me such comforting messages. Like I know a friend who did that and he's been paralyzed for five years. And I buried the senator from Maine who fell off from a ladder only eight feet tall. That was our pastor calling. Our next-door neighbor said her friend had been paralyzed for two years—she's the one who came over and closed the basement doors when the emergency ambulance carried me to the hospital.

Well, I want you to know, I'm sore. And every time I walk out and look at that [window], I get sore again, and I don't know what's the answer, 'cause I can't go in and out of my house without looking at it 'cause it's right over the garage doors. But my family, every time I mention a ladder, they really get upset.

And another good thing about it, I found out [my wife] Mary Jo still loves me, until she found out I wasn't as serious as she thought and wasn't going to collect the insurance and then it went right back to the same old Mary Jo and Fred.

But Mr. President, it's good to have you and Mrs. Carter here this morning. We talked earlier this week, and I told him that he had taught me two things. One, that honesty doesn't always pay. And secondly, that I will be able to explain and describe the Resurrection much better, because Tuesday, November the fourth, I went numb and didn't resurrect until about the sixth. So there's more than one that has resurrected now.

But I want you to know that we love you, we support you. And Rosalynn, the *World Almanac* made a mistake this week: They voted you as the second most influential woman, and in my books, you're number one and you have been a super First Lady. And Mr. President, history will record that you were a great president.

The association that we've had with President and Ms. Carter comes to a highlight every time that he agrees to teach. And this morning he has agreed to teach.

We debated over two lessons, and he said, "What are the two lessons?" And I said, "One of them's on giving," and I paused to look up the answer of the other, and he said, "Don't go any farther, 'cause the next one [will] probably be on taking and I don't want to teach that one."

So it's a delight, it's always a delight for me, and I know it is for you, to hear our President teach. So it gives me a great deal of pleasure to turn the podium over to President Carter.

PRESIDENT JIMMY CARTER:

I'm not going to get emotional because we'll be here two more months, and I can't sustain it that long.

It is always remarkable when Baptists pass something unanimously. [*Class laughs.*] That makes a beautiful message and the proclamation even more dear to us because it's so rare. I didn't have any comment to make about Fred's potential affliction. I just told him that the next time he got ready to go up on top of a roof on a ladder, not to drink anything except coffee ahead of time.

I'm very grateful for a chance to be a member of this church. It's been an exhilarating and a calming and a satisfying, gratifying experience for us to make friends here who have accepted us, not as special people who live in the White House, but as neighbors and as fellow believers in Christ.

You let me teach in the fumbling way. I was hoping that when Fred was saying what a great President history would judge me to be, that he would say something about my teaching ability, but I notice he didn't mention that.

But it has given me a chance to study and to stay in touch with God's word and my own deep faith in Christ. The Sundays that we're not here—we ordinarily are at Camp David or somewhere else—we always have church services. At Camp David, there's a chaplain who comes in from a nearby military base, and he has a service for us, our family, and just a few people. And when we're out campaigning or out traveling around the world, we always make a point to go to a church on Sunday morning to worship.

This morning, we have a lesson that I think is very interesting.

The title of it in the book is "Grace for Sinners," but as is a custom with Fred, he always says two or three other potential titles that are better. And one that I thought about this morning was "What Is Christianity?" I'm not a theologian. I'm not here preparing myself to tell you what Christianity is, but I think it's something that we ought to keep in mind, the question, as we go through this lesson. And maybe at the end of the lesson, we'll kind of jointly have some analyses of what does Christianity mean. What is Christianity?

If you were asked by the teacher, which you are going to be, what is one of your favorite verses that describes the essence of Christianity or your belief in Christ, what would you want to reply? Does anybody have a verse you'd like to mention? Yes.

CLASS MEMBER:

For God so loved the world that he gave his only begotten son that whosoever believeth in him shall not perish.

PRESIDENT JIMMY CARTER:

Very good. That reply doesn't surprise me. Yes.

CLASS MEMBERS:

Let the words of my mouth, and the meditation of my heart, be acceptable in thy sight, O Lord, my strength, and my redeemer.

He said, "Take up your cross and follow me."

Jesus loves me.

God is love.

PRESIDENT JIMMY CARTER:

God is love. What's the whole verse for "God is love"? Anybody know? Anybody remember? Somebody read 1 John 4:8.

CLASS MEMBER:

[8] He that loveth not knoweth not God; for God is love.

PRESIDENT JIMMY CARTER:

Okay. I was reading this morning a passage described as Reinhold Niebuhr's favorite verse. So anybody know what it is? Look up Ephesians 4:32. I'd rather have the old, the King James Version. Ephesians 4:32. Dr. Cranford, would you read it?

DR. CLARENCE CRANFORD:

[32] And be ye kind one to another. tenderhearted, forgiving one another, even as God for Christ's sake hath forgiven you.

PRESIDENT JIMMY CARTER:

Be kind one to another, tenderhearted, forgiving one another even as God in Christ's sake forgives you. I think that that verse plus John 3:16 kind of encapsulate as well as anything else the essence of Christianity. It's the connotation of love, mercy, the potential alienation of individual human beings, because of sin, from God. The recognition of that barrier that we ourselves build between ourselves and God and the elimination of the barrier through Christ.

And overall permeating the thought is the worth of an individual human being. It's not a broad scope about society or about war and peace. It's not philosophical dissertations, but it's that one human being, precious in God's sight, alienated because of sin, an acknowledgment of sin, and through Christ who died for us, forgiveness and reconciliation.

Those factors which I've outlined without notes are kind of a teaching that we ought to keep in mind this morning. We are studying, from Luke the fourth chapter through the ninth, Jesus' ministry in Galilee. And it kind of gives a picture of Christ's life as he related to people around him.

First of all, Christ started out an unknown person, acknowledged to be God's special son in the life of Mary and Joseph and Elizabeth and maybe a few other people, John the Baptist.

He was not scorned or despised in Nazareth when he was growing up. He began to teach, and eventually he was known as a very famous person. In the latter part of Luke 4, Christ was so pressed by the crowds around Capernaum that he was very eager to get away, and the people were clinging to him.

He went out in the desert and said, "I'm going to go to another place." And the people who lived there in Capernaum, where Simon Peter lived, right on the edge of the Sea of Galilee, said, "Don't go; stay with us. Stay with us. We need you. You have been healing the sick. You've been teaching us words of wisdom. We need you to stay with us."

And Christ said, "My ministry is broader than Capernaum. I'm going to have to move further." And then of course, he had his first encounter with some fishermen. ...

He wanted to get on the boat, move out into the Sea of Galilee, enough distance so he could separate himself from the crowd and have kind of a podium from which to speak. And then he talked to the crowd. When he got through, he said, "Take me back." He told the fishermen to catch some fish. They said they hadn't caught anything. They threw out the nets and caught more than any nets would hold.

And Peter and others were convinced that Christ had a special authority. Maybe because they caught a lot of fish. Maybe because they were impressed at the crowd that surrounded Jesus. If he's so famous, he must be great.

But that's two elements. One is the press of the crowds, and the second one is the special relationship that Christ engendered with a few people who became his disciples. What is a disciple? Anybody?

CLASS MEMBERS:

A learner. A student. Follower.

PRESIDENT JIMMY CARTER:

Follower or believer. Right. One who reveres [a] teacher. One who looks on a teacher not only as a source of wisdom, but also a source of guidance in one's life or a pattern that you would like yourself to emulate, someone you'd like to follow.

So the discipleship, the recruitment of fame through his healing and words. But there was another result of Christ's ministry around Galilee. What was that?

Very important later on in his life. Relationship with the crowd, relationship with his disciples, but another human relationship that became very important later on in his life. ... It was the relationship with power and authority in the church. But primarily what I wanted was the condemnation or the alienation or the struggle between them.

Christ became despised and hated and feared and condemned by the church leaders. This is generating, you see already in the lesson, a very complicated relationship of teaching, healing, but a certain aloofness of Christ because he couldn't be captured by the crowds. His ministry had to be broad. It had to be generic in nature. ...

[T]hat relationship with the crowd [is] kind of in contrast to his love of individuals in the crowd, his need for aloofness and not being captured, his special dependence upon and love for a few disciples, and his alienation from the church leaders. All those things in Christ's early ministry began to form the lessons or the environment within which he could teach lessons to us. What are some of the things about the Pharisees? What do you know about the Pharisees?

CLASS MEMBER:

They were separatists.

PRESIDENT JIMMY CARTER:

They were separatists. They thought it was sinful for them to deal with sinners. What else?

They almost worshipped the law itself. ... They had certain very narrow definitions of what was acceptable and what was not acceptable, right? They had prescriptions for acceptability by God, what you must do to be accepted by God. And they had proscriptions, things that you cannot do. Very narrowly defined definitions of what is an acceptable person in God's eyes.

And they made the definition. They were traditionalists. They looked back on their study of God's word, and they tried to preserve it, but they also expanded on it. There was a lot of human interpretation of what God meant in his teachings.

They defined, in effect, what is God. And in order for someone to be accepted by God in their eyes and in the eyes of the church, they had to comply with those human definitions. The personal aspect of God's love was secondary to them.

What did Jesus think of the Pharisees? They were devout people. They were sincere. They're very fervent. What did Jesus think of them? He didn't think much of them, did he? We won't dwell on it, but turn to Matthew 23, somebody. Matthew 23. ... This tells, kind of succinctly, what Christ thought about the Pharisees.

CLASS MEMBER:

[13-15] Woe to you, teachers of the law and Pharisees, you hypocrites. You shut the door of the kingdom of heaven in people's faces. You yourselves do not enter, nor will you let those enter who are trying to. Woe to you, teachers of the law and Pharisees, you hypocrites. You travel over land and sea to win a single convert, and when you have succeeded, you make them twice as much a child of hell as you are.
[16] Woe to you, blind guides. You say, 'If anyone swears by the temple, it means nothing; but anyone who swears by the gold of the temple is bound by that oath.'
[17] You blind fools. Which is greater, the gold, or the temple that makes the gold sacred?
[18] You also say, 'If anyone swears by the altar, it means nothing; but anyone who swears by the gift on the altar is bound by that oath.'

PRESIDENT JIMMY CARTER:

That gives you an indication of what Christ thought of the Pharisees. As a matter of fact, this encounter in the fifth chapter of Luke probably came before Christ said those words.

As far as Luke is concerned, this is Christ's first encounter with the Pharisees and scribes. First when he tells about them. Let's read Luke 5:12 through 16, as the first part of our lesson text this morning. Anyone? Luke 5:12 through 16. Fred, you have it?

FRED GREGG:

[12] And it came to pass, when he was in a certain city, behold a man

full of leprosy: who seeing Jesus fell on his face, and besought him, saying, Lord, if thou wilt, thou canst make me clean.

13 And he put forth his hand, and touched him, saying, I will: be thou clean. And immediately the leprosy departed from him.

14 And he charged him to tell no man: but go, and shew thyself to the priest, and offer for thy cleansing, according as Moses commanded, for a testimony unto them.

15 But so much the more went there a fame abroad of him: and great multitudes came together to hear, and to be healed by him of their infirmities.

16 And he withdrew himself into the wilderness, and prayed.

PRESIDENT JIMMY CARTER:

Very good. What was the status of lepers in those days? I think everybody knows, but I just want [to] put it on the table.

CLASS MEMBER:

Outcasts.

PRESIDENT JIMMY CARTER:

Outcasts, despised. And what was the analysis of the leper's moral status in the eyes of God?

He was not only an outcast because he was, had a contagious disease, but he was also an outcast because he was condemned by God in the eyes of the religious leaders. The reason he has leprosy is because God condemned him and because he's not worthy. And, of course, there was a morbid fear of leprosy.

If you had lived in those days, knowing what you would've known about medicine and so forth, just the approach of a leper anywhere near you would've been a reason for great consternation. You would've guarded yourself, taken your children away. And lepers had to walk along, as you know, and cry out, "Unclean, unclean," to warn people about them. What did the leper do when he saw Jesus? The leper fell on his face.

Did Jesus knock him away? What did he do?

CLASS MEMBER:

Touched him.

PRESIDENT JIMMY CARTER:

Stretched out his hand, touched him. With a feeling of condemnation or alienation? Love. It seems natural to us, doesn't it? To know that this is the way Jesus reacted. If you hadn't even read this lesson and I had said, "What was Jesus' reaction when the leper approached?" you would've said, "He reacted with love," wouldn't you?

But in those days, Jesus had been looked upon by the crowds as a great religious teacher, and they said, "Well, since he's a great religious teacher, he's probably going to be like the other religious teachers, right?" So it was a shock to people when the leper approached Christ, fell on his face, and Christ responded with love and affection and physical contact.

It was a radical departure from the religious ministry of those days. And the leper was healed. And Jesus told the leper to go to the religious authorities and have his soundness or his cure certified, because only then could the leper be accepted back in society.

Well, that lack of judgment of the leper as a condemned person in the eyes of God was really more significant than his physical healing of the sores of leprosy.

This illustrates many things. I've already covered a few of them, but I think especially it signifies Christ's care for those who are despised. I don't know how a church would respond to those who are despised.

We tend to think that people who are outcast in our society deserve it. If somebody's a drug addict, we say, "Well, he brought it on himself. He shouldn't have fooled with it. Probably had bad friends. Probably a weak person anyway. Thank God I'm not that way. Weak, sinful."

Somebody's an alcoholic, we tend to say, "Well, if they just followed the teachings of Christ, moderation, stayed away from alcohol, lived a sound life, come to Sunday School every Sunday, studied the Bible, they wouldn't be condemned to a loss of self-control. Because the person's an alcoholic, he probably wasn't good to start with. Something basically wrong with them."

A prisoner. We look on a person in prison as someone [to whom] we can demonstrate, often publicly, our Christian compassion. But we really think that person's probably not quite as good as we are, in the eyes of God. The person's committed a crime, been found guilty, sent to prison.

I visited all the prisons in Georgia when I was governor. Average education level was fifth grade. Over 40 percent were retarded, mentally retarded, with an IQ below 70. The vast majority were Black, poor. I've said many times that if my own son had committed the same act as those prisoners that I saw, my son would never have been in prison. Because my family was known to be a respectable family, and I had a lot of influence in a nice way even before I got involved in politics. The local superior court judge and I both went to the Naval Academy.

And I'm sure that if my son had been brought before the judge, in private chambers probably, having committed some crime—stealing a car, something like that, thank God he didn't—I would've probably said, "Tom, my boy's a good boy, and if you send him to prison, his life will be destroyed. And if you'll just let him go this time, I'll send him to a military school or I'll exert more discipline or I'll be personally responsible." I doubt if my son would have ever gone to prison.

But we have a tendency to despise people, not actively but kind of passively, who are different from us. Those who are poor quite often [are] looked upon as not very worthy. If they'd worked as hard as we had and studied as much as we had, they wouldn't be poor.

And I've seen in my own earlier life a strong regional, even a national, worldwide perhaps, belief that because people were Black or because people didn't speak English well or because people hadn't been living in this country very long, somehow they were not as good as we were. Homosexuality [was] looked upon as a reason for condemnation of a person in the eyes of God. ...

We read the Ten Commandments, and if they don't apply to us, we tend to think other people are despised by God because they violate the commandments and we ourselves all have sinned and come short of the glory of God and the wages of sin is death.

But point is, it's not just the Pharisees 2,000 years ago who excluded people from acceptability because they were different. And it wasn't just the Pharisees who thought that because somebody was afflicted that they didn't rank very well in the eyes of God. We tend to yield to the same temptation that afflicted the Pharisees, and that's a teaching of Christ. He went with this leper and healed him and saved him.

Let's move on. The next few verses. Luke 5. Let's read the 17th, 18th, and 19th first. Fred?

FRED GREGG:

17 And it came to pass on a certain day, as he was teaching, that there were Pharisees and doctors of the law sitting by, which were come out of every town of Galilee, and Judaea, and Jerusalem: and the power of the Lord was present to heal them.
18 And, behold, men brought in a bed a man which was taken with a palsy: and they sought means to bring him in, and to lay him before him.
19 And when they could not find by what way they might bring him in because of the multitude, they went upon the housetop, and let him down through the tiling with his couch into the midst before Jesus.

PRESIDENT JIMMY CARTER:

What's the significance of this act?

The man's sins were not the concern of his friends, were they? His friends didn't put him on the pallet because he was sinful or because he needed to be reconciled with God.

But his friends loved him to the extent that they climbed up on top of a house, tore a hole in the roof, let him down. And they had some special awareness of Christ, because you would guess that even a savior would say, "Don't tear a hole in that roof. These people are my host, they let me in the house and now you tear up the house."

They had some special feeling that Christ would put that human being even above his friend's house. And Jesus knew the man was physically afflicted, right? There he was, lying on the pallet, couldn't even walk, couldn't even move, couldn't even crawl. And Jesus didn't say, "Get up and walk." What did he say?

"Your sins are forgiven." He knew the Pharisees were there, and

Jesus was not naive. What is the significance of Christ saying, "Your sins are forgiven"? What makes it profoundly significant? Even above and beyond anything he had cone before, including healing a leper. Anybody?

FRED GREGG:

Pharisees thought God alone was only one could forgive.

PRESIDENT JIMMY CARTER:

Yes, and that is accurate, in that the Old Testament in many places—I have the verses listed here, but I won't go into them to save time—but in many places in the Old Testament, it points out that God is the one to forgive sins.

There was a contrived way for reconciliation or forgiveness. And what was that in the church, in the synagogues? What was the way to be forgiven?

To offer a sacrifice or to give an offering. Yes, a major offering. And for certain kinds of sins and certain kind of reconciliation, you had to give a certain kind of sacrifice. I'm not condemning that, but the point was that when Christ said to that man on the floor, "Your sins are forgiven you," there was a justifiable reason for the Pharisees to believe that Christ had blasphemed God because this man, Jesus, was performing an act of God, forgiving a man's sins.

Even the Pharisees didn't claim they could forgive sin. They said, "God can forgive sins if somebody does certain religious rites." But Christ had forgiven a man's sins. And I'm sure that Christ knew that there was going to be a shockwave going out when he said, "Your sins are forgiven you."

And he saw the Pharisees murmuring among themselves. He said, "What are you talking about? What are you worrying about?" Knowing what the answer would be. And then they accused him of blasphemy, and he said, "Well, if that bothers you that I have forgiven sins, let me also let the man walk." And so the man got up and took his pallet and walked away.

Do you think Christ would've healed the man if the Pharisees hadn't made a point? Speak up.

CLASS MEMBER:

Yes.

PRESIDENT JIMMY CARTER:

Right on. You're right. He would've healed him because Christ loved that man. He wasn't trying to win a debating contest with the Pharisees by healing the man. He loved the man, and he didn't say, "Your sins are forgiven. You're to preach a sermon." He wanted that person to be reconciled with God. Christ loved that man.

And as you know, several places otherwise in the Bible, Christ heals people because of the faith of someone else. He raised Lazarus from the dead because of the faith of Mary and Martha. And as you know, the centurion had so much faith that Christ healed him and a parent with a child, but faith was there, and Christ healed.

And the Pharisees murmuring among themselves, this was an embryonic beginning of the fear and the animosity of the Pharisees because they not only accused Christ of blasphemy, but they also saw the overwhelming power of Christ, the authority of Christ, the results of his words, and also the acceptability by the masses of Christ as a great religious healer.

And that was a Messianic age that was predicted in the Old Testament that Christ could have preached this sermon on then. This is the beginning of the Messianic age when sins can be forgiven. Let's move on because I want to cover the entire lesson. Read Luke 5:22 to 24. Anyone.

CLASS MEMBER:

22 But when Jesus perceived their thoughts, he answering said unto them, What reason ye in your hearts?
23 Whether is easier, to say, Thy sins be forgiven thee; or to say, Rise up and walk?
24 But that ye may know that the Son of man hath power upon earth to forgive sins, (he said unto the sick of the palsy,) I say unto thee, Arise, and take up thy couch, and go into thine house.

PRESIDENT JIMMY CARTER:

Very good. Jesus uses the words "Son of man" according to the lesson text, 80 times. And so far as we know, nobody else ever used it. His disciples, no one ever used the phrase "Son of man" except Christ.

If you read this text in other places—I read a few of them this morning—you see that there was a special connotation of it. If other people used the words "Son of man," it was a kind of common expression just for a man. Christ may have been using this phrase as the Messiah, but there's no way to know. Dr. Cranford might. Is there some special connotation that son of man should apply to us?

When we hear Christ say, "Son of man," we think in our minds the Son of God who was born a human being. and we know that Christ was the Messiah, but Christ, in order not to bludgeon people by saying, "I am the Messiah," would say, "I am the Son of man." It was a little bit obtuse, and his disciples interpreted [it] probably as we do. [For] [o]thers, it was not very contentious.

Let's move on now to the final episode in this lesson. The people looked upon Christ with this act with fear. But I would like to point out in passing that fear doesn't mean a desire to run away.

We use the meaning of the word "fear" as being contemplating punishment for ourselves or some catastrophe in our life, and we want to escape from it. But "fear" there meant an acknowledgement of, I'd say, purity or holiness, an aspect of reverence. For them, "fear" meant I want to kneel down rather than run away. "Fear the Lord" meant kneel down to the Lord, revere the Lord, accept his holiness. But we have kind of twisted the word "fear" around so that we mean escape from something, fear of punishment. But when they said they were filled with fear, it meant an awareness of holiness.

Well, they were amazed at what had happened, and then their feeling was changed to one of hostility. Let's read the next few verses. ...

FRED GREGG:

[27] And after these things he went forth, and saw a publican, named

Levi, sitting at the receipt of custom: and he said unto him,
Follow me.
[28] And he left all, rose up, and followed him.
[29] And Levi made him a great feast in his own house: and there was
a great company of publicans and of others that sat down with them.
[30] But their scribes and Pharisees murmured against his disciples,
saying, Why do ye eat and drink with publicans and sinners?
[31] And Jesus answering said unto them, They that are whole need
not a physician; but they that are sick.
[32] I came not to call the righteous, but sinners to repentance.

PRESIDENT JIMMY CARTER:

It was not just Pharisees that Jesus alienated when he went in to eat
with Levi [or Matthew]. The eating of a meal with someone was a
very intimate observance of friendship and equality and mutual
acceptance, more so even than it is with us. It was kind of a ritual.

Those of you who have visited in the homes of Jewish families on
holy days, you know that the observance of the meal has a special
part in their lives. I had the Friday meal with Prime Minister [Men-
achem] Begin at Camp David one of the nights we were there, and
there's a special religious quality about it.

When Jesus sat down in the home of Levi, who was acknowledged to be a sinner—and I have no doubt that all of his friends,
birds of a feather flock together, were outcast in the community—
they probably drank a lot. I'm sure they didn't go to the synagogue.
They were kind of alienated from the community.

The tax collectors were looked on as betrayers of the people of
Israel—Quislings, who associated with the Romans, robbers of their
own people—but they were really outcast in more ways than one.
And Jesus invited himself and went to the home of Levi. And apparently the Pharisees and others were standing around, kind of an
audience. I don't know exactly how it was. I've seen it in movies.

But there was a table with them eating at it. And these critics, the
Pharisees and the good citizens of that community, were
condemning Christ for associating with sinners. And Christ again
said, "I came to seek and to save those that are lost. The righteous
don't need me."

Well, there's several lessons to be derived in closing. First of all, that Christ ministered to human needs, material needs included, physical needs, yes. Because he saw that in a person's life, deprivation was harmful and needed to be corrected. If a person's been given a talent by God and societal obstacles prevent those talents being nurtured and used, then that is bad.

And Christ wanted to correct that badness. If somebody's deprived from an education or health, if somebody's not given equality of treatment, if someone is despised, if someone is an outcast, if someone is hungry, if someone is treated as inferior, if someone is deprived of justice, if someone is deprived of human freedom, if someone is sick and not treated, if someone is there and not loved—those human afflictions were a reason for Christ's ministry, and they should be ours.

Christ also was not concerned about religious custom or tradition as much as other leaders of that time. He saw the strict human creations of religious rules and regulations, prescriptions, proscriptions, as a substitute for God is love.

And he saw himself as someone who was a teacher. Christ taught in the synagogues. He taught in people's homes, he taught on the streets, he taught in the countryside, taught out of ships. He answered questions. Taught with his life, with his actions, his words, with his suffering, with his death, with his resurrection. Christ was a teacher.

I think that in this day and age of ours, it's good for us to remember that the Pharisaic approach is not a 2,000-year-old dead characteristic of people who profess to be Christians. The defining of what a Christian is, the defining of what is acceptable in God by human beings, the structure of complicated moral laws by human beings is not Christianity.

Which brings us to the original question we asked: What is Christianity?

One definition is the assurance of God's forgiveness toward those of us who acknowledge our sins because we believe in Christ. It's a reconciliation between sinful people, us, and God, through Christ's love.

And in all these three episodes that I've covered this morning, Christ is teaching us that. And as we study what Christ did in these occasions and the radical departure of Christ's actions from the religious teachings of that day, we should derive a lesson for ourselves.

Love, compassion, concern, forgiveness, understanding, equality, human. Those are the kinds of words that epitomize Christ's life. Humility. They're the ones that should permeate our own lives. As we depart from that and assume a Pharisaic superiority, we depart from Christ. That's something we don't want to do.

FRED GREGG:

Mr. President, thank you so much. Let's all stand and be dismissed. Every time he teaches, it really worries me how I would've cheated you had I taught.

Our Father, we thank thee for this day. We thank thee for this lesson. We thank thee for Jesus Christ. We thank thee for our President, the leadership that he gives to us, the love that he has for all mankind. We thank you for our First Lady. And Father, we just pray that thou will bless us today, may this be a glorious Lord's day. In whatever's accomplished, we'll give you the praise. We ask it in your name and for your sake. Amen.

1981

Jimmy Carter stepped to the lectern of the Couples Class for the last time on Sunday, January 4, 1981. Carter's single term in office would end 16 days later, when Ronald Reagan would take the oath of office as the 40th President of the United States.

Less than a week earlier, Carter broke his left collarbone while cross-country skiing at Camp David and was placed in a harness prescribed by the White House physician, William Lukash.

In that morning's *Washington Post*, Courtland Milloy reported that "The first lingering cold wave of the winter of '81 hung over Washington yesterday, bringing bone-chilling winds and biting temperatures to this almost Southern town, and leaving patches of ice and snow clinging tenaciously to side streets and porch steps."

Despite the pain in his shoulder and the cold outside, Carter opened the lesson by jokingly offering to arm wrestle Fred Gregg for the opportunity to lead the class. The lesson that Sunday was entitled "Following Jesus' Example" and came from Luke, Chapter 9. Just before launching his customary focused discussion of the lesson, Carter spent about three minutes talking about what the class had meant to him and to Rosalynn and about their plans for the future:

> We will be going home to Plains immediately after the inaugural ceremonies. We'll walk around the other side of the

Capitol, get on a helicopter, fly to Andrews Air Force Base and take off to Warner Robins, Georgia. And then we'll go on down to Plains from there. And we'll be living a good, private life.

Jimmy Carter's performance as president is debatable. As a predictor of his post-presidential life, he was lousy.

FOLLOWING JESUS' EXAMPLE

JANUARY 4, 1981

LUKE 9:37-62

FRED GREGG:

I know no one knew the President was teaching this morning, and I appreciate so many of y'all coming to hear me. I hate to disappoint you, though, but he's going to teach.

About four years ago, I walked through the door over on that side, and I looked in at the door here. and I saw the cutest little red-headed girl come in, and I said, "Boy, she looks familiar. I've seen her on television." And right behind her, I saw a beautiful lady, and I said, "Oh, my goodness." And then. about that time, in came the President and a whole entourage of people.

By that time, I'd worked my way to the middle aisle there, and I turned around to that cross, and I don't believe it ever looked bigger, and I said these words, "Lord, there's over 200 million Americans. Why did you put me in this position?"

Well, I want you to know that next to accepting the Lord and joining the church and saying "I do" to Mary Jo—Where are you, Mary Jo?—"I do" to Mary Jo, the greatest thrill that has come in my life in the church was the day that the President and Rosalynn Carter joined this class.

They came into this class to worship. They have been most gracious to us, the members, to the visitors, to the impositions that we've put on them. But on the other hand, the class has been super in trying to do everything in their power to give them the privilege to worship as just regular members.

The day that I first met the President, he said, "I'm looking forward to hearing you teach." I said, "Well, how about you teaching?" Well, this was only Sunday after the inauguration, and he said, "Well, after all, Fred, I have had a pretty busy week this week," but said, "I will teach." And he has, and every time that he's taught, he has really blessed our hearts.

I don't know how he's going to do a better job today than he did the last time he taught, because to me, that was just super. And I don't know what I'm going to do as a teacher when I have to look at those seats and know that they're not there, and when I need someone to read, I'm going to have to wait till somebody finds it, and I won't have Rosalynn to flip to it right quick and read it without me losing my concentration.

They've been great people; they're great friends. And there's a passage in the Bible, in this lesson today, I'm going to refer to when I close, that sums up our relationship with him. ... Mr. President, thank you so much for teaching today, and I'll turn it over to you.

PRESIDENT JIMMY CARTER:

Well, we're not dead. This is not a funeral, as you know. We're going to be living a good Christian life and staying close to all of you, cherishing the friendships and the memories. We hope to come back and visit you as often as possible.

And I can reciprocate what Fred said: One of the finest things that ever happened to us, personally, was the joining of this class and the friendship with Fred Gregg and all of you who've accepted us, not as a public official in some ivory tower, but as a human being, as a fellow Christian and as a friend.

We've never come into this class when we were treated with anything other than genuine fellowship and friendship, and on a personal basis. And it really meant a lot to us in a trying position of being President of this great country. We've also never had any unpleasant experiences in this church; everything has been fine for us.

And I know that the church has been through trying times. We are now looking for a new pastor. We couldn't possibly improve on [interim pastor] Dr. [Clarence] Cranford. If he could just stay here for the next 15 to 20 years, it would certainly suit me all right.

But I know that the church has been a strong one and a symbol of commitment and courage and dedication in this nation's capital for many generations. And I know it will continue to be that in the future.

We will be going home to Plains immediately after the inaugural ceremonies. We'll walk around the other side of the Capitol, get on a helicopter, fly to Andrews Air Force Base and take off to Warner Robins, Georgia. And then we'll go on down to Plains from there. And we'll be living a good, private life. We'll join the church in Plains, and I expect to be as active or maybe even more so than I have been in this Sunday School.

When we haven't been here on Sunday mornings, we've been to church at Camp David. We ordinarily invited the chaplain from a nearby military base to come in to give us a private church service. And then on special days, we've had several hundred military personnel there for Thanksgiving, Christmas services and so forth. But we've kept our ties with this church even on Sundays that we weren't here.

This quarter will be a continuation of our study from the New Testament, the book of Luke. I know last couple of Sundays, according to Fred's report to me, the regular classes have not been held. Special Christmas relationships have been emphasized, which I think is very fine for the church. We have a responsibility this morning to, I think, forget about goings and comings of class members and revert back to the teaching of the Bible. And if all of you would turn to Luke 9, I'll let you help me with the lesson.

I think perhaps more than any other chapter that I can remember in the Bible, this one emphasizes a sequence of events in Christ's life and also emphasizes the fact that God's ways are not our ways. The natural attributes of human beings are not God's ways.

Some of the things that Jesus did might seem strange to us. His attitudes are not predictable. The relationship with his disciples is a very interesting one in this chapter. And his disciples, predictably, are very fallible in their relationship to Christ and to people around them.

Luke perhaps took some of the activities of Christ's life out of sequence. They weren't exactly reported in a chronological way in order to emphasize the thrust from this chapter, Luke 9, all the way up to the culmination of Jesus' life with his final ascension into heaven.

And he made it look as a kind of a pilgrim's progress toward the realization of God's command for Christ's life. And the things that Jesus did on this journey are a very powerful lesson to us all.

One of the lessons that Jesus will teach us in this chapter, in the events of this chapter, is what is greatness? Is greatness being a president? Is greatness being an emperor? Is greatness being the senior executive in a major corporation? Is greatness being a very prominent, highly known news reporter or commentator? Is greatness being a powerful behind-the-scenes manipulator of current or human events?

What is greatness? What do you think Jesus teaches us in this lesson about the foundation of greatness or the definition of greatness? Anybody? Come on, speak up.

CLASS MEMBERS:

To be a servant. Do things for those who can't return what you do for them.

PRESIDENT JIMMY CARTER:

That's right. Christ will teach us throughout his life, but particularly in this chapter, that the foundation of greatness is service to others.

Another thing that we'll learn today is how to accept people who are different from us.

It's very difficult for a human being to accommodate, as an equal, another person who is different. I don't know if it's more difficult for us to accept those that are more exalted than we are in public opinion or those who are inferior to us in public opinion. But it's a challenge to a human being, living ostensibly in accordance with God's laws. to treat other human beings with tolerance, with acceptance, with friendship, with love.

Another thing that we will learn today is how to accommodate these intense pressures put on us by the world in which we live, our milieu. Transient emphases in our lives, transient circumstances that we face, transient pressures on us, transient decisions to be made with things that never change, with the really important facts, with the really important events, with the really important circumstances, with the really important relationships.

Those important ones, the permanent ones, are the ones embedded in God's teachings to us. The best lesson to us taught by God is the life of Christ itself. When you try to imagine in your own mind, "What does God want me to do in a circumstance like this?" almost invariably there is an event in Jesus' life about which we have been taught since we were tiny children that vividly demonstrates what I should do.

Sometimes we don't want to see it. It's much easier for us to ignore it or pretend not to remember or rationalize some alleged or imagined difference between what Christ would have done and what we try to figure out what we ought to do. But when we come down and face the facts in a courageous fashion, putting our faith in God and say, "Jesus would have done this because I know Jesus did this in a similar circumstance," it opens up an avenue for proper decisions to be made by us—not often the natural decision that a human being would want to make.

So the acceptance of others is something that Christ will teach us in this chapter, and the development of an inward attitude that makes every decision that we have to face not be an extraordinary circumstance.

We don't have the mental capacity and we don't have the physical stamina to face a series of a hundred crises every day. If every time we face something that's difficult, we have to make a brand new analysis of that particular subject and go through a torturous assessment of the situation and a screening out of the factors and finally come to a conclusion, that's a very trying experience, isn't it? And we'd be torn one way or another and we'd be in a mental and even a physical turmoil.

So what Christ teaches us and what we as Christians have as a great reservoir of strength is an inner attitude, hopefully based on a constant relationship with God. And that inner strength based on faith is what sustains us and lets us live our life, not from one crisis to another, but dealing with rare crises when we genuinely face an unpredictable circumstance or perhaps one that we haven't experienced before.

But the underlying commitment to God, the underlying faith in Christ, the underlying knowledge of God's teachings as applicable to our lives, lets us avoid that tension and that constant dashing from one trying experience to another as we set a tone in our lives.

If we are inherently honest, then every time we have a business transaction, we don't have to decide, do we cheat this customer or not? Another thing that we have to do is to prepare for hostility. You have to make a choice. All of us have to make a choice.

Do we serve God, or do we try to accommodate with a wishy-washy, flexible human life, the accommodation of whoever happens to be in front of us at a particular time? Are we so malleable, just soft clay that can be molded to suit every circumstance, to try to look good in the eyes of the immediate beholder?

Or do we stand firm and say, "I want to look good in the eyes of God, and let the immediate beholder see in me a Christian," and sometimes be willing to take the displeasure of the person with whom we are dealing at that time or the group that we are dealing with that time, which may be a very large group. It may sometimes include those that are our circle of friends who demand from us or expect from us an acceptable human action that we feel is not acceptable as a godly action.

So those are the kind of things that we'll be looking at this morning, and I've taken up a lot of time, but in Luke 9, before our lesson begins today, we've already seen that Christ gave the disciples power and authority and instructions to go out in the surrounding territory and preach the gospel. And they did so, with remarkable success. They performed miracles, they healed people.

They were exemplars of God's teachings as instructed by Christ. And then later they came back to Christ to make a report to him, and they went off and sought and found some temporary solitude, following which, predictably, the multitudes descended on them, and they had to accommodate large crowds of people.

The disciples wanted to slip away again. That's when Christ fed the 5,000. And then, later on, Jesus turned to them, the disciples, and said, "Who am I?" And his disciples made a response that's reported in several of the Gospels, I think two others. But in this, in Luke 9, is when Peter said ... did anybody remember what Peter said Christ was?

DR. CLARENCE CRANFORD:

The Christ of God.

PRESIDENT JIMMY CARTER:

He didn't say Christ, the Son of God, though. He said, "The Christ of God." That's at least in the King James Version. I guess it means the Messiah of God, prophet of God, the Son of God for whom everyone had been waiting. And then Christ said, "Don't tell anybody about this."

You know, it was an extraordinary thing when you consider it, that Peter was able, and the other disciples I'm sure, accepted the analysis that this man was a messiah, was in effect God, was the Christ, because the expectations of Jesus' life as a ruler, as a god, had not really been observed.

They saw the healing of some physical ailments, restoration of broken or diseased bodies. That was not adequate for them to know that this leader of theirs, this teacher of theirs, was Christ.

What else had they observed in this man?

[I]n addition to the miracles, to make an eye see again or to make an ear hear again or to make a limb walk again, what else was there that let them know this was not just a healer?

His miracles obviously transcended that of a fakir, an F-A-K-I-R, or a magician or a great physician or a prophet. But there was something, some inner quiet strength, authority, that was there, and that was another, almost unique characteristic of Christ.

CLASS MEMBER:

He was humble.

PRESIDENT JIMMY CARTER:

Absolutely. He was humble. A humble leader. Gee, how rare that is. Even today, right? It's almost unknown. But here was a man when they tried to say, "What is exaltation? What is superiority? What is leadership? What is greatness?" Christ said, in this chapter, that greatness is service.

And right after Jesus told his disciples that he was going to go to Jerusalem and be killed and be persecuted and fall into the hands of man, the disciples didn't understand it. And immediately according to Luke, they started an argument among themselves, what was it?

CLASS MEMBER:

Who'll be the greatest.

PRESIDENT JIMMY CARTER:

Who's going to be the greatest in the kingdom of God? Which one of us 12 is going to be the greatest man? And do you remember what Jesus did?

He reached and got a little child and stood the child alongside him. This was a unique thing. I don't remember it in the case of Moses or David or the great prophets, this extraordinary demonstration of service or humility.

But there was no absence of strength, and there was no absence of leadership in forming a guide for others or in instructing as a superb teacher.

This is a new concept in Christ's life, which he tried to embed in the hearts and minds of his disciples, and which he therefore is trying to embed in the hearts and minds of Dr. Cranford and Fred Gregg and Jimmy Carter and all of you.

What is greatness? No one in this room fails to want to lead a great life. We want our lives to be significant. God created us in a unique way. We are different from everybody else. We want our lives to be meaningful. And if we are not rich, then in order to salve our own self-esteem, we look around and say, "Well, maybe I can be a good tennis player or maybe I can be a good father or maybe I can build a beautiful house or maybe I can be a good artist or maybe I can write a book or maybe I can serve my neighbors."

And eventually we come around to the realization that the grasping for things that make us look great in the eyes of other people is really a fruitless exercise. Because quite often the richest people on earth, we know from accurate reports, are the most unhappy, the most frustrated, committed to frequent infidelity in marriage and despair and suicide and so forth. So richness in material wealth is not a measure of greatness.

And the same thing with world leaders. The acquisition of power as measured in human terms is not greatness in the eyes of God.

The disciples just didn't understand why Jesus had to suffer. Why should a leader have to suffer? Why should a great person have to suffer? Why should the Son of God have to suffer? Why should Christ have to suffer?

When they were brought face to face with that fact, the natural inclination for the disciples was to turn away. Often they denied it. They said, "Oh, Jesus, you know you're not going to suffer." Or sometimes they would, just as in this case in Luke 9, they just didn't want to know any further. They were afraid to ask further what Christ meant.

The aspect of suffering in Christ's life is also a pattern in ours. We don't, many of us, expect to suffer as much as Christ suffered. A perfect person weighted down with all our filthy sins: great suffering, physical torture with briars penetrating his forehead and with nails in his hands and feet, dying with thirst, even doubting God, feeling that God had forsaken him.

We don't expect to suffer that much. But each of us, if we are true to God's commands, must expect and accept the fact that we will suffer, and we cannot expect all our prayers to be answered.

Jesus taught his disciples how to pray, but he never told them all their prayers would be answered the way they expected the prayers to be answered. Were all of Jesus' prayers answered? Were they?

CLASS MEMBER:

NO.

PRESIDENT JIMMY CARTER:

How can we expect all our prayers to be answered if Jesus' prayers were not even answered? When he faced Calvary, he said, "God, if it be your will, take this bitter cup from me. Don't make me go through this." But he said, "Thy will be done."

Philosophers and theologians and others for centuries have argued back and forth about free will of human beings versus predestination or the ordering of human events, or the under-standing of predictability of human events as known by God. We know that God's omniscient, he knows everything. He's omnipresent, everywhere. Omnipotent, all powerful. If God is all these things, then how can a human being like me lead a free life?

Why does God let me sin? Why did God let my daddy die when he was a young man? Why does God let suffering go on? Why does God let there be wars?

There's an extraordinary sentence, it's not in [the] Bible, but there's an extraordinary sentence in the teacher's manual, in expla-nation of verse 51. It explains Jesus going toward Jerusalem knowing that he would die. It says he chose this path voluntarily in obedience to the Father.

He chose this path voluntarily in obedience to the Father. That's really an interesting sentence to me. I thought about it a lot this morning when I was getting ready to teach this lesson. And that's really our relationship with God. As we make our decisions volun-tarily, God gives us a right to decide good versus evil. We make our choices voluntarily, but in obedience to the Father.

And the realization that those two clauses in a sentence are not incompatible, there's a very profound discovery: We can act volun-tarily with complete free will, in obedience to God. The choice is ours.

Well, I think it might be good for us to read the verses. We've just got five more minutes. Rosalynn, would you read? Start with the 43rd verse and read through the 56th verse.

ROSALYNN CARTER:

[43] And they were all amazed at the mighty power of God. But while they wondered every one at all things which Jesus did, he said unto his disciples,
[44] Let these sayings sink down into your ears: for the Son of man shall be delivered into the hands of men.
[45] But they understood not this saying, and it was hid from them, that they perceived it not: and they feared to ask him of that saying.
[46] Then there arose a reasoning among them, which of them should be greatest.

^{47} And Jesus, perceiving the thought of their heart, took a child, and set him by him,

^{48} And said unto them, Whosoever shall receive this child in my name receiveth me: and whosoever shall receive me receiveth him that sent me: for he that is least among you all, the same shall be great.

^{49} And John answered and said, Master, we saw one casting out devils in thy name; and we forbad him, because he followeth not with us.

^{50} And Jesus said unto him, Forbid him not: for he that is not against us is for us.

^{51} And it came to pass, when the time was come that he should be received up, he steadfastly set his face to go to Jerusalem,

^{52} And sent messengers before his face: and they went, and entered into a village of the Samaritans, to make ready for him.

^{53} And they did not receive him, because his face was as though he would go to Jerusalem.

^{54} And when his disciples James and John saw this, they said, Lord, wilt thou that we command fire to come down from heaven, and consume them, even as Elias did?

^{55} But he turned, and rebuked them, and said, Ye know not what manner of spirit ye are of.

^{56} For the Son of man is not come to destroy men's lives, but to save them. And they went to another village.

PRESIDENT JIMMY CARTER:

The last few verses in Chapter 9—you might want to read it when you get home—concerned people that came up to Christ and said, "I want to serve you, Jesus. I've heard these great things about you. I want to be one of your disciples. But first I've got to get my family affairs in order. But first I've got to go bury my father." And other occasions people said, "I want to serve you, but I want to cling to the money that I've earned or inherited."

So suffering in our human life or deprivation in our human life or unselfishness in our human life or quote "excessive" unquote service to God in our human life doesn't result in a belittling of this one life on earth that God gives us. All these things contribute to the greatness of humility and service.

The disciples all thought that they, chosen almost arbitrarily by Christ, were certainly greater than any other person could possibly be outside their own immediate circle. One person was healing in the name of Christ. And John said, "What should we do? I've already told this guy to lay off." And Jesus said, what?

ROSALYNN CARTER:

He who is not against us is for us.

PRESIDENT JIMMY CARTER:

That's right. Said, leave him alone. Let him teach. And I can't dwell on this part of a lesson—it's a complicated long lesson—but it means that as we serve Christ, let's don't belittle others who serve Christ in a different way. Let's don't exalt ourselves because we think that worship in the First Baptist Church in Washington is perhaps the ultimate in God's eyes in Christian service.

Christ taught that lesson very quickly and very profoundly, and it was a shock to his disciples. And when he finally decided to go to Jerusalem, there were really two ways to go. If there's one part of the world's history or geography with which I'm familiar, it's this particular area of the world. I probably know it as well as I do my own farm in Webster County, Georgia. And that is the East and West Bank along the Jordan River.

But one route was, from where Jesus was on the Sea of Galilee, was more direct, up the West Bank of the Jordan River, through where the Samaritans lived. And the other one was across the Jordan River, go down to Jericho, and then come on up the mountain toward Jerusalem. Rosalynn and I have been there. And I've been there in spirit many times.

And when the disciples said, "Which way are we going to go?" Jesus said, "Let's go through Samaria." The Samaritans were hated by the Jews, and vice versa. In the synagogues, the Jews would pray against the Samaritans. A common prayer then was that the Samaritans would not have eternal life. And the hatred or distrust was reciprocal.

Jesus said, "Let's go through Samaria." Jesus looked with special favor, for some reason, on the Samaritans. Or maybe he just used them as examples because they were the despised people in those days.

Perhaps if you lived in a modern day, he would look on Blacks or poor people or Hispanics as special persons. But he picked out the Samaritans: the parable of the Good Samaritan; the visit to the Samaritan woman; he told his disciples to go get food in the Samaritan village, when their food was looked on as filth by most.

And after this generous gesture on Jesus' part, to go through this despised country, he sent his advance team out, which kind of struck me between the eyes, because Jesus had a large entourage when he traveled with him, and he had to make special preparations when he went into a village, because he had several hundred, sometimes several thousand, people who would descend on a village, traveling along with him. People followed him.

And what did the Samaritans say? "No way. We don't want you in our village." And what did his disciples want to do—anybody remember? They wanted to bring down fire from heaven and strike those Samaritans dead. It just proved how filthy, lowdown, bums they were. This shows Jesus, that you were wrong. You were trying to be nice to these lowdown people, and see how they reacted to your trust in them? And what did Jesus do? What did he say?

He said, "You can't bring down fire and destroy these people. You got to love them. And if they don't want us in that village, let's go to another village."

Well, there are so many lessons in Luke 9. I hope when you get home after church, that you will read the whole chapter. I've not been able to do it justice. But the fact is that this is a part of Jesus' life where he demonstrates vividly with personal events—facing human challenges and human temptations—how God wants us to act, with humility, service, love, forgiveness, understanding, tolerance, compassion, obedience, courage.

If we'll just act like Jesus, we'll be good Christians. And if we try hard, God will understand when we fail.

FRED GREGG:

I said there was a verse in here that I'll always remember President Carter by. It's the 32nd verse of Luke 9, and I've told you many times, sometimes I quote them my way and sometimes I interpret them my way. This says, "And when they were awake, they saw his glory."

I want to repeat: In time, history, people will wake up to what a great president they had [*Applause*] and what a great First Lady. Let's all stand and be dismissed.

Our Father, we thank thee for this day. We thank thee for the privilege that we have to come into thy house and to study your word. We thank thee for the privilege that we have to assemble together, and we thank thee so much for this lesson today, and so much for the one who brought it to us.

Father, we pray that thou will bless him, that thou will guide him as he continues to direct our country. Be with our First Lady as she stands beside him. We pray for our pastor. We pray for our class. And Lord, what we fail in asking, fail not in giving. These favors we ask in thy name it for thy sake. Amen.

AFTERWORD

Three weeks after President Jimmy Carter taught his final Sunday School lesson at First Baptist D.C., in January 1981, he joined Maranatha Baptist Church in Plains, Georgia.

The "good, private life" he had predicted to his class at First Baptist lasted less than two years. In September 1982, the Carters founded the Carter Center at Emory University in Atlanta with the slogan: "Waging Peace, Fighting Disease. Building Hope." In 1984, the Carters added another kind of building to their to-do list by forming a partnership with Habitat for Humanity.

On October 11, 2002—just shy of 41 years after Carter lost the presidency—a news release issued in Oslo, Norway, summed up a career that might have been busier outside the White House than in:

> The Norwegian Nobel Committee has decided to award the Nobel Peace Prize for 2002 to Jimmy Carter, for his decades of untiring effort to find peaceful solutions to international conflicts, to advance democracy and human rights, and to promote economic and social development.
>
> During his presidency (1977-1981), Carter's mediation was a vital contribution to the Camp David Accords between Israel and Egypt, in itself a great enough achievement to qualify for the Nobel Peace Prize. At a time when the cold war between East and West was still

predominant, he placed renewed emphasis on the place of human rights in international politics.

Through his Carter Center, which celebrates its 20th anniversary in 2002, Carter has since his presidency undertaken very extensive and persevering conflict resolution on several continents. He has shown outstanding commitment to human rights, and has served as an observer at countless elections all over the world. He has worked hard on many fronts to fight tropical diseases and to bring about growth and progress in developing countries. Carter has thus been active in several of the problem areas that have figured prominently in the over one hundred years of Peace Prize history.

The former president collected the Peace Prize in December 2002 and went back to Plains, where he continued his humanitarian and habitat work for another 20 years and—of course—taught Sunday School at Maranatha Baptist Church.

Through it all, Jimmy Carter's name remained on the official rolls as an associate member of the First Baptist Church of the City of Washington, D.C.

ACKNOWLEDGMENTS

Thank you, President Carter, for being part of my church family at the First Baptist Church of Washington, D.C., and for demonstrating that people with difficult jobs can find room and time to both give and receive spiritual nourishment.

Readers and historians should share my gratitude for the work of Chip Hailey and Ed Fry in recording and preserving the Sunday School lessons taught by President Carter at First Baptist D.C. May they rest in peace with the crowns of stars they richly deserve.

For their invaluable work sorting and cataloging the history of a 222-year-old congregation, I thank 'Our Ladies of the Archives": Janice Osborn, Ellen Parkhurst and Sadye Doxie, as well as their predecessors and every member (and there were lots) who clipped an article from *The Washington Post* or *Washington Star* and donated it to the archives.

Keeping a congregation together for more than two centuries is no mean feat, and I'm grateful to the current and former members and pastors who have contributed to the continuum of First Baptist D.C.

My thanks to every friend, family member, grocery clerk, cab driver, waiter, waitress, health care professional and complete stranger on the street who has listened to me talk about this project. You helped more than you could ever know.

Finally, my thanks to those who made the project a reality: foremost, my book coach and editor Cyndi Hughes of Booktique Consulting in Austin, Texas; photographer Jay Brousseau of Dallas, Texas; and design guru Tom Molinaro of Bethesda, Maryland. You are pros, and it shows.

SOURCES

The bulk of the material in this book comes from verbatim transcripts of recordings of 14 Sunday School lessons taught by President Jimmy Carter at the First Baptist Church of the City of Washington, D.C., between November 1977 and January 1981.

Bible verses read during the lessons are from the versions used by the class members when audible on the recordings and from the King James Version when the readings are not audible.

The events of Carter's presidency described in the introductions to each year are drawn primarily from government sources, most notably from the website of the Jimmy Carter Presidential Library and Museum, including the archives of the official White House Diary, documenting each day of the presidency; Carter's State of the Union addresses to Congress; and timelines of events. The website is www.jimmycarterlibrary.gov.

The sources of specific details in the yearly overviews are listed on the following pages.

OPENING QUOTES

In His Words: The quotations are from transcripts of Jimmy Carter's Sunday School lessons, First Baptist Church of the City of Washington, D.C.

About President Jimmy Carter Teaching Sunday School: Zachary B. Wolf, "After negotiating a peace deal, Jimmy Carter taught this Bible class," *What Matters* (CNN), April 1, 2023, https://www.cnn.com/2023/04/01/politics/jimmy-carter-religion-what-matters/index.html

About Christi Harlan and First Baptist D.C.: Janis Johnson, "At DC's First Baptist Church With President Jimmy Carter," *WomanTraveler,* September 24, 2023, https://womantraveler.info/at-dcs-first-baptist-church-with-president-jimmy-carter/

THE SUNDAY SCHOOL CLASS

History of the First Baptist Couples Class: Unknown author, Archives of The First Baptist Church of Washington, D.C.

Couples Class banquet: Caspar Nannes, "President & Mrs. Carter Attend Church Banquet," *Capital Baptist,* November 10, 1977

President and Mrs. Carter attend Sunday School: Diary entry, January 23, 1977, The President's Daily Diary, Jimmy Carter Presidential Library, https://jimmycarterlibrary.gov/sites/default/files/pdf_documents/assets/documents/diary/1977/d012377t.pdf

1977

1977 inauguration: "Inauguration at the U.S. Capitol: Jimmy Carter Inauguration, January 20, 1977, " Architect of the Capitol, https://www.aoc.gov/what-we-do/programs-ceremonies/inauguration

History of the Department of Energy: Office of Legacy Management, "Brief History of the Department of Energy," Department of Energy, https://www.energy.gov/lm/brief-history-department-energy

1978

Jimmy Carter State of the Union Address, January 19, 1978, Jimmy Carter Presidential Library, https://www.jimmycarterlibrary.gov/the-carters/selected-speeches/jimmy-carter-state-of-the-union-address-1973

Panama Canal treaty: "The Panama Canal and the Torrijos-Carter Treaties," Milestones: 1977–1980, Office of the Historian at the U.S. Department of State, https://history.state.gov/milestones/1977-1980/panama-canal

1978 Nobel Peace Prize: The Nobel Peace Prize 1978 award ceremony speech by Aase Lionaes, Chairman of the Norwegian Nobel Committee, December 10, 1978, Oslo, Norway, https://www.nobelprize.org/prizes/peace/1978/ceremony-speech/

1979

Jimmy Carter State of the Union Address, January 23, 1979, Jimmy Carter Presidential Library, https://www.jimmycarterlibrary.gov/the-carters/selected-speeches/jimmy-carter-state-of-the-union-address-1979

Television premieres and new world leaders: "Historical Events in 1979," *On This Day* website, https://www.onthisday.com/events/date/1979

"Malaise" speech: "Jimmy Carter Energy and National Goals: Address to the Nation," July 15, 1979, Jimmy Carter Presidential Library, https://www.jimmycarterlibrary.gov/the-carters/selected-speeches/jimmy-carter-energy-and-national-goals-address-to-the-nation

First Baptist attendance: White House Diary entries, The President's Daily Diary, Jimmy Carter Presidential Library & Museum, https://www.jimmycarterlibrary.gov/research/daily-diary

Russian Pastor Georgi Vins: Marjorie Hyer, "President Likens Soviet Dissident to Bible Figure," *The Washington Post*, April 30, 1979, page A1

Three Mile Island: "Backgrounder On The Three Mile Island Accident," NRC Library of the U.S. Nuclear Regulatory Commission website, https://www.nrc.gov/reading-rm/doc-collections/fact-sheets/3mile-isle.html

SALT II Treaty: "Treaty Between the United States Of America and the Union of Soviet Socialist Republics on the Limitation of Strategic Offensive Arms," U.S. Department of State Archive, https://1997-2001.state.gov/www/global/arms/treaties/salt2-1.html

1980

Jimmy Carter State of the Union Address, January 23, 1980, Jimmy Carter Presidential Library, https://www.jimmycarterlibrary.gov/the-carters/selected-speeches/jimmy-carter-state-of-the-union-address-1980

Mariel Boatlift: "Cuban-Haitian Task Force," July 15, 1980, through June 1, 1981, Jimmy Carter Library, https://www.jimmycarterlibrary.gov/sites/default/files/pdf_documents/assets/documents/findingaids/Cuban_Haitian_Task_Force.pdf

Mount St. Helens eruption: "1980 Cataclysmic Eruption," November 7, 2023, U.S. Geological Survey, U.S. Department of the Interior, https://www.usgs.gov/volcanoes/mount-st.-helens/science/1980-cataclysmic-eruption#overview

Olympic boycott: "The Olympic Boycott, 1980," U.S. Department of State Archive, https://2001-2009.state.gov/r/pa/ho/time/qfp/104481.htm

Other disasters in 1980: "Disasters and Other Declarations," Federal Emergency Management Agency, https://www.fema.gov/disaster/declarations

1981

President Carter's broken collarbone: Norman D. Sandler, "Carter recuperates from broken collarbone; meets Algerians," UPI Archives, December 28, 1980, https://www.upi.com/Archives/1980/12/28/Carter-recuperates-from-broken-collarbone-meets-Algerians/3411346827600/print/

Weather conditions: Courtland Milloy, *The Washington Post*, January 4, 1981

ABOUT THE AUTHOR

Christi Harlan is a writer and communications consultant in Washington, D.C. During a 20-year career as a reporter, her articles appeared on the front pages of *The Wall Street Journal*, *The Dallas Morning News* and the *Austin American-Statesman*.

After newspapers, she held top communications jobs at the Senate Banking Committee, the Federal Emergency Management Agency, the Securities and Exchange Commission and the Public Company Accounting Oversight Board.

Beginning with Hurricane Katrina, Christi spent six years as a volunteer and consultant in disaster public affairs with the American Red Cross, providing media interviews and writing eyewitness accounts of the Red Cross's response to hurricanes, ice storms, flooding and the deadly tornadoes in Enterprise, Alabama, and Joplin, Missouri.

A native of Manhattan, Kansas, Christi attended junior and senior high school in Houston and earned a bachelor's degree in journalism and English from Stephen F. Austin State University in Nacogdoches, Texas. She was accepted to the Knight Fellowship in Law for

Journalists and earned a Master of Studies in Law from Yale Law School.

In August 1993, Christi joined the First Baptist Church of the City of Washington, D.C., where her journalistic skills of taking notes and writing suited the jobs of church clerk and volunteer communications director. She is owned by two cats who think every computer screen is occupied by magical nests of squirrels.

WAIT. THERE'S MORE.

Thank you for reading *Mr. President, The Class Is Yours*. I hope you enjoyed President Carter's Sunday School lessons as much as I did. If you did, I'd appreciate a tout on Amazon (or your favorite online bookseller), on your Facebook page, in your church newsletter, with your book club and/or your entire family. If you didn't enjoy the book, please deposit it responsibly where someone might find it and be grateful for its insight and historic significance.

If you're writing positively, you don't have to get mushy or go gushy (not that there's anything wrong with that), but you can simply borrow an old journalism trick by referring briefly to what somebody already said. Example: "I loved how President Carter described the political machinations of Queen Jezebel! She could be in Congress today!" Don't give a page number; don't give a date or a Scripture citation; somebody will be curious enough to buy the book and look it up.

ENGAGING WITH ME

I was trained as a newspaper reporter to keep myself out of the story. I did that for 20 years before I went into government public affairs, where other people got credit for the quotes and speeches I wrote. After a career of working behind the scenes, I'm having trouble with what feels like full-frontal engagement with readers.

That said, I feel so strongly about the historic importance of Jimmy Carter's time at the First Baptist Church of Washington, D.C., that I will engage with my readers and anyone who will listen. I welcome opportunities to speak to your book club, church, library or retirement home—even your family reunion, provided the potato salad doesn't sit outside in the heat for too long.

Check out my website: www.christiharlanwriter.com
Email me: christi@christiharlanwriter.com

in linkedin.com/in/christiharlan

A PREVIEW

NORMAL LIVES: PRESIDENT JIMMY CARTER AND HIS CHURCH

As I mentioned in the Introduction, there is a lot of historic "stuff" in the archives of the First Baptist Church of the City of Washington, D.C.—enough to fill another book. The companion volume to this book of Sunday School lessons is *Normal Lives: President Jimmy Carter and His Church*, which tells the back story of First Baptist and President Carter's time there.

Normal Lives is based almost entirely on original sources found only in the church archives, from the diary of an usher who hauled protestors out of the sanctuary to the reports filed by a former tennis editor hired by the church to handle publicity about the Carters.

Normal Lives contains lots of excerpts from the now-defunct *Washington Star* and from histories of First Baptist written by former members and pastors. Good researchers could track down those sources, but I include excerpts so you don't have to work to learn that Jimmy Carter and the rest of the congregation were (1) lucky to have pews to sit in and (2) didn't have to pay to rent them every Sunday.

The title of the book comes from a quote in the account of the Sunday School banquet the Carters attended in October 1977:

> "You have made our lives normal lives," President Carter told his classmates. "You have given us stability in a position that

is inherently sometimes unstable. A president of our country can be an isolated person. You have taken us in, and we are indebted to you. Thank you very much."

———

Normal Lives will be published in 2024. Please join my mailing list at **www.christiharlanwriter.com** so you'll be among the first to know the book's release date.

FROM NORMAL LIVES: THE INVITATION

Baptists, like all Christians, base their religion on concepts that are sometimes recited as the "mystery of our faith": Christ has died, Christ has risen, Christ will come again.

For other matters, like eligibility for church membership, Baptists rely less on faith and more on documentation.

So it was for a family attending worship at the First Baptist Church of the City of Washington, D.C., on January 23, 1977. At the end of the service, the pastor issued the traditional "invitation," or altar call, encouraging anyone who wanted to join the church to walk to the front of the sanctuary.

The family stood and walked forward, where ushers gave them little blue cards to write their names and check the means by which they sought membership. The young girl indicated she was seeking baptism; the adults checked the line for "transfer of letter" from a prior church.

The pastor introduced the family to the congregation, asking "all you who join the pastor in recommending them to the membership committee raise your hand," reported William Willoughby in the now-defunct *Washington Star* newspaper.

It was up to the membership committee of First Baptist D.C. to affirm the bona fides of the new members, which included obtaining a letter of recommendation from their prior church.

A small white card arrived at First Baptist D.C. in May 1977. In handwriting and typewriting, the church clerk of Plains Baptist Church in Plains, Georgia, attested that "Pres. and Mrs. Carter, Chip (James Earl III) and Caron Carter" were members in "regular standing ... and, in compliance with your request, are given this letter cordially recommending them to your fellowship."

With those formalities—a public expression of intent, a background check and a letter of recommendation—Jimmy Carter, the 39th President of the United States, officially became a member of the First Baptist Church of the City of Washington, D.C.

www.ingramcontent.com/pod-product-compliance
Lightning Source LLC
Chambersburg PA
CBHW030410130626
46549CB00004B/1705